GOING TO MARKET

For Karin

Going to Market

Women, Trade and Social Relations in Early Modern English Towns, c. 1550–1650

DAVID PENNINGTON
Webster University, St. Louis, USA

Routledge
Taylor & Francis Group
LONDON AND NEW YORK

First published in paperback 2024

First published 2015 by Ashgate Publishing

Published 2016 by Routledge
4 Park Square, Milton Park, Abingdon, Oxon OX14 4RN

and by Routledge
605 Third Avenue, New York, NY 10158

Routledge is an imprint of the Taylor & Francis Group, an informa business

Publisher's Note
The publisher has gone to great lengths to ensure the quality of this reprint but points out that some imperfections in the original copies may be apparent.

British Library Cataloguing in Publication Data
A catalogue record for this book is available from the British Library

The Library of Congress has cataloged the printed edition as follows:
Pennington, David, 1977–
Going to market : women, trade and social relations in early-modern English towns, c. 1550–1650 / by David Pennington.
pages cm.—(The history of retailing and consumption)
Includes bibliographical references and index.
ISBN 978-1-4724-4370-0 (hardcover)
1. Women merchants—England—History—16th century.
2. Women merchants—England—History—17th century. 3. Women merchants—England—Social conditions. 4. Women—England—Economic conditions. 5. Markets—England—History. 6. Households—Economic aspects—England—History. 7. City and town life—England—History. 8. England—Commerce—History—16th century. 9. England—Commerce—History—17th century. 10. England—Social conditions. I. Title.
HF3515.P36 2015
381.082'0942—dc23

2015009330

ISBN 13: 978-1-4724-4370-0 (hbk)
ISBN 13: 978-1-03-292759-6 (pbk)
ISBN 13: 978-1-315-58539-0 (ebk)

DOI: 10.4324/9781315585390

Contents

List of Tables

The History of Retailing and Consumption
General Editor's Preface

It is increasingly recognized that retail systems and changes in the patterns of consumption play crucial roles in the development and societal structure of economies. Such recognition has led to renewed interest in the changing nature of retail distribution and the rise of consumer society from a wide range of academic disciplines. The aim of this multidisciplinary series is to provide a forum of publications that explore the history of retailing and consumption.

Gareth Shaw, University of Exeter, UK

Acknowledgments

This project began its life as a rather hastily written, and not entirely convincing, graduate seminar paper. That it has reached its current incarnation as a book is testimony to the wonderful support I have received over the years. Research and writing was made possible by funds provided by a Washington University dissertation writer's grant, various Washington University summer research grants, and professional development funds provided by Webster University, St. Louis. Washington University's Dissertation Writers' Workshops and Early Modern Reading Groups have provided pleasant and collegial forums for me to share chapter drafts at various stages of development. I also thank the journal *Seventeenth Century*, through its website www.tandfonline.com, for allowing me to republish a slightly modified version of my article "Three Women and Goose Make a Market" as Chapter 2 of this book. At early stages of research, Alice Wolfram, Alexandra Shepard, and Craig Muldrew provided advice on how to navigate the archives; and the impeccable helpfulness and efficiency of the staffs of various English archival offices and, in particular, the Cambridge University Archive, made research a productive and rewarding experience. I'd also like to thank my colleagues at Webster University in the department of History, Politics, and International Relations for their friendliness and encouragement. Our department is located in a big, old house built by the inventor of Tums, but our departmental atmosphere is such that I take surprisingly few antacids.

A number of individuals have been crucial in helping me improve this book. Christine Johnson provided advice on several chapters; she and Tim Parsons taught me much about the craft of historical research and writing. Daniel Bornstein generously provided detailed editorial commentary on the dissertation upon which this book is based. Above all, my greatest intellectual debt is to Derek Hirst, who was unflagging in his willingness to read and comment on chapter draft after chapter draft. Without his advice, my writing would have much less clear, and my arguments would have been much less sharp. I can hardly thank him enough. I alone am responsible for any lingering mistakes.

I also owe a great many debts to family and friends for providing much needed moral support. Matt Brown, Jill Storm, and Chris Pepus helped make scholarly endeavors fun at a crucial time. My parents were my first, and remain, my greatest teachers; this book would not be possible without them. My sons, Henry and Oliver, remind me that there are things in life even more important than finishing a book. Finally, my wife Karin knows all too well the perils of living with an anxious, distracted author. Throughout she has provided me with love and support for what many times I feared was a quixotic quest. That's why I dedicate the book to her.

List of Abbreviations

APC	Acts of the Privy Council
BL	British Library
Bodl. Lib.	Bodleian Library, Oxford University
BrRO	Bristol Record Office
c.	*contra*
CKS	Centre for Kentish Studies, Maidstone
CUA	Cambridge University Archive
DRO	Dorset Records Office, Dorchester
EcHR	*Economic History Review*
ERO	Essex Record Office, Chelmsford
ESRO	East Suffolk Record Office, Ipswich
HampRO	Hampshire Record Office, Winchester
HertRO	Hertfordshire Record Office, Hertford
HMC	*Historical Manuscripts Commissions, Reports*
JP	Justice of the Peace
LMA	London Metropolitan Archives
OED	*Oxford English Dictionary*
OUA	Oxford University Archive
P&P	*Past and Present*
Pepys Ballads	Hyder Edward Rollins (ed.), *The Pepys Ballads* (8 vols, Cambridge, Mass.: Harvard University Press, 1929–1932)
PRO	Public Record Office, Kew
Rox. Ballads	W.M. Chappell and J. Woodfall Ebsworth (eds), *The Roxburghe Ballads* (8 vols, London and Hertford: The Ballad Society, 1871–1897)
SCA	Southampton City Archives
SRO	Somerset Record Office, Taunton
WRO	Wiltshire Record Office, Trowbridge

Chapter 1
Introduction: Households, Marketplaces, and Neighborhoods

This book argues that women traders were central to the commercial life of early modern English towns. It attempts not only to reconstruct the types of work trading women did, but also their business practices, mentalities, and relationships with town authorities and neighbors. As Pamela Sharpe has argued, the study of women's working roles can reveal more than the nature of gender inequality; it can also teach us much about the operation of the early modern economy.[1] We should therefore be as interested in what the experiences and activities of tradeswomen tell us about the commercial culture and social life of urban communities as we are in what they tell us about the gendered division of labor.

The contention that women could wield influence over commerce would have been unsurprising to contemporary observers of the early modern marketplace. An early seventeenth-century penny-priced ballad entitled "An excellent new Ditty" proposed that "women the best Warriers be, for they made the Devill from earth … to flee."[2] Looking for merriment, "Old Beelzebub" visits the marketplace in order to offer leases of eternal life. He makes deals with a cast of greedy characters—tradesmen and their wives; gallants and disobedient "roaring sons"; usurers and corn-hoarding landowners—before finally being driven away by the fishwives of Billingsgate market in London. The women terrify the Devil by raising a ferocious "noyse"; they "brabled with [each] other/ [over] which first should have choise" of his offering. The Devil concludes:

> "I must [flee] from them,
> for, should I stay here,
> In pieces, among them,
> My body they'd tear!"
> (Quoth he) "I am willing
> to deale among men,

[1] Pamela Sharpe, "Continuity and Change: Women's History and Economic History in Britain," *EcHR*, new series, 48 (May, 1995): 353–69.

[2] *Rox. Ballads*, vol. 1, pp. 331–6, quote from p. 336. For other examples, see Martin Parker, "Have among you! Good women," in *Rox. Ballads*, vol. 1, pp. 436–7, and "The Country-Man's Kalender, Or, His Astrological-Predictions for the ensuing Year, 1692," in *The Bagford Ballads: Illustrating the Last Years of the Stuarts*, (ed.) Joseph Woodfall Ebsworth (2 vols, Hertford: Stephen Austin and Sons, 1878), vol. 1, p. 188.

> But nere will have dealing
> 'mongst women agen!"

The anonymous author of this ballad was hardly alone in claiming that market women were too forceful, too "warrior-like" in their dealings. Ballad writers and dramatists clearly spotted a commercial opportunity in gendered anxieties, for they populated their tales with caricatures of aggressive working women. Learned authors of household conduct books may have had less of an eye for sales, but they too accused trading women of breaches of feminine decorum.[3] Moreover, trading women's aggressive pursuit of profits worried moralists who believed that the rapacious pursuit of wealth and possessions—signified in the ballad by their attempts to purchase immortality, that priceless item—undermined the provision of necessities to consumers at a fair price, the proper purpose of commerce. The prescriptive and popular printed sources of the sixteenth and seventeenth centuries reflected a desire for a commercial and gendered order which seemed troublingly out of reach. So too did the emerging architecture of sixteenth- and seventeenth-century market towns. Many of these towns invested in new town halls to house market officials. These halls sometimes featured "surveillance" galleries on the second story from which market officials could observe the traders below; they were testimony to the contemporary belief that the urban moral, economic, and gender order would fall apart without proper oversight.[4]

Gender historians have often cited early modern women's trading activities to complicate the simplistic notion that women were confined to a separate domestic "sphere."[5] But they have rarely been as curious about early modern trading women as they have been about these women's contemporary critics and regulators.[6] Since the 1919 publication of Alice Clark's landmark *Working Life of Women in the Seventeenth Century*, scholars have offered competing theories about women's loss of occupational opportunities in the sixteenth and seventeenth centuries. This debate has largely overlooked trading women. Overviews of the subject emphasize women's lack of access to high-paying and high-status craft and mercantile

---

[3] See below, Chapter 2.

[4] Robert Tittler, *Architecture and Power. The Town Hall and the English Urban Community c. 1500–1640* (Oxford: Clarendon Press, 1991), pp. 14, 134–5.

[5] Amanda Vickery, "Golden Age to Separate Spheres? A Review of the Categories and Chronology of English Women's History," *Historical Journal* 36 (1993): 408–9; Bernard Capp, "Separate Domains? Women and Authority in Early Modern England" in *The Experience of Authority in Early Modern England*, (ed.) Paul Griffiths, Adam Fox and Steve Hindle (London: Macmillan, 1996), pp. 121, 128; Anthony Fletcher, *Gender, Sex and Subordination in England 1500–1800* (New Haven: Yale University Press, 1995), pp. 244–6.

[6] For an important exception which focuses on plebeian women's engagement in credit networks and pawnbroking, see Beverly Lemire, *The Business of Everyday Life: Gender, Practice and Social Politics in England, c. 1600–1900* (Manchester: Manchester University Press, 2005).

trades.[7] Studies of specific occupations have focused on those jobs—commercial brewing and baking, midwifery, and dairy farming—from which women were gradually excluded.[8] Because most early modern trading women operated on the retail level, often on behalf of male householders, it has been easy to assume that their activities merely confirm gloomy interpretations of women's earning power and economic agency.[9]

If the long-running focus on working women's occupational status has deflected our attention from trading women (whose activities often did not fit neatly with early modern conceptions of occupation), so too has the common, but tacit, assumption that women's involvement in urban commerce has little to tell us about the practice of a broader business and commercial culture. Historians of plebeian protests, most famously E.P. Thompson, once emphasized the role of the female shopper turned rioter. And yet Thompson and others considered women's commercial interests only in terms of the experience of buying, not in terms of selling.[10] Poor women were, in such accounts, merely reacting to the failure of

---

[7] Sara Mendelson and Patricia Crawford, *Women in Early Modern England 1500–1720* (Oxford: Clarendon Press, 1998), chs 5–6; Susan Cahn, *Industry of Devotion. The Transformation of Women's Work in England, 1500–1660* (New York: Columbia University Press, 1987); Marjorie Keniston McIntosh, *Working Women in English Society, 1300–1620* (Cambridge: Cambridge University Press, 2005).

[8] For example, see Judith Bennett, *Ale, Beer and Brewsters in England. Women's Work in a Changing World, 1300–1600* (Oxford and New York: Oxford University Press, 1996); McIntosh, *Working Women in English Society*, ch. 6 (on brewing) and ch. 7 (on baking); Jean Donnison, *Midwives and Medical Men: A History for the Control of Childbirth* 2nd edn (Stroud: Phillimore, 1999); Deborah Valenze, "The Art of Women and the Business of Men: Women's Work and the Dairy Industry c. 1740–1840," *P&P*, 130 (1991): 142–69. In addition to tracking women's exclusion from the brewing trades, Bennett has also contested the narrative of decline—what she calls the "familiar backbeat" of early modern women's history—by highlighting the common challenges late medieval and seventeenth-century working women faced across the centuries. Thus, Bennett argues, women were only excluded from brewing once it became a more lucrative, high-status trade. Her research has had the salutary effect of undermining the notion that a "golden age" of women's work is somewhere to be found in the middle ages or the early modern period; gender inequality in working roles was persistent across the centuries. For her most recent formulation of the case for continuity, see *History Matters: Patriarchy and the Challenge of Feminism* (Philadelphia: University of Pennsylvania Press, 2006), ch. 5, quote from p. 85.

[9] For example, see McIntosh, *Working Women in English Society*, pp. 122–32.

[10] E.P. Thomson, "The Moral Economy of the English Crowd," *P&P* 50 (1971): 115–17; Peter Clark, "Popular Protest and Disturbance in Kent, 1558–1640," *EcHR*, new series, 29 (1976): 376–7; Mendelson and Crawford, *Women in Early Modern England*, pp. 44, 385–6; Bernard Capp, *When Gossips Meet: Women, Family, and Neighbourhood in Early Modern England* (Oxford: Oxford University Press, 2003), pp. 316–17. The latest study of food riots questions how instrumental female consumers were in participating in riots: John Bohstedt, *The Politics of Provision: Food Riots, Moral Economy, and the Market Transition in England, c. 1550–1850* (Farnham and Burlington: Ashgate, 2010), p. 45.

local officials to enforce paternalistic custom and law. Historians have seen female retailers as having even less influence over the norms of commerce than riotous consumers. Hemmed in by market regulators on the one hand, and by the practices of wealthy male wholesalers on the other, they were, according to one of the few studies of market women, facing a marketplace which they "never regulated; could rarely influence; but to whose changing structures they were required to adjust."[11] When historians have turned to how women conducted business, they have often limited their investigations to poor women attempting to patch together an "economy of makeshifts."[12] Of course poor women, out of necessity, often broke commercial rules or dealt dishonestly with customers. As one scholar has put it, "self-preservation was the name of the game and any means of accomplishing this was justified."[13] Early modern trading women appear resilient, yet always on the defensive; they reacted to, but could scarcely shape, the commercial culture of their communities.

Contemporary observers would have been surprised to learn that market women were largely powerless in the face of commercial change. Indeed, the influence of early modern women over the marketplace made many uneasy. It is, after all, the fishwives who swarm the market in the "Excellent New Ditty." Drawings and woodcuts depicting the marketplace almost always included women as both retailers and consumers. In his 1598 pamphlet on Londoners' sharp trading practices, Hugh Alley populated his sketches of London markets with female stallholders and hucksters.[14] In the illustrated broadside *Tittle-Tattle; Or the Several Branches of Gossiping*, a satirical attack on female sociability, women dominate the marketplace—trading, gossiping, and sharply observing the delivery and weighing of foodstuffs.[15] The gendered stereotypes in these images are easy to identify. Often unregistered is that they also reflect the power women could wield in the world of local commerce. The fact that many women combined their roles as managers of household resources, consumers and retailers, placed them in a strategic position from which they could, if not regulate, at least shape how traders conducted business. Trading women didn't need to riot to exert pressure. Detailed knowledge of prices, customs, and regulations; friendly contacts with officials and neighbors; an ability to spread information that could make or break

[11] W. Thwaites, "Women in the Market Place: Oxfordshire *c.* 1690–1800," *Midland History* 9 (1984): 23.

[12] The term was coined by Olwen Hufton in *The Poor of Eighteenth-Century France, 1750–1789* (Oxford: Clarendon Press, 1974).

[13] Penelope Lane, "Work on the Margins: Poor Women and the Informal Economy of Eighteenth and Early Nineteenth-Century Leicestershire," *Midland History* 12 (1997): 85–99 (quote from p. 94).

[14] Hugh Alley, *Hugh Alley's Caveat: Markets of London in 1598*, (ed.) Ian Archer, Caroline Barron, and Vanessa Harding (London: London Topographical Society, 1988).

[15] *Tittle-Tattle; Or the Several Branches of Gossiping*, British Museum.

a rival's reputation: these were intangible assets, but possession of them gave women considerable influence over the conduct of local commerce.

This book focuses on the late sixteenth and early seventeenth centuries, a period in which England experienced the birth pangs of a commercial revolution.[16] It is commonplace to observe that every period is one of both continuity and change; nevertheless the century—which followed several centuries of steady demographic and economic growth and preceded the relative prosperity of the late seventeenth and eighteenth centuries—was one of awkward transition. The moralists, economic thinkers, and policy makers of the period took a particularly dim view of profiteering.[17] Suspicions of covetousness were not unique to the time, but they were given urgency by economic crises and threats of social upheaval. Several decades of abundant harvests were punctuated by the severe dearths of the 1590s.[18] Trade disruptions and harvest failures in the 1620s and 1630s brought another round of misery.[19] In the face of rising poverty and uncertainty—and the protests they provoked—it is unsurprising that authorities worried that the paternalistic order, in which commerce was to be regulated for the good of the commonwealth, was in danger of fraying.

And yet the late sixteenth and early seventeenth centuries were marked by new opportunities as well as perils. Population growth and new consumer demands prompted manufacturing and commercial entrepreneurship. The rise of rural industries to satisfy demand for novel consumer goods—including such items as playing cards, tobacco pipes, and glassware—was one response; the growing

---

16 The most recent overviews of the economy of the period stress both economic growth and new uncertainties: Keith Wrightson, *Earthly Necessities. Economic Lives In Early Modern Britain* (New Haven and London: Yale University Press, 2000); C.G.A. Clay, *Economic Expansion and Social Change: England 1500–1700* (2 vols, Cambridge: Cambridge University Press, 1985).

17 A persuasive corrective to the claim that the godly invariably celebrated the pursuit of wealth was offered some time ago by Laura Stevenson O'Connell: "Anti-Entrepreneurial Attitudes in Elizabethan Sermons and Popular Literature," *Journal of British Studies* 15 (Spring 1976): 1–20. For the assumptions of economic thinkers and policy makers, see Andrea Finkelstein, *Harmony and Balance: An Intellectual History of Seventeenth-Century English Economic Thought* (Ann Arbor: University of Michigan Press, 2000).

18 On dearth in the 1590s, and the fears of authorities which accompanied it, see Jim Sharpe, "Social Strain and Social Dislocation, 1585–1603," in *The Reign of Elizabeth I: Court and Culture in the Last Decade*, (ed.) John Guy (Cambridge: Cambridge University Press, 1995), pp. 192–211.

19 Barry Supple's *Commercial Crisis and Change in England, 1600–1642* (Cambridge: Cambridge University Press, 1964) remains the classic account of disruptions in the seventeenth-century overseas cloth trade and the resulting unemployment. For food riots and workers' protests during the period, see Buchanan Sharp, *In Contempt of All Authority: Rural Artisans and Riot in the West of England, 1586–1660* (Berkeley: University of California Press, 1980).

number of retail shops in sixteenth- and seventeenth-century towns was another.[20] The growth of English provincial towns is another indication of adaptation and resilience. The spectacular expansion of London once overshadowed studies of early modern urbanity, but more recent studies have highlighted the robustness of late sixteenth- and seventeenth-century provincial towns.[21] As Penelope Corfield has found, "A more complex and polycentric urban society was emerging, with a concomitant growth in the number of large towns and a broadening range of economic specialization."[22] Early modern England, of course, remained a predominately agrarian society, but the importance of provincial towns cannot be measured by size alone, for they brought commercial development to the countryside.[23] The demographic recovery and expansion of English towns after the contraction of the fourteenth and fifteenth centuries certainly brought social problems, including higher rates of disease, vagrancy, and poverty. Nevertheless, migration from rural to urban areas suggests that economic opportunities were to be had for both men and women in England's provincial towns. This book explores women's commercial work in the context of three institutions which shaped the early modern commercial economy: the household, the marketplace, and the urban neighborhood.

---

[20] For new rural industries in the sixteenth and seventeenth centuries, see Joan Thirsk, *Economic Policy and Projects: The Development of a Consumer Society in Early Modern England* (Oxford: Clarendon Press, 1978). For a pioneering study which shows the increasing prevalence of shops in the late sixteenth and seventeenth centuries, see Nancy Cox, *The Complete Tradesman: A Study in Retailing, 1550–1820* (Burlington and Farnham: Ashgate, 2000).

[21] For the classic pessimistic account of early modern towns, see Peter Clark and Paul Slack, "Introduction," in *Crisis and Order in English Towns 1500–1700: Essays in Urban History*, ed. Peter Clark and Paul Slack (Toronto: University of Toronto Press, 1972), pp. 1–56. For more optimistic appraisals which stress the resilience and adaptability of town economies, see Nigel Goose, "Economic and Social Aspects of Provincial Towns: A Comparative Study of Cambridge, Colchester and Reading, c. 1500–1700" (PhD diss., Cambridge University, 1984); Nigel Goose, "English Pre-Industrial Urban Economies," and Penelope Corfield, "Urban Development in England and Wales in the Sixteenth and Seventeenth Centuries," both in *The Tudor and Stuart Town: A Reader in English Urban History 1530–1688*, ed. Jonathan Barry (London and New York: Longman, 1990). For the growth of provincial urban communities, see Clay, *Economic Expansion and Social change*, vol. 1, ch. 6.

[22] Corfield, "Urban Developments in England and Wales," p. 58.

[23] Christopher Dyer, "The Consumer and the Market in the Later Middle Ages," *EcHR*, new series, 42 (Aug., 1989): 305–27. See also Richard Phillips, "Grassroots Change in an Early Modern Economy: The Emergence of a rural Consumer Economy in Berkshire," *Southern History* 11 (1989): 23–39.

Household, Marketplace, Neighborhood

Early modern writers and urban authorities assumed that the stable, economically autonomous patriarchal household was the foundation of the urban social order. They likened households to little commonwealths in which the male householder, his wife, children, servants, and apprentices all had their places within a hierarchy. Sir Thomas Smith, drawing upon Aristotle's classification of political regimes, described the household as an aristocracy—"one of the best kindes of a common wealth"—in which "a few and the best [of the household] doth governe" the matters for which they are best fit. Thus, male heads of household—possessing the greatest strength, courage, and powers of reason— were public representatives of the household, and worked abroad to supply the needs of the household; the wife managed the house and its resources, though she was to get her way through her beauty and persuasive "sweete words" rather than by physical force or strength of mind.[24] While Smith invoked Aristotle, clergy turned to biblical exegesis to legitimate the patriarchal household and its accompanying gendered division of labor. With their different sets of ancient sources, Smith and the clerics underscored the timelessness, and permanence, of properly structured household relations.

Town officials imagined urban communities as "confederations" of such households, and so it is little wonder that when they considered economic activity, they continued to think in terms of the household *oeconomy* rather than of an impersonal market *economy*.[25] The assumptions of early modern thinkers have leaked into historians' accounts. Most historians have continued to envision the household *oeconomy* as a pre-modern institution: traditional, resistant to change, and supportive of the social and gender hierarchy. Social historians have thus argued that work patterns in ordinary households had less to do with building wealth than with pursuing traditional methods of insuring survival and household respectability.[26] Feminist interpretations of the household economy have focused on how patriarchal precepts and the legal privileges of husbands entrenched a gendered "dual labor market" which relegated women to unskilled, low paid or unpaid domestic working roles, thus ensuring the status of male householders; the implication is that proper patriarchs could not suffer their women to do work which required skill and brought a certain status.[27]

---

[24] Sir Thomas Smith, *De Republica Anglorum*, (ed.) Mary Dewer (Cambridge: Cambridge University Press, 1982), p. 59.

[25] Jonathan Barry, "Bourgeois Collectivism? Urban Association and the Middling Sort," in *The Middling Sort of People: Culture, Society and Politics in England, 1550–1800*, ed. Jonathan Barry and C.W. Brooks (New York: St. Martin's Press, 1994), p. 95; Keith Wrightson, *Earthly Necessities*, p. 30.

[26] Wrightson, *Earthly Necessities*, p. 56.

[27] The phrase is from Katrina Honeyman and Jordan Goodman, "Women's Work, Gender Conflict and Labour Markets in Europe, 1500–1900," *EcHR*, new series, 44 (Nov. 1991): 608–28.

Do early modern women's trading activities fit historians' vision of the patriarchal, hidebound household economy? Women workers did not trade only because they were excluded from apprenticeships in skilled crafts. Significant "pull" factors made trading more attractive than gender-specific occupations such as the work done by charmaids, spinners, and nurses. As Jan de Vries has argued, early modern households were not so wedded to autarky that they were unresponsive to emerging market forces; male householders, and their wives, were opportunistic. During the course of what de Vries calls the "industrious revolution," the expansion of markets prompted workers—and rural women in particular—to spend less time producing goods for home consumption, and to spend more time specializing in producing goods for sale in the market, the proceeds from which they used to purchase household necessities previously (and less efficiently) produced at home.[28] A similar dynamic was at work in late sixteenth- and seventeenth-century urban communities. Population growth, rising consumer demand, and the decline in real wages made paid work less attractive than trading. Women, whether selling the goods produced by their husbands or trading on their own, were attentive to the commercial opportunities open to them. The profits they brought in gave husbands a powerful incentive to make accommodations for their wives' commercial activities.

The tensions which accompanied new commercial opportunities were supposed to be mitigated by the town marketplace.[29] In the sixteenth and seventeenth centuries, marketplaces were more than convenient sites to do business. They were institutions intended to impose a moral—and a social and gendered—order upon commercial activity. The regulations of the marketplace reflected, according to Keith Wrightson, "the values of an economic culture in which the benefits of commercial exchange were fully recognized, but regarded nonetheless as subordinate to the need to exercise control in the interests of the wellbeing of the immediate community."[30] Markets were held on specific days of the week, and governed by a corps of market officials who tried to curb dishonest and sharp dealing by inspecting weights and measures, doling out fines for shoddy goods or rotten foodstuffs, and capping prices of necessary commodities. They also banned or curtailed the practices of middlemen, which included forestalling

---

[28] Jan de Vries, "Between Purchasing Power and the World of Goods: Understanding the Household Economy in Early Modern Europe," in *Consumption and the World of Goods*, (ed.) John Brewer and Roy Porter (London: Routledge, 1993), pp. 85–132.

[29] The following description of the rules and regulations of markets is based on Alan Everitt, "The Marketing of Agricultural Produce," in *The Agrarian History of England and Wales* vol. 6, *1500–1640*, (ed.) Joan Thirsk (Cambridge: Cambridge University Press, 1967); Alan Dyer, "Small Market Towns 1540–1700," and Michael Reed, "The Urban Landscape 1540–1700," both in *The Cambridge Urban History of Britain* vol. 2, *1540–1840*, (ed.) Peter Clark (Cambridge: Cambridge University Press, 2000), pp. 429, 438–40, 302; Alley, *Hugh Alley's Caveat*, pp. 5–7.

[30] Wrightson, *Earthly Necessities*, p. 111.

(the interception and purchase of producers' goods before they reached the market), regrating (the purchase of market goods for resale), and engrossing (the attempt through purchases to corner the market in a particular good in order to drive prices higher). These regulations were meant to ensure that producers sold directly to consumers at a just price.

The spatial organization of the marketplace and its surrounding architecture underscored the regulatory ambitions of its officials. Markets were held at designated sites—usually a triangular or square space at the center of town. In order to make business easier to monitor, officials designated each type of commodity and its traders an assigned place, specified which goods could be sold at which hours, and often used a bell to signal when certain types of commodities could be traded. Officials attempted to keep undesirable traders away by enforcing regulations which allowed only those with the freedom of the town, or their representatives, to trade freely; other respectable householders, or their representatives, could trade, provided that a market fee was paid. Women retailers were supposed to be qualified widows in charge of their own households or wives or servants trading on behalf of qualified male householders. The officials who regulated the market kept the official weights and measures in the town hall. In an interesting but, as Phil Withington has shown, common inversion of the usual association of men with public spaces and women with private spaces, the owners of the marketplaces usually found it to their advantage to allow women to trade in the public space, but they reserved the private deliberations on how to regulate the marketplace to male officials within the enclosed chambers of the town hall.[31] Late sixteenth- and seventeenth-century towns invested heavily in marketplaces, a development which helped bring markets within walking distance of many rural producers and consumers. England in the late sixteenth century had a little fewer than 650 markets; by 1700, it had 750.[32] By this measure, the town marketplace and the values it embodied seemed triumphant.

But, as women's commercial activities suggest, the importance of the marketplace was more apparent than real. In urban communities, markets were not dominant commercial institutions but rather loose foci around which men and women conducted business. Paradoxically, because marketplaces attracted producers and their goods they were also magnets for traders, both men and women, whose commercial activities undermined the very principles upheld by the market regulations. Buyers regularly intercepted suppliers on their way to the market; others bought goods in the marketplace with the expectation of selling them later and elsewhere at a higher price. Profits from such activities were made possible by the fact that the marketplace was not the only commercial venue. As that piece of contemporary wisdom "three women and a goose make a market"

---

31 Phil Withington, *The Politics of Commonwealth: Citizens and Freemen in Early Modern England* (Cambridge: Cambridge University Press, 2005), ch. 7.

32 Dyer, "Small Market Towns," p. 431.

suggests, women did business almost anywhere they pleased.[33] Women bought and sold in shops, streets, alleys, and even alehouses and taverns.[34] The private house itself, even if unattached to a shop, was a common business site, with women trading inside, at the front doorstep, or at the kitchen backdoor. In these varied places, they often traded in defiance of marketplace rules and prohibitions. This presented few difficulties because their dealings were unlikely to be observed by town officials who were badly overstretched. What is surprising about women's commercial activities was not the level of restrictions they faced, but the ease with which they navigated and traversed both private and public spaces in the pursuit of profit.[35]

The early modern urban "market" was thus far more expansive than the legal, spatially circumscribed marketplace. The period did not, of course, witness the rise of an impersonal "free market" dreamed of by University of Chicago economists, in which the unfettered play of supply and demand alone determines the decisions of cool-minded, rational agents. Indeed, it was precisely by cultivating amiable relations with their neighbors, customers, and creditors—by building what social scientists term "social capital"—that trading women succeeded in business.[36] Nevertheless the dealings of women outside the marketplace suggest that even as towns and villages were building new marketplaces, England's commercial culture was outgrowing traditional institutional structures and strictures.

If the needs of the household encouraged women to engage in trading, the urban neighborhood, an informal institution often ignored by historians of early modern working women, provided a crucial environment within which women could profitably pursue business. In the crowded early modern urban environment,

---

33 William George Smith (ed.), *The Oxford Dictionary of English Proverbs* (Oxford: Clarendon Press, 1935), p. 491; Morris Palmer Tilley (ed.), *A Dictionary of Proverbs in England in the Sixteenth and Seventeenth Centuries: A Collection of Proverbs Found in English Literature and the Dictionaries of the Period* (Ann Arbor: University of Michigan Press, 1950), p. 746.

34 For shops, see Cox, *The Complete Tradesman*, ch. 2. For an attempt to explore street trading, see David Pennington, "Taking it to the Streets: Hucksters and Huckstering in Early Modern Southampton, ca. 1550–1652," *Sixteenth Century Journal* 39, no. 3 (2008): 657–79. Amanda Flather has shown that women visited public houses with surprising frequency, though she does not discuss their business dealings in these venues: *Gender and Space in Early Modern England* (Woodbridge: Boydell, 2007), p. 112.

35 Compare with the more pessimistic picture presented by Laura Gowing, "'The Freedom of the Streets': Women and Social Space, 1560–1640," in *Londinopolis. Essays in the Cultural and Social History of Early Modern London*, (ed.) Paul Griffiths and Mark S.R. Jenner (Manchester and New York: Manchester University Press, 2000), pp. 130–53.

36 For an account of early modern German women which emphasizes their lack of social capital, see Sheilagh Ogilvie, *A Bitter Living: Women, Markets, and Social Capital in Early Modern Germany* (Oxford: Oxford University Press, 2003). Ogilvie, however, focuses on women's exclusion from formal institutions such as guilds and town governments, rather than their connections with the informal networks of the neighborhood.

households were linked by proximity, friendships, rivalries, credit arrangements, and business relationships. Neighborhoods were the sites of interlocking networks within which people spent their working and social lives. These communities were defined by a set of mores which determined standing not just in terms of class or gender, but also in terms of personal or household credibility, honesty, and morality. "Good neighborliness" was thus a set of "horizontal" obligations which stressed not just deference to superiors but also honest living, creditworthiness, and Christian neighborly love.[37] Within the context of the neighborhood, a trading woman's success often had less to do with her adherence to the conventional code of feminine decorum and more to do with the respectability of her household and the honesty of her trading practices.

Because trading women were often important commercial agents in their own right they played important roles in the disputes which marked England's transition toward a commercial economy. Social historians have already suggested the power women could wield in the micro-politics of the neighborhood. While these historians have remained attentive to power imbalances between men and women, they have nonetheless come to recognize the ways in which women could at times exploit gaps and tensions within patriarchal culture. Historians in the new field of masculinity studies have led the way in questioning simplistic assumptions about the nature of patriarchal authority. Elizabeth Foyster and Alexandra Shepard have pointed out that for many the ideal of the patriarchal master—economically self-sufficient and in firm control of the women of his household—was out of reach.[38] When issues of household respectability and communal moral norms were at stake, the deference wives owed to husbands was not always assumed to be applicable to relationships between male and female neighbors. When it came to disputes over sexual honesty, local women regularly confronted offenders, both male and female. Many were the women who identified and shamed local men and women who failed to live "chastely."[39] Local women also denigrated men who

---

[37] Keith Wrightson, *English Society 1580–1680* (London: Routledge, 1982), pp. 50–57; Jeremy Boulton, *Neighbourhood and Society: A London Suburb in the Seventeenth Century* (Cambridge: Cambridge University Press, 1987), chs. 9–10.

[38] Elizabeth Foyster, *Manhood in Early Modern England: Honour, Sex and Marriage* (London and New York: Longman, 1999), ch. 4; Alexandra Shepard, *Meanings of Manhood in Early Modern England* (Oxford: Oxford University Press, 2003), chs 4, 7.

[39] Male "whoremasters" and fornicators may have suffered less communal opprobrium than women who gained a reputation for incontinence, but their activities did engender communal disapproval. See Bernard Capp, "The Double Standard Revisited: Plebian Women and Male Sexual Reputation in Early Modern England," *P&P* 162 (1999): 70–100; Foyster, *Manhood in Early Modern England*, ch. 3. Compare with Laura Gowing, *Domestic Dangers: Women, Words, and Sex in Early Modern London* (Oxford: Clarendon Press, 1996) which discusses women's disputes over sexual honesty in much detail, though she is skeptical of women's abilities to substantially damage the reputations of male enemies because, Gowing argues, sexual honesty was central to a woman's reputation in a way that it wasn't for men.

drank too much, were cruel to their wives, or were too lazy to provide for their families. Studies of social networks and neighborhood conflicts have revealed plentiful evidence of female assertiveness.[40] But what has yet to be uncovered are the ways in which women's participation in disputes shaped commercial culture.

Sources and Definitions

However prominent to contemporary observers of urban life, trading women have remained liminal to historians' understanding of women and work. A major difficulty is presented by the record-keeping practices of local authorities, practices which reflected the ideal of a structured, gendered labor market that did little justice to the complex reality of early modern urban commercial life. While court clerks and town officials regularly recorded the occupations of male artisans, merchants, laborers, and husbandmen, they most commonly designated trading women by marital status, not their work roles. Furthermore, they regularly failed to describe the work of traders who worked in service industries outside regulated crafts and trades. The closest some medieval and early modern authorities came to labeling some trading women by occupational status was their designation of women street traders as "hucksters"—the feminine counterpart to the word "hawker," which referred to male street sellers (just as a "brewster"—as opposed to a "brewer"—referred to a woman who brewed drink). This study uses the terms "market women" and "trading women" as convenient ways to designate those women who vended goods in, or around, the marketplace—either on their own or as agents of male householders.

Such trading and market women are less visible in the historical record than guild members or wealthy male merchants, but they can be found if we know where to look. Particularly informative for reconstructing the goods women traded and the kinds of commercial practices they engaged in are the records of courts leet, petty courts which were sometimes charged with prosecuting offenders against marketplace rules. The detailed records of the courts leet of Cambridge University (which oversaw the market of the town), Southampton, Manchester, Liverpool, and Carlisle reveal much about women who sold goods on behalf of men or on their own.[41] An important reason to focus our study on Cambridge in particular is

---

40 Bernard Capp, *When Gossips Meet*; R.A. Houlbrooke, "Women's Social Life and Common Action from the Fifteenth Century to the Eve of the Civil War," *Continuity and Change* vol. 1, no. 2 (1986): 171–89.

41 In Southampton and Manchester, the court leet was presided over by the mayor. The origins of Cambridge University's proctors' court leet was somewhat different from other leets. The University had dominated the economic administration by right of a 1382 royal grant in response to the town's disloyalty during the Peasant Revolt. Thus, the Vice-Chancellor presided over the town's leet, and also held the right to set prices, hold the assizes of bread and ale, and license victualers. See Alexandra Shepard, "Contesting

the survival of the University's court records charged with overseeing the town's two major fairs, Midsummer (or Barnwell) Fair and Stourbridge Fair (held for three weeks in September). These records provide considerable information on women's commercial activities in the fairs. Midsummer Fair, the less important of the two, drew most of its traders from Cambridgeshire and neighboring counties, and its most important commodities were wholesale goods, such as timber, coal, groceries, and hops.[42] Stourbridge Fair was early modern England's largest fair, and drew visitors from all of England eager to trade in foodstuffs, malt, cloth, and all manner of manufactured wares. The playwright Thomas Dekker, hinting at a rapacious commercial culture, observed in 1608 that Stourbridge Fair was where "from all other partes men [and, he should have added, women] in Multitudes repayre to Suck the sweetness of honest gayness and so to increase theyr wealth."[43] A study of prosecutions of women traders who evaded or defied the regulations governing markets and fairs exposes the divergence between the ideology of the moral economy—enshrined in local regulations and parliamentary statute—and the actual practice of commerce.

The records of fair courts and courts leet are invaluable in reconstructing market women's tactics, but they reveal little about how these traders were able to persist in the face of prejudices, or how they succeeded in balancing the values of charity and good neighborliness with the increasingly commercial culture of the era. In order to fill out the social context within which women traders operated, this study will explore the records of civil disputes heard by the Oxford University chancellor's court and the Cambridge University courts of the vice-chancellor and his commissary. These courts of course held jurisdiction over university members, but they were also entitled to hear cases involving any resident, and that resident's spouse, who in some way did business with the university. The university courts records are, as Alexandra Shepard has shown, "particularly informative" for any reconstruction of the social and economic life of these two commercially vibrant towns because much of the business done revolved around the economic disputes of ordinary townspeople.[44]

The legal peculiarities of the university courts make them a rich source for the study of women's involvement in the commercial urban economy. Because of their jurisdiction over the marketplaces, the university courts, in much the same way as the courts leet, prosecuted traders who broke commercial regulations.

Communities? 'Town' and 'Gown' in Cambridge, c. 1560–1640," in *Communities in Early Modern England: Networks, Place, Rhetoric*, (ed.) Alexandra Shepard and Phil Withington (Manchester: Manchester University Press, 2000), pp. 218–19.

[42] Mary Christine Siraut, "Some Aspects of the Economic and Social History of Cambridge Under Elizabeth I" (M.Litt thesis, Cambridge University, 1978), p. 111.

[43] Quoted in Siraut, "Economic and Social History of Cambridge," p.89. See also p. 114, table 4.

[44] Alexandra Shepard, "Litigation and Locality: the Cambridge University Courts, 1560–1640," *Urban History* 31, no. 1 (2004): 7–8, 21, table 4.

In addition, they heard a broad range of civil disputes, including the types of debt and defamation cases heard by the borough courts of other towns. Unlike most borough courts, however, the university courts accepted written and depositional evidence in their hearing of debt and injury cases; as a result, their archives contain an unusually rich written record of the testimony of women plaintiffs, defendants, and witnesses, regarding a wide variety of commercial disputes. The university courts, like borough courts, observed the common law doctrine of coverture, which designated husbands as the legal representatives of their wives and as caretakers and controllers of the common property of the household. But, as the depositional evidence from the university courts shows, many debt suits that ostensibly involved only male litigants actually stemmed from the transactions conducted by the litigants' wives. Furthermore, women frequently gave depositions on behalf of plaintiffs and defendants; these records illuminate their working lives and their commercial relationships with their neighbors.

A final set of sources for the study of women's involvement in commerce is popular literature and entertainments—cheap broadsides, penny-priced ballads, and the city comedies of the seventeenth century. These works were meant to cater to the appetites of as wide an audience as possible. While it would be foolhardy to use such sources in lieu of archival records, cheap print and city comedies can nevertheless help us recapture the assumptions and the mental world of everyday people, at least as it was imagined by the authors and playwrights who catered to popular tastes. Consumers of popular literature—men and women—enjoyed representations of transgressive, combative, scheming trading women because such characters reflected on the often absurd contradictions between contemporary gender rules and the circumstances of everyday life. The next chapter explores these contradictions.

Chapter 2

Prescription, Anxiety, and Acceptance: Representations of Market Women in Popular Culture

The early modern proverb "A spaniel, a woman, and a walnut tree: the more they're beaten, the better they be" suggests that there was scarce tolerance for assertive women in early modern England.[1] Authors of godly household conduct guides advised men to use softer means to discipline combative women, but they were no less insistent in their claim that women's honor should be defined by the passive virtues of reticence, chastity and obedience to male superiors.[2] But if loquacious, forceful women were objects of derision and disrepute, how can we explain the active commercial roles women played in early modern towns? After all, the ideal wife of patriarchal teaching—quiet, meek and mild—could hardly have fared well in the early modern marketplace, in which (as we shall see) sharp practices and hard bargaining were the norm. This chapter explores how early modern townspeople grappled with the evident tensions between patriarchal ideals and the everyday practice of commerce. A reconsideration of popular literature—broadsides, ballads and the city comedies performed in seventeenth-century London's theaters—reveals an anxious, popular misogyny, but also a grudging acceptance of the necessity of female assertiveness in the household and marketplace.

As scholars have grown to appreciate the ways in which gendered texts constitute a "primary way of signifying power,"[3] they have become more sensitive to the ways in which such sources reflected and reinforced the gender hierarchy. It is commonly argued that popular literature reflected and bolstered patriarchal

---

1 Tilley, (ed.), *Dictionary of the Proverbs*, p. 742.

2 Scholarship on this literature is extensive, but see the particularly important studies of Kathleen Davies, "Continuity and Change in Literary Advice on Marriage," in *Marriage and Society: Studies in the Social History of Marriage*, (ed.) R.B. Outhwaite (New York: St. Martin's Press, 1981); Susan Dwyer Amussen, *An Ordered Society: Gender and Class in Early Modern England* (Oxford: Basil Blackwell, 1988), ch. 2; Jacqueline Eales, "Gender Construction in Early Modern England and the Conduct Books of William Whately (1583–1639)," in *Studies of Church History*, (ed.) R.N. Swanson, 34 (1998), pp. 163–74; Alexandra Shepard, *Meanings of Manhood*, ch. 3.

3 The phrase is Joan Scott's in her classic essay "Gender: A Useful Category of Historical Analysis," *American Historical Review*, 91 (1986): 1053–75.

values, reinforced stereotypes against assertive women, and spurred authorities to constrain their social and economic activities.[4] Elizabeth Foyster, for instance, has asserted that published works "from household conduct books to broadside ballads prescribed specific gender roles. Women were to be chaste, silent, and obedient ... According to this literature, it was essential to the operation of patriarchy that women were to be confined to the 'private' sphere of the home and excluded from the male 'public' world."[5] Literary scholars have explored this aspect of popular culture in their analyses of unflattering portrayals of shrewish, lascivious, and vain citizen wives in the city comedies of the period. According to these scholars, city comedies inculcated the notion that respectable women of the middling sort should confine themselves to housework, serve their husband as private 'adjuncts' and not meddle with the household shop or public marketplace.[6] Such studies support the theory, first advanced by Alice Clark and more recently espoused by Peter Earle, that capitalistic specialization in the seventeenth century pushed married women out of positions of economic partnership and cooperation with their husbands.[7] And yet, as a close study of seventeenth-century popular literature suggests, the ideal of marriage as an economic partnership survived longer than Clark or Earle suggest.

It is as easy to find evidence of misogynistic attitudes in popular literature as in the learned discourses of churchmen; nevertheless, rather than reading popular texts as mere patriarchal prescription, we should analyze them as contemporary commentary upon a socio-economic environment marked by a wide gap between prescriptions of gender norms and actual behavior. Popular notions of how husbands and wives, and female traders and their male competitors, should resolve their disagreements have yet to be explored. What characterized the cheap print and city comedies which dealt with these issues was not an unbending patriarchal

4 An argument advanced most forcefully by Bennett in *Ale, Beer and Brewsters*, ch. 7.

5 Foyster, *Manhood in Early Modern England*, p. 2. See also Joy Wiltenburg, *Disorderly Women and Female Power in the Street Literature of Early Modern England and Germany* (Charlottesville and London: University of Virginia Press, 1992); Sara Mendelson and Patricia Crawford, *Women in Early Modern England*, pp. 58–74.

6 Simon Shepherd, *Amazons and Warrior Women: Varieties of Feminism in Seventeenth-Century Drama* (New York: St. Martin's Press, 1981), ch. 4; Karen Newman, *Fashioning Femininity and English Renaissance Drama* (Chicago and London: University of Chicago Press, 1991), ch. 8; Douglas Bruster, *Drama and the Market in the Age of Shakespeare* (Cambridge: Cambridge University Press, 1992), pp. 48–57, 90–96.

7 Alice Clark, *Working Life of Women in the Seventeenth Century* (1919; repr., London: Routledge & Kegan Paul, 1982); Peter Earle, *A City Full of People: Men and Women of London 1650–1750* (London: Metheun, 1994), pp. 107–13, 122. Earle bases his conclusion that married couples increasingly refrained from working in partnership with one another on married women's answers to the London church courts when asked how they earned their living. But there is evidence that suggests that women who worked in partnership with their husbands often found it adequate to answer a court's question of how they had their living by answering they "lived by their husbands." See below, chapter 6.

prejudice, but rather a multivocality, in which men and women, rich and poor, the godly and the profane, are all given speaking parts. It was common for city comedies to satirize both citizens and gallants, and husbands and wives at once, and for dueling ballads to voice contradictory opinions in playful response to one another.

There are compelling reasons to look toward plays and cheap print, rather than learned conduct books, to reconstruct popular attitudes toward women traders. Tomes such as William Gouge's *On Domestical Duties*, William Whately's *A Bride-Bush*, and John Dod and Robert Cleaver's *A Godly Form of Household Government* had a limited readership; these lengthy and expensive exegeses of the Biblical foundations of patriarchal authority would have been most attractive to godly gentry, particularly pious artisans, and, above all, to other clergy.[8] Authors of popular literature and entertainments strove to attract a much wider audience than the writers of patriarchal household conduct books. The gradual rise of literacy rates and the expansion of London and provincial towns in the late sixteenth and early seventeenth centuries led to an explosion of demand for cheap print.[9] By 1641, almost three hundred ballad sellers plied the streets of London, and innumerable chapmen sold ballads throughout the counties. These vendors sold ballads and broadsides primarily to the humbler sorts.[10] Cheap print was not just accessible to the literate minority of working people, for reading was often a communal, oral activity performed in homes, alehouses and other sites of conviviality.[11]

The plays performed in London's theaters also catered to a mass audience. Andrew Gurr estimates that between the 1560s and 1642, "well over fifty million visits were made to playhouses."[12] While aristocrats, gentry and wealthy London citizens sat in balconies and seats, artisans, laborers, apprentices and hucksters

---

[8] John Dod and Robert Cleaver, *A Godly Forme of Houshold Gouernment for the Ordering of Priuate Families, According to the Direction of Gods Word* (London, 1630); William Gouge, *Of Domesticall Duties* (3rd edn, London, 1634); William Whatley, *A Bride-Bush or, a Direction for Married Persons* (London, 1619). On readership, see Davies, "Continuity and Change in Literary Advice on Marriage," pp. 76–7. Of course, clergymen reiterated from the pulpit celebrations of patriarchal rule and female domesticity found in these books. However, we underestimate the level of popular indifference to godly values if we imagine that those in the pews accepted preachers' teachings without question. See, for instance, the frustrations of godly reformers in the aftermath of the civil war detailed in Derek Hirst, "'The Failure of Godly Rule in the English Republic," *Past and Present* 132 (1991): 33–66.

[9] For literacy rates, see David Cressy, *Literacy and the Social Order: Reading and Writing in Tudor and Stuart England* (Cambridge: Cambridge University Press, 1980).

[10] Bernard Capp, "Popular Literature," in *Popular Culture in Seventeenth-Century England*, ed. Barry Reay (New York: St. Martin's Press, 1985), pp. 200–202.

[11] Capp, "Popular Literature," pp. 198–203; Natalie Zemon Davis, *Society and Culture in Early Modern France* (Stanford: Stanford University Press, 1975), pp. 212–15.

[12] Andrew Gurr, *Playgoing in Shakespeare's London* (2nd edn, Cambridge: Cambridge University Press, 1996), p. 4.

dominated the penny-priced standing room sections of theaters. Because they were meant to appeal to a broad audience, popular print and plays may better represent popularly held attitudes toward female involvement in commerce than godly conduct books; they certainly reflect different attitudes. The first section of this chapter discusses representations of relationships between husbands and wives, while the second part examines how market women and hostesses were perceived as traders and members of their neighborhoods.

Popular Attitudes Toward the Household Economy

However deeply rooted patriarchal conceptions of household authority were, few would have disagreed that the authority of the husband had to be tempered by mutual love and a sense of common purpose between husbands and wives. As all moralists and advice book writers stressed, while the primary duty of the wife was obedience to her husband, the husband had a duty to "love his wife as Christ loved the church."[13] As these writers argued, of the three types of relationships within the household—husband and wife, parent and child, master or mistress and servant—the relationship between husband and wife was the one closest to equality.[14] While almost all advice book writers condemned wife beating, suggesting instead that the husband should correct a disobedient wife with gentle persuasion rather than corporal punishment, wives also had a right to offer husbands counsel and direction, provided that it was offered humbly and in private. An emphasis on mutual love and regard was not novel to godly conduct books; frequent descriptions of marriage as a partnership between "yoke fellows" testify to the consensus that the ideal marriage was companionate as well as patriarchal.[15] It must, however, be noted that clergy saw no contradiction between describing marriage as constituting mutual labor and upholding the ultimate authority of the husband. For instance, William Whatley, along with other moralists, advocated against husbands allowing a separate purse for their wives; while the notion that the household should have a common purse might indicate a certain equity between husband and wife, Whatley and his colleagues could have had no doubt that such an arrangement left the husband, imbued with the rights of covert baron, securely in charge of the household resources.[16]

The image of marriage as constituting a mutual labor underscores the belief that understanding and love between husband and wife was a necessary precondition for household prosperity. Clergymen invariably described the prosperous household

---

[13] This frequently cited quote from Ephesians 5: 25.

[14] For example, see Gouge, *Domesticall Duties*, pp. 259–61.

[15] Thomas Gataker, *Marriage Duties Briefely Couched Togither*, 2nd edn (London, 1620), p. 21; Wrightson, *English Society*, p. 91.

[16] Whately, *A Bride-Bush*, pp. 82–3; Gouge, *Domesticall Duties*, pp. 255–7; Mathew Griffith, *Bethel: Or, A Forme for Families* (London, 1633), pp. 331–3.

as one in which husbands and wives pursued separate, complementary work, with the husbands going abroad to their work and wives occupied with housewifery and domestic labor.[17] A similar theme occupied two ballads which were marketed to both husbands and wives as New Year's gifts during the hard years of the 1620s and 1630s. In these two dialogues, the husband and wife get past their disagreements and resolve to pursue their complementary duties with renewed fervor. In "A new Ballad" by Francis Coules, the "careful wife" advises her husband to avoid lending money or standing surety to cheating "foxes," but instead to labor and pay his debts dutifully; in exchange, she shall "be a huswife, to husband your purse," and supplement the household income by spinning. Thus, she concludes, "Even you, my good husband, and I, your good wife,/ Will passe this hard yeere, man, without any strife." In "The Householder's New Yeere's Gift" the wife consoles her husband, who is distraught over a downturn in their fortunes: "The Lord will never leave them/ where true love doth appeare: And God send a merry new yeare ... Goe thou and ply thy labour,/ and I will work with thee ... I will not be idle,/ I but I will card and spin;/ I will save together/ that thou bringest in."[18]

Ballads celebrating harmonious marriages were rare: domestic strife made better copy, if only because cuckolds, drunkards, and scolds offered more comedic potential than conscientious spouses. But the numerous ballads excoriating shrewish wives and browbeaten husbands illustrate no less powerfully than do depictions of dutiful husbands and obedient, careful wives the importance of the wife to the household's prosperity. The stock figure of the combative wife who insisted on "junketing abroad," buying fine clothes or drinking with her gossips represented a dire threat to the prosperity of the household.[19] One ballad writer went so far as to advise husbands that "He that hath a drunken wife,/ that spends all at the Alehouse,/ Were better take a Cord in hand,/ and hang himselfe at the Gallowes."[20] Balladeers and pamphlet writers frequently attacked shrews who battled their husbands over the household purse: as one drunken wife declares to her friends in a tavern in Samuel Rowland's *A whole crew of kind Gossips, all met to be merry* (1609), "I scorne to take allowance like a child,/ There's nothing got, when women be too mild."[21] If bullying did not work, spendthrift shrews invariably picked their husbands' purses.[22] At the very worst, the shrew inverted

---

17 Edmund Tilney, *A Brief and Pleasant Discourse of the Duties of Mariage* (London, 1571), sig. C2; Dod and Cleaver, *A Godly Forme of Houshold Gouernment*, sig. L3v–L4; Whately, *A Bride-Bush*, p. 84; Griffith, *Bethel*, pp. 413–14; Patrick Hannay, *A Happy Husband or, Directions for a Maide to Choose Her Mate* (London, 1619), sig. C3^v.

18 *Rox. Ballads*, vol. 1, pp. 122–8.

19 See for example *Rox. Ballads*, vol. 1, pp. 297–9; vol. 2, 35–7, 188; vol. 6, p. 332; vol. 7, pp. 20–21, 188–9, 192–3, 431, 432; vol. 8, pp. 14–15, 103.

20 "Choice of Inuentions," in *Rox. Ballads*, vol. 1, p. 107.

21 Samuel Rowlands, *Tis Merrie When Gosips meete* (London, 1602), reprinted in *The Complete Works of Samuel Rowlands* (3 vols, Glasgow: Hunterien Club, 1880), vol. 1, p. 5.

22 For example, see "Have among you! good Women," in *Rox. Ballads*, vol. 1, p. 436.

the patriarchal order, cuckolding her husband and forcing him to do the housework while she drank with her gossips and her gallant at the tavern.[23]

Demands that wives concern themselves with their domestic duties and anxieties about their social activities and spending were common enough. But that hardly means that householders believed that a good wife was a cloistered wife. Indeed, good housewifery required that the wife go abroad, at the least to obtain household provisions and necessities. As the "careful wife" of the "A new ballad" cited above reminded her husband, "I must provide, man, for many an odde thing/ That you neuer looke to buy or to bring."[24] It was a foolish husband who refused to allow his wife some discretion in provisioning the household as she saw fit.[25] Ballad writers derided husbands who interfered too directly in the business of buying provisions or housewifery, and not just because such meddling was beneath the dignity of a patriarch. Men were widely regarded as bumbling incompetents when it came to performing "women's work." "The St. Giles's Broker," published sometime between 1682 and 1688, recounts the misfortunes of a London broker who has to purchase provisions in the market for a feast because he had a falling out with his wife. When the broker, intent upon buying a "green" goose, rejects the first goose offered, the market woman, recognizing his ignorance, sells him a goose which is literally green; the subsequent cooking of rancid flesh drives the family out of the house.[26] Such humorous stories reinforced the notion that it was the wife's particular role to provision the household.

Stories of untrustworthy, spendthrift wives are thus marked more by a bemused resignation than an insistence on the patriarch's duty to control the household purse. The everyday, necessary excursions of women to the marketplace inevitably gave wives the chance to tarry and drink with gossips in alehouses or buy fripperies. In *The Gossips Meeting, Or The merry Market-Women of Taunton* (1674), one wife brags to her compatriots that she obtains her drinking money by telling her husband that "my money it would not hold out,/ For all things so dear in the

---

[23] The possibility of the inversion of the gendered social and moral order was a subject of endless fear and fascination, as reflected in popular rituals and beliefs in witchcraft. See Davis, *Society and Culture* chs 4–5; Stuart Clark, *Thinking With Demons: The Idea of Witchcraft in Early Modern Europe* (Oxford: Oxford University Press, 1999).

[24] "A new Ballad," in *Rox. Ballads*, vol. 1, p. 123. See also "The New and True Touch of the Times," in *Pepys Ballads*, vol. 7, p. 168. One advocated that young men marry widows, for an experienced widow "will always,/ looke well to her home … [and] Sheele buy what is needfull/ to serue her owne vse;" Hyder Edward Rollins (ed.), *A Pepysian Garland: Black-Letter Broadside Ballads of the Years 1594–1639* (Cambridge: Cambridge University Press, 1922), p. 263. See also Bridget Hill, *Women, Work, and Sexual Politics in Eighteenth-Century England* (Oxford: Basil Blackwell, 1989), p. 119.

[25] "A Hee-Diuell," in Rollins (ed.), *Pepysian Garland*, pp. 334–6, esp. p. 336; the song was sung to the tune of, and thus a response to, "The shee-diuell."

[26] *Rox. Ballads*, vol. 7, p. 52–4. See also in the same volume "The Woman to the Plow, And the Man to the Hen-Roost," pp. 185–7; R.B., *The Description of a good Wife: Or, A rare one amongst Women* (London, 1619), sig. B4; Gouge, *Domesticall Duties*, p. 372.

Market row be." The wily twice-married woman responds that if her husband "give[s] me money to buy meat to roast, Be sure I will reckon him more than the cost;" thus, her "husband shall ne[ve]r know what money I spend."[27] The need to trust wives to fulfill their duties despite such temptations meant that, as another writer put it, a "husband must ask his wife if he shall thrive," underscoring the agency many wives enjoyed in managing the household economy.[28]

Were complaints against excessive consumption gender-specific? Historians have argued that attacks against luxury consumption were aimed particularly at city women, and such interpretations would support the notion that there was a growing unease regarding female economic activities in the public market.[29] But gender was only one of the axes along which contemporary observers of society plotted portrayals of conspicuous consumption.[30] Indeed, in many ballads and city comedies it is the dichotomy between honest country folk and depraved city dwellers, the healthy pastoral life versus the corruption of urban living, which is more evident than the contrast between patriarchal prudence and feminine excess. Ballad writers throughout the seventeenth century contrasted profligate, "wanton" city wives and shop girls of the New Exchange with the hard-working, humble, and sexually honest country "maid."[31] Condemnations of greed and covetousness were aimed at both men and women, for both men and women were vulnerable to the temptations of the urban market. In ballads in which a country girl muses about whom to marry, the maid invariably chooses the honest plowman or yeoman and the simple joys of pastoral life over the grasping, ambitious tradesman and the wealth and corruption of city life.[32]

The playwright Thomas Shadwell explored the differences between idealized pastoral values and urban profligacy and corruption in his 1689 *Bury Fair*. Shadwell characterized cities as "Pens of Wild Beasts upon two Legs, undermining,/ lying in wait, preying upon informing against, and hanging one/ another: A Crowd of Fools, Knaves, Whores, and Hypocrites."[33] With as much vehemence as any

---

27 Anon., *The Gossips meeting, or, The Merry market-women of Taunton* (London?, 1674).

28 "A Good Wife is a Portion every Day," *Rox. Ballads*, vol. 6, p. 333.

29 Cahn, *Industry of Devotion*; McIntosh, *Working Women in English Society*, ch. 9.

30 For instance, in Italy, aristocratic display, as much as feminine excess, provoked city authorities to restrict consumption. See Diane Owen Hughes, "Sumptuary Laws and Social Relations in Renaissance Italy," in *Disputes and Settlements: Law and Human Relations in the West*, (ed.) John Bossy (Cambridge: Cambridge University Press, 1983), pp. 69–99.

31 *Rox. Ballads*, vol. 1, pp. 165–70; 7: 27–8, 29–30; *Pepys Ballads*, vol. 1, p. 48–50.

32 For example, see "Sure my Nurse was a witch," in *Pepys Ballads*, vol. 2, pp. 65–9, esp. p. 69. In the late seventeenth-century, such maids preferred brave, honest sailors to corrupt citizens; no doubt such ballads resulted from the patriotic fervor which accompanied the Anglo-Dutch wars, e.g. "The Fair Maids Choice; or, The Seamans Renown," in *Bagford Ballads*, (ed.) Ebsworth, vol. 1, pp. 289–91.

33 Thomas Shadwell, *Bury Fair: A Critical Edition*, (ed.) John C. Ross (New York and London: Garland Publishing, 1995), 1.2.68–70.

attack on city ladies, observers such as Shadwell derided impecunious gallants who preened and festooned themselves in finery. The response of Gertrude to Mrs. Fantast's disdain for the traders who visit this provincial fair is telling: "I have no such contempt for the common People: they come/ near Nature, and have no Art or Affectation; and there are a thousand/ Fops made by Art, for one Fool by Nature."[34] Quite often for writers engaged in attacks against profligate women, it was not that they were *women*, but the fact that they were *city women*—just as corrupt as many *city men*—that gave London women a bad name.

There was thus a measure of commensurability between the economic expectations of husbands and wives. Both husbands and wives were obligated to preserve the resources of the household; and either could waste them. Some ballad writers were just as willing to take the part of distraught wives married to wasteful, lazy, and cruel men as they were to console husbands married to spendthrift shrews. Significantly, they chastised these bad husbands for the very same sins for which they condemned bad wives.[35] Martin Parker, the most prolific ballad writer of the early 1600s, may have thought it only fair after composing a song about a bad wife entitled the "She-Devil" to take up the cause of long-suffering wives in "A Hee-Diuell: or, If this Womans Husband vse her well, Ile say somme kindnesse may be found in Hell" (c. 1630). At the very least, he saw a commercial opportunity in publishing a ballad that appealed to disgruntled wives. The complaint of the poor wife in Parker's song is that "While [her husband] doth to the Ale-house goe,/ I worke to get his dyet. Though my labour earnes the meat,/ I nor my little daughter,/ Till he hath done, dare nothing eate,/ but dine (like seruants) after."[36] Parker was not alone in trying to appeal to the constituency of suffering wives. The complaint of the wives in "The Country-man's new Care Away!," published during the reign of James I, was typical in its pessimism regarding bad husbands:

> If spendthrifts were carefull,
> And would leaue their follies,
> Ebriety hating
> Cards, Dice, Bowling-Alleyes,
> Or with wants to dally
> By night or by day,
> Their wiues might be merry,
> And sing "Care away!"[37]

---

[34] Shadwell, *Bury Fair*, 2.2.13–15.

[35] In doing so, they echoed the conduct book writers.

[36] Rollins (ed.), *Pepysian Garland*, p. 334; Parker explored a similar theme in "Knauery in all Trades," (c. 1632); see p. 414.

[37] *Rox. Ballads*, vol. 1, p. 113; see also vol. 6, pp. 337, 340–41, 343–5, 480–81, 483; vol. 7, pp. 147–8; *Pepys Ballads*, vol. 2, pp. 170–73.

Gambling and whoring were seen as distinctly male activities which threatened the household economy.[38] But ballad writers also censured husbands for engaging in activities usually associated with lazy female gossips. In one ballad, a nurse advises her charge to avoid marrying the "giddy headed Shopkeeper" who "loues gadding here, and there,/ And of his businesse at home/ hath no respect and care;" such loquacious men, the nurse warns, are destined to become beggars.[39] In one ballad about a shrewish wife, the wife answers the charge of scolding that she must maintain her "sovereignty" over her husband to keep him from "prating about."[40] In a similar response to complaints about scolds, the wife explains:

> If I do blame your gadding,
> It is for love, be sure;
> Bad company doth alwaies
> Ill counsell still procure;
> The man that will be thrifty,
> Must at his worke endure.[41]

For both husbands and wives neighborly sociability had to be controlled if the household was to thrive; husbands and wives had an obligation to tend to the needs of the household first.

Demands that householders spend more time at home were therefore not just limited to wives. One ballad from the late seventeenth century counseled husbands to avoid wasting money by standing drinks for alehouse friends: instead, "A cup of good liquor at home with thy wife,/ Will chear up your hearts and prevent further strife."[42] Perhaps not coincidently, palatable spirits had just begun arriving in England in considerable amounts, and large quantities of domestically manufactured gin were soon to follow. In any case, undisciplined and uncontrollable men were believed by many moralists to constitute as much a threat to the ideal patriarchal order as profligate, disobedient women.[43]

Just as husbands had the obligation to discipline shrewish wives, so wives had a duty to reform wayward husbands. Moralists invariably argued that the efforts of wives to reform drunken, wasteful, or lazy husbands should be limited to gentle advice offered humbly and in the privacy of the home. The wisdom of accepting the wise counsel of responsible wives was underscored in "Wade's Reformation,

---

38 In all of the ballads I have studied, I have not found an instance of a woman who gambled; gambling seems to have been perceived to be a male-specific vice.

39 "Sure my Nurse was a witch," *Pepys Ballads*, vol. 2, pp. 67–8.

40 "The Wife's Answer to the Hen-peckt Cuckold's Complaint" (c. 1688), in *Rox. Ballads,* vol. 7, p. 432.

41 "The Lamentation of a new-married man," in *Rox. Ballads*, vol. 2, p. 39

42 "The Poor Man's Counsellor" (c. 1672–1685), in *Rox. Ballads*, vol. 8, p. 104.

43 Alexandra Shepard, "Manhood, Credit and Patriarchy in Early Modern England c. 1580–1640," *P&P* 167 (2000): 75–6, 78, 82–90; Shepard, *Meanings of Manhood*, ch. 3.

To all good fellows of this nation" (printed c. 1670–1680), sung to the tune of "'Tis old Ale has undone me." The narrator of the song laments that if he had only listened to his wife, who advised him to refrain from beer and tobacco, he would not have become impoverished, scorned by his friends, and harried by the alehouse hostess impatient for the repayment of his debt.[44] However, the advice that wives limit themselves to gentle admonishments was cold comfort to women whose husbands were unwilling to listen to reason. And it was in the context of husbands so dissolute as to threaten the very survival of the family that a few ballad writers contemplated the merits of physical discipline by wives. Plebeian and middling attitudes toward domestic violence were more flexible than the attitudes of godly moralists, almost all of whom condemned wife beating, and none of whom would have condoned wives beating wayward husbands.[45] In the ballad "Choice of Inuentions," it is only after his wife beats him with a broomstick that a drunken cobbler comes to his senses and resolves to drink only water or small beer. In another ballad, a wife resolves to no longer "scold and brawle" as long as her husband honors his vow not to drink to excess.[46] In such ballads, good behavior on the part of the husband is the price that must be paid for a quiet wife.

The contradictions which arose from patriarchal precepts and the notion of marriage as a partnership of mutual dependence were dramatized with especial urgency in the city comedies which became popular in the first half of the seventeenth century. Many scholars have extrapolated from these plays a conventional, unbending defense of patriarchy and feminine domesticity. According to such interpretations, the vulnerability of market women to sexual temptation and innuendo[47] and descriptions of unmarried maids such as Moll in Thomas Middleton's *A Chaste Maid in Cheapside* (c. 1613, published 1630) as commodities to be bought and sold off as wives to the highest bidder reflected declining female social and economic agency during the period.[48] Furthermore,

---

44 Ebsworth (ed.), *The Bagford Ballads*, vol. 1, pp. 6–9.

45 For example, see Gouge, *Domesticall Duties*, pp. 394–400. Very different attitudes toward marital violence are expressed in ballads such as "Roaring Dick of Dover" (c. 1632), which excused attacks upon wives by husbands as the result of scolding; the song concluded by asking wives to keep silent, even as their husbands spend the household purse on drink: *Pepys Ballads*, vol. 2, p. 237. We should note, however, that even though husbands were legally empowered to punish disobedient wives by corporal punishment, and that middling and lower sorts were much more tolerant of spousal abuse than conduct book writers, especially cruel, violent husbands did risk censure from their neighbors: see Elizabeth Foyster, "Male Honour, Social Control and Wife Beating," *Transactions of the Royal Historical Society*, 6th Series, vol. 6 (1996).

46 *Rox. Ballads*, vol. 1, p. 107; and "A merry discourse" (c. 1603–1625), pp. 249–53.

47 For example, Thomas Dekker, *The Roaring Girl* (1611), in Fredson Bowers (ed.), *The Dramatic Works of Thomas Dekker* (4 vols, Cambridge: Cambridge University Press, 1953–1958), vol. 3, 2.1.

48 Shepherd, *Amazons and Warrior Women*, ch. 4; Bruster, *Drama and the Market*, pp. 48–57, 90–96.

the lampooning of mild citizen husbands and their shrewish, socially ambitious wives can be seen as an attempt to appeal to coterie disdain for lowly citizens. But such misogynistic strands should not be mistaken for serious moral instruction, for much of the humor generated by these plays had to do with their exposure of the limits of patriarchal authority. Citizens in the audience—or at the very least their wives—would have recognized that in everyday practice, an assertive wife was necessary to the household economy, and this fact is reflected, and not always lamented, in these plays.

The household shop was a frequent scene of contention between husbands and wives in city comedies. In Dekker and Middleton's *The Honest Whore, part I* (published 1604), a comedy set in Milan, much of the humor of the play is generated in one subplot by the machinations of a shrewish wife, Viola, to goad her incredibly patient husband, Candido, to anger. In a reversal of the usual notion that shrews create browbeaten husbands, Dekker and Middleton place the blame of the wife's shrewishness squarely on the shoulders of Candido, illustrating the proverb that the calmest of husbands can make the stormiest of wives.[49] Distraught that her husband does not have "all things/ belonging to a man," namely the emotions of choler and jealousy, she frets to her brother "I am ready to bite off my tongue, because/ it wants that vertue which all womens tongues haue (to anger their/ husbands:) Brother, mine can by no thunder turne him into a/ sharpnes."[50] Part of her complaint is sexual: she wishes to make her husband as "horne mad[d] e" as a jealous cuckold, and to make his mustache stand up like a porcupine's quills. To arouse her husband's jealousy and lust, she enlists her brother to play the role of her gallant. Her scheme is unsuccessful, and results in her brother receiving a beating at the hands of the shop apprentices loyal to Candido. But Candido's infuriating passivity also means that Viola must assume the role of sole protector of the household economy. Particularly galling to Viola is her husband's casual tending of "her shop." She is outraged when a group of gallants, making sport of Candido's patience, offer to buy a penny's worth of lawn which, they demand, must be cut from the center, thus ruining the entire cloth. After the sale, they make off with one of Viola's gilt cups, provoking Viola to exclaim to her husband: "I had rather haue/ a husband that would swaddle me thrice a day, then such a one,/ that will be guld twice in halfe an hower, Oh I could burne all the/ wares in my shop for anger."[51]

The relationship between a tailor-citizen, master Openwork, and his wife, in Middleton and Dekker's *The Roaring Girl*, is just as tense. Openwork has lost control of his shop. His wife claims to be the better workman, and she, angered by his supposed sexual infidelity, dictates which clothes her husband is allowed

49 Edition of Dekker and Middleton's *The Honest Whore, part I* here is in Bowers (ed.), *Works of Dekker*, vol. 2. For the proverb, see Smith (ed.), *Oxford Dictionary of English Proverbs*, p. 422.

50 Dekker and Middleton, *Honest Whore, part I*: 1.2.58–9, 75–9.

51 Dekker and Middleton, *Honest Whore, part I*, 1.5.193–6.

to tailor just as she attempts to circumscribe his sexual dalliances: "Dare you presume to noble womens linnen,/ Keepe you your yard to measure sheepeheards holland."[52] Mistress Openwork's contempt for her husband is spurred by a false rumor that Openwork keeps whores in the suburbs. Significantly, she frames her complaints in terms of the threat his infidelity poses to the prosperity of their shop. She complains that while Openwork is about his supposed whoring, "I'me/ seru'd with good ware byth shift, that makes it lye dead so long/ vpon my hands, I were as good shut vp shop,/ for when I open it/ I take nothing."[53] Openwork's reputation for sexual incontinence is no less damaging to his status as patriarch than Candido's puzzling patience; in both cases, the failure of these husbands to satisfy their wives sexually is conflated with their economic impotence.

It would go too far to suggest that Dekker and Middleton were questioning the legitimacy of patriarchy, for at the end of both plays husbandly authority is restored. It is Openwork himself who has spread the rumor of his whoring in order to test the loyalty of a young Mr. Goshawke, whom he suspects of having intentions upon his wife; when Openwork reveals his scheme and gently admonishes Goshawke, both Goshawke and Openwork's wife are chastened and beg his forgiveness. Candido, sent to the madhouse by his wife in her final scheme to try his patience, is also restored to his rightful place at the conclusion of the play when the Duke commands a chastened Viola to accept her husband's authority, however mild he might be. Both wives (unlike the common caricature of the gossiping shrew) want not independence, but a reasonable governor. These two representations of marriage thus speak at once to both the wide, if nominal, acceptance amongst both men and women of patriarchal tenets, and the very real frailty of patriarchal authority in many households. Contemporary observers recognized that patriarchal authority could not be taken for granted: it had to be earned.

In such depictions of deficient patriarchies, citizens' wives had to assert their authority over the apprentices and journeymen of the workshop as well as their husbands. Even authors of domestic conduct books recognized that wives had to act as subaltern magistrates, enforcing discipline upon the children, servants, and apprentices of the household when the husband himself was unable or unwilling to do so. The response of George, Candido's apprentice, to Viola's demand that he put on her husband's best apparel in yet another scheme to provoke Candido's anger is telling: he agrees to do so as long as she metaphorically puts him "vnder couert/ barne," a legal term which referred to the subsuming of the wife's legal identity under that of her husband's.[54] Earlier in *Honest Whore I*, Viola, while upbraiding the apprentices for not putting her shop wares in good order, wishes "I would your maister or I/ could be a note more angry: for two patient folks

[52] Dekker, *Roaring Girl*, 2.1.149–50.

[53] Dekker, *Roaring Girl*, 2.1.203–6. These lines of course are also a metaphorical complaint against her husband's unwillingness to fulfill his conjugal duties.

[54] Dekker and Middleton, *Honest Whore, part I*, 3.1.251–2.

in the house/ spoyle all the seruants that euer shall come vnder them."[55] Dekker dealt with a similar theme in *The Shoemaker's Holiday* (1600), a play loosely based upon an episode in Thomas Deloney's proto-novel *The Gentle Craft* in which Simon Eyre, a London shoemaker, rises to a position of wealth and gains the office of mayor. In the play, Eyre regularly upbraids his wife for questioning his judgment, but his constant calls for her to be a silent "midriff," to "vanish," to "melt like/ kitchen stuff" into the interior of the home are boisterous hyperbole, and to little effect.[56] Despite his harsh words, Eyre, like Candido, is a lax master, and his wife, for all of her preening and pretensions to social respectability, is the only one who has a watchful eye on the shop. Particularly galling to Eyre's wife is the habit of Eyre and his journeymen and apprentices to sing and drink on Monday—that they "loiter and tipple thus" on the "shoemaker's holiday."[57] While she relents whenever her husband demands her silence, she nevertheless finds time to harry his workers for their lethargy. Simon Shepherd's argument that this play's depiction of a shrewish shop wife reinforced the notion that women had no proper place in the "capitalistic" workshop of early modern London is overdrawn. Shepherd highlights the fact that Eyre's journeymen threaten to quit if they have to bear any more verbal assaults from this shrewish woman.[58] But how seriously could early modern audiences have taken the loafing journeyman Firke's exclamation that he would rather have his "guts ... be turnd to shoo-thread" than bear the insults of Eyre's wife when immediately afterward Eyre placates him with a tankard of beer?[59] Elements of early modern audiences might well have sympathized with Eyre's wife when she complained that she "must be cald rubbish, kitchinstuff, for a/ sort of knaues."[60]

Citizens' wives are depicted in city comedies no less often than in ballads as social climbers, but conspicuous consumption was only one facet of female ambition. Writers often portrayed ambitious city wives as being the real brains behind successful household businesses. In his popular work *The Gentle Craft*, Deloney described women as being "for the most part very couetous." Thus, while Simon Eyre's ambitions are limited to repaying his debts on time and eking out a living, his wife is "inflamed" with the desire to become a lady. Upon hearing that a valuable shipment of Holland cloth is available for sale and could bring significant profit if bought and resold, she promises her husband that she will "procure friends to borrow one forty shillings, and beside that, rather then you shall lose so good a bargain, I haue a couple of crowns that saw no sun since we were first maried, and

---

55 Dekker and Middleton, *Honest Whore, part I*, 1.5.6–8.

56 Thomas Dekker, *The Shoemaker's Holiday*, in *Works of Dekker*, (ed.), Bowers, 1.1.135; 2.3.43–4.

57 Dekker, *Shoemaker's Holiday*, 2.3.91.

58 Shepherd, *Amazons and Warrior Women*, p. 45.

59 Dekker, *Shoemaker's Holiday*, 2.3.53–4. Yet another crude metaphor seems to be at play here.

60 Dekker, *Shoemaker's Holiday*, 2.3.45–6.

them also shall you haue" as a down payment for the goods. This deal establishes him as a wealthy man.[61] In Dekker's version of the story, the journeymen rather than Eyre's wife arrange the deal. But, as indicated in her continual efforts to discipline the "festive capitalism" of Eyre's shop, Dekker did retain the wife's eye toward profit.[62] Equally grasping is the character of Mistress Mulligrub, a crafty tavern hostess and wife of a vintner in John Marston's *The Dutch Courtesan* (published 1605). In business, Mrs. Mulligrub "must bear/ a brain for all."[63] She reassures her foolish husband after he is cheated out of fifteen pounds by a gallant that she can easily make the money back by selling weak wine: indeed, the money is "but a week's cutting in the term."[64] But Mr. Mulligrub's position is not enviable, for his wife gulls him as well as their customers. Unbeknownst to him, she lends money to gallants and has affairs with her customers; and when his gallant-provocateur succeeds in getting him sentenced to death for theft, she betroths herself to the gallant before her husband is even hanged. The play was unusual amongst city comedies in that it did not soften its critique of citizen households in the concluding act; indeed, so scathing is Marston's portrait of this citizen couple that he felt the need to add this defensive postscript addressed to the audience:

> … and you, my/
> worshipful friends in the middle region:
> If with content our hurtless mirth hath been,
> Let your pleas'd minds at our much care be seen;
> For he shall find, that slights such trivial wit,
> 'Tis easier to reprove than better it.[65]

Ending the action of the play with the foolish Mulligrub barely escaping the noose, but still very much in the clutches of his scheming wife, obligated Marston to smooth some ruffled citizens' feathers.

But despite anxieties regarding the ability of cunning, assertive, and shrewish wives to undermine patriarchal authority, husbands were occasionally thankful for—or at least tolerated—sharp, crafty wives, for the survival of the household often depended on their acuity and assertiveness in the marketplace. Candido, Mulligrub, and Deloney's Simon Eyre all rely upon the commercial acumen of their wives for their profit. As depictions of such dependent husbands would suggest, popular wisdom regarding the advantages and disadvantages of having a

---

61 Thomas Deloney, *The Works of Thomas Deloney*, (ed.) Francis Oscar Mann (Oxford: Clarendon Press, 1912), pp. 143–4.

62 For this characterization of Eyre's shop, see Shepherd, *Amazons and Warrior Women*, ch. 4.

63 John Marston, *The Dutch Courtesan*, (ed.) M.L. Wine (Lincoln: University of Nebraska Press, 1965), 3.3.26–7.

64 Marston, *Dutch Courtesan*, 2.3.107–8.

65 Marston, *Dutch Courtesan*, 5.3.155–60.

"shrewish" wife was divided. Two popular, contradictory adages—"it is better to marry a sheep than a shrew" and "it is better to marry a shrew than a sheep"—indicate that there was no consensus on who had the more enviable position: the husband whose wife was unfailingly passive, or the husband whose wife might contend with his will at home but also fiercely guarded household interests in the course of her business abroad. Yet another early modern proverb contended that "A shrew profitable may serve a man reasonable."[66] As this adage suggests, shrewishness was often associated with shrewdness in commerce; indeed, the words have a common etymology.[67] Furthermore, there was some recognition that women who adopted a shrewish, aggressive demeanor in the public market did not necessarily act that way at home with their husbands. As one ballad writer noted, wives who behaved with perfect mildness and decorum in public could turn out to be the worst of scolds at home. But, on the other hand:

> … shall I griue when I behold,
> The picture of a parfect scold:
> Be her tongue so truly euill,
> That well might tire the very Deuill:
> *Yet if she be not such to me,*
> *What care I how curst she be.*[68]

Claims that an assertive wife could be valuable to the household indicate that many men recognized that the patriarchal ideal of clear husbandly authority and female passivity was indeed detrimental to the running of the household economy. Just as fanciful to writers as the image of the passive, deferential wife was the meek market woman or alehouse hostess.

Representations of Female Traders

We might be tempted to ascribe the public commercial activities of women to atypical evasions of patriarchal authority, for proponents of patriarchy were no less adamant in advocating the circumscription of the roles of women in public commerce than they were in advocating husbandly authority over the household. Such learned authorities did not go so far as to advocate the seclusion of women, but they did contend that the proper wife was like a snail or the tortoise: she should only venture out of the protective shell of the household with good reason, and

---

66 Smith (ed.), *Oxford Dictionary of Proverbs*, pp. 27, 231; Tilley (ed.), *Dictionary of Proverbs*, pp. 603, 604.

67 *OED*, s.v. "shrew" and "shrewd."

68 "A new Song of a Young mans opinion, of the difference betweene good and bad women" (c. 1615) in *Pepys Ballads*, vol. 1, pp. 61–3.

then preferably under the close supervision of the husband.[69] Household conduct writers of course joined ballad and broadside writers in condemning wives who frittered away their time and money socializing with "gossips," and thus neglected household duties. Furthermore, they advised husbands to accompany their wives whenever possible to public events such as church services, markets, fairs, and feasts, for, as Dod and Cleaver warned, "it would seeme strange to behold the household go diuided: and it were a thing that would much be marked."[70] With the exception of wives who under *specific* orders from their husbands ventured out to markets and shops to buy necessary provisions, Dod and Cleaver saw as inherently disordered households that arrived at public places "not together but scattered, and one droping after another in a confused manner."[71] And, of course, when in public, women were to conduct themselves as they should in the privacy of the household, being either reticent or at least mild in their speech. Depictions of market women and hostesses of drinking and eating establishments, however, underscore that such precepts were noted more often in the breach than in the observance. Many contemporaries recognized that expectations of female meekness in the public markets and drinking establishments were no less far-fetched than idealistic portrayals of the docile housewife.

We can be certain that contemporaries expected to see women frequent shops and marketplaces. The forbearance of good wives to attend markets on their own as either buyers or sellers are more apparent in the wishes of the clerical advice book writers than in perceptions of reality. Ballads recording the calls of chapmen selling clothes, kitchen stuff, and other household items almost always have these traders imploring city women to peruse their goods; and one 1698 ballad lamenting the deleterious economic effects of the decay of coinage poignantly described the distress of poor London wives unable to use debased (but hard-earned) coinage to buy enough bread and meat in the markets to feed their families.[72]

But shopping was only part of a city wife's commercial duties. Balladeers and playwrights assumed that women who married tradesmen would sell their husbands' goods in shops and markets. According to such writers, the vending of the workshop's goods became a de facto professional identity for citizens' wives. Thus, in Chapman, Jonson, and Marston's comedy *Eastward Ho* (1605), the goldsmith's daughter Gertrude, full of aristocratic pretension after having married an impecunious knight, contemptuously dubs her sister Mildred, who made the more sensible decision of marrying her father's industrious apprentice, "Mistress

69 For this common analogy of wife as a snail or tortoise, see for instance Griffith, *Bethel*, p. 413.

70 *A Godly Forme of Houshold Gouernment*, sig. C3.

71 *A Godly Forme of Houshold Gouernment*, sig. P, C1v.

72 "The Trader's Medley; or, Cries of London," in *Bagford Ballads*, (ed.) Ebsworth, vol. 1, p. 115; Thomas Joy, "The New and True Touch of the Times" (c. 1696), in *Pepys Ballads*, vol. 7, p. 168.

What-lack-you?," after the common call of London shopkeepers.[73] In emphasizing the lack of defensible motive of a "bloody butcher" of London who was executed in 1667 for murdering his wife, a ballad writer noted that the butcher's wife "did keep a Seat I'th Market-place to sell her Meat; And was by all report that's made, A careful house-wife in the Trade."[74] A 1692 ballad recounting the complaints of tradesmen at the decline of commerce because of the war with France similarly hints at the vocational duties of tradesmen's wives:

> Our Wives which did large Portions bring,
> a splendid life to lead,
> They now a woful Ditty sing,
> which makes our Hearts to bleed:
> For in their Shops they sit all day,
> while takings are but small,
> And then at Night they sighing say
> *we must a Begging all.*[75]

This passage underscores the point that a dowry was only one of the advantages women betrothed to tradesmen were expected to bring to the marriage: the ability of wives to sell was seen as crucial to the success of the household.

Unmarried women (who of course enjoyed *feme sole* status) were also prominent in representations of commercial London. Ballad writers often mentioned the multitude of country "maids" who brought fruit, pies, and dairy products to the capital to sell; and fashionable young women were widely regarded to be the most successful vendors for the shops which sold the high-end clothes and imports of London's New Exchange, for many of these shops' customers were women of means.[76] As figures of popular literature, the shop-keeping wife, the huckster, and the Exchange girl were more mundane than controversial.

As contemporaries recognized, sites of commerce such as the marketplace, shop, and tavern—in which the ability to buy or sell was prized above all—rendered conventional notions of social and gender hierarchies problematic. If a "rough and ready" equality between the sexes existed anywhere in early modern England,

---

[73] George Chapman, Ben Jonson, and John Marston, *Eastward Ho* in *The Roaring Girl and Other City Comedies*, (ed.) James Knowles and Eugene Giddens (Oxford: Oxford University Press, 2001), 3.2.85–86; compare with "A merry discourse," in *Rox. Ballads*, vol. 1, p. 252.

[74] Anon., *The Bloody Butcher, And the two wicked and cruel Bawds* (London, 1667); for a similar story, in which a butcher kills his wife in her market stall in front of his mother-in-law, see "The Inhumane Butcher of Leaden-Hall Market" (1692), in *Pepys Ballads*, vol. 7, pp. 259–61.

[75] "The Shop-keeper's Complaint" (1692), in *Pepys Ballads*, vol. 6, p. 293.

[76] For instance, see "Turner's dish of Lenten stuffe" (1612) in Rollins (ed.), *Pepysian Garland*, p. 33; and "Michaelmas Term," in Ebsworth (ed.), *Bagford Ballads*, vol. 1, p. 405.

it was in boisterous fair grounds and marketplaces. Certainly there was little expectation that market women would show the deference which in other contexts women were supposed to give to male householders. In Ben Jonson's *Bartholomew Fair*, the relationship between two stallholders, Joan Trash, a gingerbread seller, and Lantern Leatherhead, a hobbyhorse seller, is revealing. When Leatherhead accuses Trash of selling adulterated goods and demands that she move away from his stall so that she will not "hinder" his commerce, she stands her ground, pointing out that she has paid for her plot just as Leatherhead had. Goading the "too-proud pedlar" to do his "worst," she warns that "I'll find a/ friend shall right me, and make a ballad of thee."[77] Later, when Leatherhead threatens to bring Trash to the piepowder court for distracting a foolish customer, Trash maintains that her purchase of space in the fair gives her as much right to display her wares as Leatherhead. That Leatherhead feels the need to threaten Trash with legal action underscores the point that men could expect no especial consideration by neighboring female traders on the grounds of patriarchal convention.

Gentlemen and gallants were not immune to the barbs of assertive, plebeian female characters. Perhaps the most outstanding portrait of the assertive market woman is Jonson's Ursula. Ursula dominates her unruly pig and ale stall, shows no respect for her (male) superiors, and delights in verbal combat, exercising what Knockem, one of her customers, calls her "Bartholomew-wit."[78] When the two crafty gallants, Winwife and Quarlous, have the temerity to mock her in her tent, she easily wins the contest of insults, provoking a quarrel which drives the two from her stall. Jonson was not alone in conjuring the combativeness of market women to humorous effect. In the opening scene of George Etherege's *The Man of Mode*, the orange woman[79] is polite enough to Mr. Dorimant, from whom she can expect to profit by selling her oranges spiced with news of a young woman who fancies the gallant, but she has no such patience with Medley, Dorimant's caustic companion, who accuses the fruit seller of keeping a house of bawdry. She responds to Medley's insults: "Good Mr Dorimant, pay me; gad, I had rather give you/ my fruit than stay to be abused by that foul-mouthed rogue … such a dirty fellow does/ one more disgrace [than good]."[80] The numerous ballads warning men of the perils of the alehouse and tavern also dramatized the notion that commerce muddled conventional understandings of the social and gendered order. These ballads were ostensibly moralistic in tone, serving as reminders to male readers to place the needs of their families before drink and diversion. And yet surely

---

77 Ben Jonson, *Bartholomew Fair*, (ed.) Simon Trussler (London and New York: Methuen, 1986), 2.2.13–17.

78 Jonson, *Bartholomew Fair*, 2.5.94.

79 A character perhaps based on Orange Moll (Mrs. Mary Meggs), who held a profitable monopoly to sell oranges and sweetmeats, and who was a noted distributor of gossip outside Etherege's rival theater, the Theatre Royal, Drury Lane; see Robert Lawrence (ed.), *Restoration Plays* (London: Everyman, 1994), p. 109.

80 George Etherege, *The Man of Mode* in *Restoration Plays*, (ed.) Lawrence, 1.1.46–9.

some of the popularity of these ballads came from their display of the inversion of social relationships between the humble hostess and the respectable householder, the latter being in due course laid low. The prodigal drunkard ballads invariably followed the same plot: the formerly prosperous householder falls deeply into debt to his provider of drink, and the once deferential, polite alewife, now clothed in expensive silks and finery bought with the proceeds of her trade, is empowered to treat the impoverished drunkard with contempt; she has him thrown out of her house and harries him for the repayment of the rest of his tab.[81]

Contemporaries thus recognized that the characteristics which made a woman successful in the rough-and-tumble world of the marketplace and tavern were very different from the behavior expected from the ideal of the modest, retiring housewife. A talent for verbal and sometimes even physical combat was necessary, as was an ability to aggressively advertise wares and bargain hard in order to find the best deal. Thus one ballad (c. 1620) which lists common London characters who merit punishment makes note of the "oyster-wench" who deserved to ride the cucking stool, for she by her terrifying "scolding" somehow "payes all her debts."[82] The pudding-pie woman of another ballad (c. 1674–1681) uses her well-practiced voice not only to advertise her pies, but also to loudly cajole her baker to lower his prices, warning him that he will lose her custom if he does not accept her price:

> "O Baker!" quoth she, "I prethy do not me cozen;
> I am an Old wife, *tell fifteen to the dozen*;
> For by that means my profit doth fairly rise,
> Or else I must never more cry Pudding-pyes."[83]

The frightful noise female vendors made in the markets and the streets was notorious, a common complaint of men uneasy with female loquaciousness; and it was thus fitting that the silence-loving character Morose in Jonson's *Epicoene* is compelled to bribe the hucksters of London to refrain from bellowing their calls when they pass his residence.[84] That only the promise of a bribe could convince these imagined women traders to keep silent is suggestive of the little regard hucksters had for elite notions of female propriety.

---

81 For such songs, see Rollins (ed.), *Pepysian Garland*, pp. 166–9, 194, 363; *Rox. Ballads*, vol. 1, p. 107; vol. 6, pp. 337, 340–41; vol. 7, pp. 147–8, 821; Ebsworth (ed.), *Bagford Ballads*, vol. 1, pp. 6–9; vol. 2, p. 910.

82 *Pepys Ballads*, vol. 1, p. 193.

83 "The Old Pudding-pye Woman," in *Rox. Ballads*, vol. 7, p. 77; italics in the original. That a discount on the price of bread rather than "cozenage" was this pudding-pie seller's real concern is apparent in her demand of fifteen loaves for the price of a dozen. Such demands by hucksters were hardly uncommon.

84 Ben Jonson, *Epicoene*, (ed.) L.A. Beaurline (Lincoln: University of Nebraska Press, 1966), 1.1.140–43.

When writers of popular literature turned from the streets to the marketplace, they depicted it not as part of a publicly dominated part of the male "sphere," but instead as contested space, in which women could wield considerable power. Misogynistic stereotypes of disordered, shrewish women aplenty mark the descriptions found in ballads. For instance, the prolific balladeer Martin Parker called for harsh punishments to be meted out to scolding market women who kept browbeaten husbands and female neighbors in thrall. But that does not mean that the purpose of most authors was to warn public officials of the need to control women in the public market.[85] Martin's work aside, the tone of these ballads is more often one of amused resignation rather than patriarchal scandalization. The oyster vendors of London's Billingsgate market in particular were famed for their combativeness, and they therefore served as a common point of reference in descriptions of aggressive market women. The picture which emerges is not one of market women's solidarity in the face of patriarchal prejudice, but rather one of fierce competition amongst profit-oriented traders. In the ballad "An excellent new Ditty" described in the introduction, the devil is intimidated by the fierceness with which the market women fought amongst themselves to purchase his offer of eternal life. A 1692 spoof of country almanacs elevated the aggressiveness of these vendors to the status of a predictable force of nature: "Morning and Night, like Tygers they'll fight/ Before they'll be wrong'd in the least of their right,/ in their Oysters."[86] Observers may have recognized that such combativeness with customers and competitors alike was necessary if these vendors were to turn a profit.

Hostesses too had to be assertive in their dealings. Indeed, few people could have doubted that these women had to be commanding and cunning if they were to deal with rowdy or unreliable customers. Contemporaries recognized that complaints of alewives and tavern hostesses wringing as much as possible from poor customers were only half the story, for hostesses were often the victims of cozenage as well as the perpetrators. One ballad, for instance, reveals the plan of an unsavory customer who owes a sizable tab at a tavern near London:

> With hony words I will screw her,
> And many a fine tricke shew her;—
> Ile keepe me away
> When she is to pay
> Her Baker and her Brewer.[87]

In his 1632 *London and the Country Carbonadoed and Quartred into Severall Characters*, Donald Lupton noted that the alehouse hostess had to be on guard against "tinkers and poor soldiers most, not that they will not drink soundly, but

85 *Rox. Ballads*, vol. 1, pp. 436–7.
86 Ebsworth (ed.), *Bagford Ballads*, vol. 1, p. 188.
87 "The kind beleeving Hostesse," in *Rox. Ballads*, vol. 1, p. 520.

that they will not pay lustily."[88] These women had to maintain their authority over their customers if they were to prosper.

It is thus significant that an alternative image of the honest, noble-minded, formidable hostess who insisted on fair remuneration for her services counterbalanced the common stereotype of the hostess as dissolute, cozening bawd. As Simon Shepherd has observed, the example of Queen Elizabeth as an extraordinary, virtuous female ruler with the body of a woman but with the heart of a man provided an apt metaphor for contemporaries' descriptions of women able to rule over their victualing and tippling houses.[89] Elizabethan imagery is most obvious in Heywood's *Fair Maid of the West*.[90] The heroine, Bess, owner and hostess of the Windmill tavern in Foy, Cornwall, supposedly shares with her namesake the virtues of honesty, frugality, and chastity; but just as significantly, she keeps order over her tavern just as Elizabeth kept order in the realm. When Roughman, a local tough, "tyrannizes" her house by beating her customers and servants, Bess dons male clothing and, posing as her brother, challenges the gallant to a duel in a field. The cowardly Roughman yields without a fight, and when he later brags in her tavern that he had won a closely fought duel in the open field, she reveals to all that it was she who had bested him, humiliating Roughman in front of his lackeys and re-establishing order in the tavern. Similarly commanding, if less refined, was the popular character of Long Meg. The heroine of several chapbooks from the early seventeenth century, the character was supposedly based on a woman from Lancashire who migrated to Westminster and became first a tavern hostess, then a cross-dressing soldier in the English army in France, and finally the owner of her own tavern.[91] Though Long Meg stories date back to the reign of Henry VIII, her exploits—especially the two beatings she gives to Sir James, an arrogant Spanish knight who frequents her tavern—could hardly have failed to remind early seventeenth-century readers of England's victories during the Elizabethan wars with Spain.[92] Besides serving meat and drink, Meg's chief duty as hostess is to use her brawn to collect money from the many "swaggering fellowes" who fail to pay for their food and drink.[93] One of those who receive a beating at her hands is a boisterous vicar who rashly provokes Meg by refusing to pay fully for his meal and drinks, accusing her in her reckoning of being a "cozening queane."[94] Meg, as the enforcer of the tavern, shows no more deference

88 Joan Thirsk and J.P. Cooper (eds), *Seventeenth-Century Economic Documents* (Oxford: Clarendon Press, 1972), p. 348.

89 Shepherd, *Amazons and Warrior Women*, pp. 105–6.

90 Thomas Heywood, *The Fair Maid of the West*, (ed.) Katharine Lee Bates (Boston, New York, and Chicago: D.C. Heath, 1917).

91 Shepherd, *Amazons and Warrior Women*, 96.

92 Anon., *The Life of Long Meg of Westminster* 2nd edn (London, 1635), pp. 5, 9.

93 Anon., *Life of Long Meg*, pp. 5–7, 14–15; her mistress, after appraising Long Meg's great physical strength, tells her that any unpaid bills will be taken out of her wages.

94 Anon., *Life of Long Meg*, pp. 6–7.

to legal authorities than she does toward the vicar. Declaring her bar a "sanctuary" for debtors for the sake of good neighborliness, she cudgels and throws into a pond a bailiff who attempts to arrest a debtor in her mistress's tavern.[95] As the popularity of heroines such as Bess and Long Meg suggests, instances of gender inversion, in which assertive women gain the upper hand over men, were not confined to the popular rituals of misrule or economic protest, but were common in the everyday rough-and-tumble environments of the marketplace and tippling house.

So we have much evidence of market women and hostesses standing up for themselves in popular literature. But to end our analysis of representations of commercial women with conflicts between female vendors and customers, women and men, would be to omit a crucial point: cooperation amongst men and women as well as conflict colored representations of the early modern marketplace and fair. Relations amongst the fair folk in Jonson's *Bartholomew Fair* illustrate this point most sharply. Despite their bickering over pride of place within the fair, Trash and Leatherhead refer to each other as "brother" and "sister," denoting a common sense of identity as market traders. They show an ability to work together when they spy the foolish young gentleman Cokes approaching their stalls, and they quickly hatch a plan to gull him of his money. The terrifying Ursula is also not without her male allies in the fair. When hot grease is spilled upon her, Knockem comes to her aid, bidding her to "sit i' thy chair, and give directions, and shine Ursa/ major."[96] Jonathan Haynes's argument that we can detect a Bakhtinian sense of primitive, plebeian communism in *Bartholomew Fair* perhaps overstates the case, for these alliances are ones of temporary convenience. Trash and Leatherhead, after all, only work together when there is the prospect of mutual profit; and we can be sure that Ursula's customers want to keep her stall open, so that the pig platters and ale bottles keep coming.[97] But the play nevertheless speaks to the fact that in the context of the fair, patriarchal conceptions of the social order could count for very little.

The popular literature and city comedies of the day give us a strikingly different picture of gender relations than the one upheld by moralists and clergymen. But there are reasons to doubt that balladeers and playwrights give us any more insight into women's commercial activities than the stern admonitions of godly advice literature. Ballads and city comedies were meant primarily to entertain. Authors were not engaging in anthropology; they were catering to their customers' appetite for humorous or intriguing stories about stock characters: aggressive market women, scheming female fair booth holders, and heroic barmaids. Furthermore, much of the material in this chapter comes from London, a metropolis which, as Eleanor Hubbard has recently shown, offered women a surprising degree of

95 Anon., *Life of Long Meg*, pp. 12–13.

96 Jonson, *Bartholomew Fair*, 2.2.3–4, 7–8; 2.5: 178–9.

97 Jonathan Haynes, *The Social Relations of Jonson's Theater* (Cambridge: Cambridge University Press, 1992).

social and economic agency.[98] Was women's prominent role in commerce peculiar to London, or did it reflect how a wider commercial culture was shaping gender relations? Literary sources suggest that urban women were surprisingly active in participating in trade. The following chapters turn toward the actual dealings and disputes of women in Cambridge, Oxford, and other provincial cities in order to chart their commercial roles.

98 Eleanor Hubbard, *City Women: Money, Sex, and the Social Order in Early Modern London* (New York: Oxford University Press, 2012).

Chapter 3
Cooperation and Conflict: Women, Commerce, and the Household Economy

We have seen how prescriptive and popular literature emphasized the ideal of cooperation between husbands and wives, how couples ought to behave as "yoke fellows," each pulling alongside each other for the common good of the household. Did this ideal translate into practice? After all, commercial expansion and the growth of towns in the late sixteenth and seventeenth centuries hardly eroded the institution of the patriarchal household. Indeed, England's demographic and commercial revival was accompanied by renewed efforts by guilds and town governments to bolster the position of male artisans and traders, and circumscribe the participation of women in production and high status trades.[1] However, the standard picture of the patriarchal household as an institution which constricted female economic opportunities is overdrawn. The economic contributions of women to the early modern household were hardly limited to the unpaid labor of childcare, cooking, and cleaning. In fact, many wives residing in early modern towns had a great deal of influence over the running of the early modern household economy. Women did much of the purchasing and often managed household consumption. Furthermore, they tended their husbands' shops and marketplace booths. Male householders, dependent upon the extra money and the commercial services their wives provided in managing consumption and retailing household goods, were often obliged to allow their wives some degree of independence in commercial matters.

It is not the argument here that women in early modern provincial towns enjoyed a "rough-and-ready" economic equality with men, or that the early modern period constituted a "golden age" for female workers.[2] While in the

---

1 For the argument that the fourteenth-century plague opened economic opportunities to women see P.J.P. Goldberg, *Women, Work, and Life Cycle in a Medieval Economy: Women in York and Yorkshire c. 1300–1520* (Oxford: Oxford University Press, 1992), esp. pp. 336–7; and McIntosh, *Working Women in English Society*, pp. 30, 154, 188, 251–2. Conversely, periods of overpopulation and increased unemployment led to fewer opportunities for female laborers: see Honeyman and Goodman, "Women's Work, Gender Conflict and Labour Markets."

2 The former phrase is Eileen Power's; the latter is Caroline Baron's, both cited in Judith Bennett, *Ale, Beer and Brewters*, p. 147.

medieval period some married women living in towns enjoyed *feme sole* status, the right of married women to run businesses legally on their own had been done away with in most towns, with the exception of London—and even there few wives in the early modern period claimed *feme sole* status.[3] Furthermore, as Judith Bennett and Marjorie McIntosh have shown, the re-organization of old industries such as brewing along capitalist lines, which required producers to have access to large reserves of credit in order to compete, could often close down economic opportunities for women operating independently of male householders.[4] Thus, historians such as Bennett, McIntosh, and Susan Cahn have argued that the early modern period saw a constriction of women's economic independence, though Bennett would add that their low economic status remained unchanged from the medieval to the early modern periods. The work of these scholars has been valuable in uncovering the enduring role patriarchal values played in limiting economic opportunities open to women throughout the late medieval and early modern periods.[5] But in focusing primarily on the disadvantages women faced vis-à-vis established male householders—when many men also failed to become householders in a period marked by overpopulation, and rising rates of vagrancy and underemployment—in the early modern labor market, these scholars risk imposing a frame of reference that would have been quite foreign to contemporaries of the period. In practice, men and women alike saw the household primarily as a cooperative enterprise necessary for prosperity or—at the least—everyday survival, rather than as yet another institution erected with the intent to exclude women from commerce and production.

The everyday commercial agency of wives is altogether evident in accounts of marital conflicts which occasionally appear in depositions from debt cases heard by the university courts of Cambridge and Oxford. Such conflicts were sometimes of material interest to the debt cases heard by these courts, for if it could be shown that a wife made a transaction without the consent of her husband, the transaction could be rendered void. Such domestic conflicts between husbands and wives, however, do not invariably confirm the notion that because husbands held ultimate legal authority over household property, they felt free to exercise overbearing control over their wives' commercial activities. Wives were occasionally able to turn coverture to their advantage against their husbands by making transactions for which their husbands were legally accountable. In other instances, in the course of marital disputes, women were able to use their indispensable commercial roles as leverage over their husbands.

---

3 Marjorie Keniston McIntosh, "The Benefits and Drawbacks of *Femme Sole* Status in England, 1300–1630," *Journal of British Studies* 44 (July, 2005): 410–38.

4 Bennett, *Ale, Beer, and Brewsters*; McIntosh, *Working Women in English Society*.

5 An endurance mirrored in the very similar advice medieval and early modern moralists gave regarding the proper structuring of the household; see Davies, "Literary Advice on Marriage," pp. 60–61.

To what extent did notions of the proper gendered division of labor determine the commercial role of wives in urban communities? As Alexandra Shepard has demonstrated, the expectation that the male householder provide for the household, through either wage labor or by practicing a craft or trade, was a fundamental tenet of patriarchy; husbands who failed to support their households through labor were objects of derision.[6] Reserved for wives, or the female servants under their direction if they had them, were the jobs of childcare, housecleaning, and food preparation.[7] It might seem at first glance that these roles consigned women's work to the "private sphere" of the household, but even these gender-specific domestic duties did not limit the economic role of women to the confines of the household.

The consigning of the care of the household goods and provision of meals for the family to women, in fact, demanded that they frequent public markets, shops, and streets to purchase victuals, clothing, and other necessities. A large number of debt cases heard by the Cambridge University courts involved disputes regarding a wide variety of consumer goods purchased by women.[8] But management of household provisions did not simply entail taking orders from the husband; wives had some independence in determining the needs of the household. Agnes Lockwood of Cambridge was very much in charge of her own kitchen when in 1580 she ordered her husband to go to Hellen Fryer, a baker's wife, and "bye hir fleshe withall," a chore he duly performed.[9] The management of household resources, expertise in judging the price of daily necessities, and an ability to "cheapen"—that is, the skill of bargaining for the lowest price—were considered

---

6 Shepard, "Manhood, Credit and Patriarchy," pp. 82–7.

7 For discussions of these roles, see Mendelson and Crawford, *Women in Early Modern England*, pp. 303–13; Hill, *Women, Work and Sexual Politics*, ch. 7.

8 For examples, see *John Bowrne c. Marmaduke and Joan Rise*, CUA, Comm.Ct.I.1, fo. 226^{v}, regarding spoons Joan Rise purchased from Bowrne; *Richard Newmarshe c. John Borne*, CUA, Comm.Ct.II.3, fo. 181, for victuals sold and money loaned to Borne's wife; *Gregory Dawson c. Leonard Glascock*, CUA, Comm.Ct.III.9, no. 12a: regarding money Glascock's wife borrowed from the miller in order to purchase bread; *Jonas Weelkes c. John and Elizabeth Hytch*, CUA, Comm.Ct.III.14, no. 6: regarding a debt in part for draper's wares bought by Elizabeth; *Roger Butterham c. John and Phillipa Ward*, CUA, Comm. Ct.III.17, no. 23: regarding a hat band bought by Phillipa Ward; *Robert and Margaret Smyth c. Richard and Annah Beamont*, CUA, Comm.Ct.III.17, no. 95: for cheese bought by Annah Beaumont; *Radulphus Draper c. William Kinge*, CUA, Comm.Ct.V.9, fo. 214^{v}: regarding the purchase of a hat; *John Scott c. Thomas Watson*, CUA, Comm.Ct.V.3, fo. 41: regarding the purchase of lace; *Francis Baldwin c. Edmund Ivory*, CUA, V.C.Ct.II.25, fo. 73: regarding the purchase of tobacco from the plaintiff by the defendant's wife. For instances from other towns, see: BrRO, JX/1/3, fo. 83^{v}, and *A Calendar to the Records of the Borough of Doncaster* (4 vols, Doncaster, 1900–1902), vol. 2, p. 183, vol. 3, pp. 116, 119.

9 *Agnes Lockwood c. Thomas Gillam*, CUA, Comm.Ct.II.1, fo. 1.

valuable skills.[10] Young, unmarried women in towns often served apprenticeships in "housewifery" under married women and widows; once they had obtained competence in bargaining and the trust of their mistresses, they were allowed to purchase food for the household. As we shall see, a good working knowledge of prices for household goods and bargaining skills opened opportunities for women in informal, unregulated trades such as pawnbroking and the selling of used goods.[11]

That women often practiced such informal trades suggests that housework and the management of household consumption did not occupy many a householder's wife full time. Middling households often found it to their advantage to employ female servants or charmaids to cook, clean, and watch the children, leaving the wife free to devote much of her time to household production and commercial activities. But even wives of humbler households would have had time to devote to jobs other than domestic work. As Keith Wrightson has pointed out, most middling and poor households were too small and contained too few household goods to preoccupy wives full time with cleaning. Child rearing undoubtedly occupied significantly more time, but working women could turn to older children or servants for assistance.[12] And, of course, children, once they were old enough, were expected to assist their parents in the work of the household. Married women often had enough free time available to pursue remunerative work, casting doubt on the notion that the oft-repeated early modern adage "a woman's work is never done" referred exclusively to domestic drudgery.

Indeed, many women married to skilled craftsmen and tradesmen assisted their husbands in household production, and it was this work experience which enabled some widows to carry on their husbands' businesses, in a few cases long after the death of the husband. The longevity of Cambridge's widow business owners is illustrated by the records of several cases regarding the inability or unwillingness of St. Catherine's College of Cambridge University to repay the hefty debts it accrued in obtaining provisions in the last decade of the sixteenth century. Agnes Scott, a widow and a baker, continued to sell bread to the college after her husband's death, and had to bring a case against the college in order to obtain payment.[13] Alice Holmes, who, along with her husband, sold beer to the college, operated as a brewer for at least 20 years after her husband's death.[14]

---

10 For example, see Sheila D. Thomson (ed.), *The Book of Examinations and Depositions Before the Mayor and Justices of Southampton 1648–1663*, Southampton Record Series 37 (Southampton: Southampton University Press, 1994), p. 64.

11 See below, Chapter 4.

12 Wrightson, *Earthly Necessities*, pp. 44–5, 48–9; for a persuasive critique of the argument that women's domestic and child-rearing duties precluded their involvement in early modern labor markets, see Ogilvie, *A Bitter Living*.

13 *Agnes Scott c. William Forster, MA*, CUA, V.C.Ct.II.1, fo. 224. For similar cases, see *Michael Homes c. Katherine Hall*, CUA, V.C.Ct.II.3, fos 44ᵛ–5; and OUA, Hyp/B/1, fo. 257.

14 *Michael Homes c. John Overall, MA*, CUA, V.C.Ct.3, fo. 13; Alexandra Shepard, "Litigation and Locality," p. 18 and n. 43.

It might be expected that trades involving the production of food and drink were especially open to widows, for wives were of course expected to supervise the family kitchen and often baked and brewed in order to supplement household provisions. But there are instances of widows practicing trades usually associated with male tradesmen. Dorcas Swetson of Cambridge, for instance, ran her husband's apothecary shop after his death.[15] Elizabeth Crossley, sued in 1618 by a creditor in the Chancellor's court of Oxford University, operated a book and stationery shop in Oxford.[16] Widow Smart, who had married a miller, was able to continue her husband's business in Cambridge; she, like her husband before, was fined by the University's leet for charging excessive tolls for milling grain.[17] Some husbands evidently planned for their wives to take over the household business. Phillipe Delamotte, a prominent clothier and minister of the Huguenot church of Southampton, turned his workshop over to the supervision of his wife in his declining years. Though wives could not become officers of the guild, Judith Delamotte nevertheless assumed a position of leadership in the guild in representing the clothiers' interests. She went on to operate her clothier's workshop for at least 21 years after her husband's death in 1617.[18] Because apprentices in skilled crafts were almost invariably male, it is certain that widows such as Delamotte learned their craft in the course of assisting their husbands in the shop.[19]

Production was only one aspect of the household business, and for a household to thrive, it had to have competent retailers. Women were necessarily involved in the vending of goods at the shop counter. Commentators often remarked upon the prominence of shopkeeper's wives in London's centers of fashionable consumption and among the "shop girls" of the Royal Exchange. Such observers usually noted that attractive women dressed in the latest fashions could only increase custom. For instance, a ballad written around 1690 which conjured wives' responses to recent squibs that attacked the popular but expensive fashion of "top-knots" asked:

> What Man would not have his Wife richly Array'd?
> When as he well knows it enlarges his Trade;
> Come, come, I must tell ye, 'tis fit we should wear
> *Rich Towers and Top-Knots, with Powdered-Hair.*[20]

---

[15] CUA, Comm.Ct.III.20, no. 3.

[16] *John Fennell c. Elizabeth Crossley*, OUA, Hyp/B/4, fos 333–4.

[17] CUA, CUR 17, fo. 23 (1574).

[18] In 1638, she was presented by the Southampton court leet for using light weights: SCA, SC 6/1/49, fo. 20.

[19] On this point, see also Ilana Krausman Ben-Amos, "Women Apprentices in the Trades and Crafts of Early Modern Bristol," *Continuity and Change* 6 (Aug., 1991): 227–52.

[20] "The London Ladie's Vindication of Top-Knots," in *Pepys Ballads*, vol. 6, p. 17. Italics in the original text.

Appearances, however, were not the only, or even the most, important attribute fashionable wives and shop girls were expected to bring to the shop counter. Such vendors also had to be able to keep the shop books in order to account for who owed what.

Townswomen were hardly confined to those shops which pushed fineries upon fashionable passersby. Many women tended shops which sold mundane goods, such as bread, linen, candles, coal, and beer. Male householders, of course, were engaged to some extent in selling their own goods. For instance, Shakespeare's father, a glover, found it convenient to hand his gloves out of a ground floor window to customers as he worked, if only because it allowed him to close his shop quickly when he spied the approach of a creditor. But because male artisans had to (or, at least, were supposed to) devote much of their working day to their craft, they often had to leave the tending of the shop counter to their wives. For instance, the wife of Walter Metcalfe, a chandler, assumed the role of tender of the shop counter in the 1590s.[21] Similarly, John Ellyson, a brewer and former apprentice to William Medcalf recalled in a debt case that both William and his wife regularly sold beer and collected money from St. John's College, Cambridge.[22] The impression that wives were often the ones who made sales in the household shop is bolstered by several cases from the Cambridge University courts in which wives were reported to be involved in reckonings with customers or to have kept the shop book which recorded the debts of customers.[23]

Wives of tavern keepers and inn-holders had similar commercial responsibilities. In addition to serving food and drink and making up rooms, wives of publicans collected payment for sales and services and supervised servants, duties which were central to the profitability of these establishments. Indeed, it is likely that many married women ran alehouses while their husbands, who held the license, pursued other lines of work. In 1614, the constables of Nottingham highlighted women's de facto control over the alehouse business in their warning to the town assembly that "some order" needed to be imposed on "all the alewyfes of this town, for we thinke that never an alewyfe dothe as hir husband is bownd to."[24] Evidence of transactions also suggests the central roles women played in running alehouses. In several cases heard before the university courts, men sued on behalf of their wives against those customers who failed to pay for food, drink, and

[21] *Office c. Walter Metcalfe*, CUA, V.C.Ct.I.3, fo. 224^{v}.

[22] *Master and fellows of St. John's College c. Thomas Smithe, MA*, CUA, V.C.Ct.II.2, fo. 87^{v}.

[23] *Robert Bales c. Alan Hall,* CUA, V.C.Ct.I.3, fo. 228r; *Michael Homes c. John Overall, MA*, CUA, V.C.Ct.II.3, fos 13^{v}–14^{v}; *Richard Leichfild c. Adam Gantlett,* CUA, V.C.Ct.II.14, fo.9^{v}; *John Ward c. Roger Bartram,* CUA, V.C.Ct.II.32, fo. 33.

[24] W.H. Stevenson, et al. (eds), *Records of the Borough of Nottingham* (9 vols, Nottingham and London: Thomas Forman & Sons and Bernard Quaritch, 1889), vol. 4, p. 325.

lodging.[25] That the selling of drink carried with it risks less likely to be faced by women tending artisans' shops failed to dissuade many husbands from allowing their wives to run rowdy tap rooms. In 1632, when Peter Yate's wife tried to collect payment from two youths for 8d. worth of cake and beer, she was confronted by six "scholars"—friends of the youths—who shouted "fowle threatninge wordes," which prompted her, with the help of a customer, to bar the alehouse door. After the attackers fled, Yate's wife, with her maidservant, pursued the youths as they made their escape, only to be assaulted by the young men, now bearing cudgels, in a university quadrangle. Yate's wife, finding herself outnumbered, unarmed, and her maidservant "strooke ... downe" with a club, continued the fight until the affray was dispersed by University proctors.[26] As the injury case brought by Yate's husband against one of the attackers suggests, there had to have been, for the survival of many a public house, an understanding between many husbands and wives that when wives or servants were cheated or assaulted in the trying to collect payment, husbands would bring suits for debt or damages on behalf of their wives.

Dealing with shifty or violent customers was just one aspect of a hostess's business; they also had to oversee servants and tapsters. Two cases from the Cambridge University courts suggest that wives who served in their husbands' alehouses and taverns had a say in the hiring of help. In 1595, John Nashe, a baker, persuaded both Thomas Knights and his wife, proprietors of "the signe of the wrastlers" in Cambridge, to hire John Harrison as a tapster by promising to repay them in beer if Harrison proved untrustworthy.[27] Similarly, Richard Stevenson, the patron of an aspiring tapster, felt the need to convince Roger Hylls, owner of the "Sign of the Anteloppe," and his wife of the young candidate's trustworthiness. As Elizabeth Hylls recalled, Stevenson, after asking both Elizabeth and Roger Hylls to hire the tapster, sought to seal the deal by clapping her "uppon hir shoulder once or twice," declaring "hostes you have here A good fellow & a very honest man ... I praye you be good to him." Then, perhaps sensing some remaining doubt, he promised her and her husband, according to Elizabeth Hylls, four or five barrels of beer if the tapster cheated them.[28] What is most intriguing about this encounter was Stevenson's friendly, familiar gesture—the claps on Elizabeth Hylls's shoulder. Just as today deals are often sealed with a handshake, so in the early modern period agreements were solemnized by gestures of physical intimacy: claps upon the shoulder, embraces, the taking of drinks out of the same cup. That Stevenson

---

[25] *Thomas Hayes c. Nevel Haies*, CUA, Comm.I.1, fo. 140^{v}; *Peter and Joan Joanes c. John Symond*, CUA, Comm.Ct.I.1, fo. 168; *John Harvey c. James Moreley*, CUA, Comm. Ct.I.2, fo. 76, Comm.Ct.II.3, fo. 12^{v}; *John Cutchye c. Richard Warryn*, CUA, Comm.Ct.II.1, fo. 38^{v}; *Francis Gibbonsen c. James Cowley*, CUA, Comm.Ct.II.1, fos 54, 63, Comm. Ct.II.2, fol. 2^{v}; *Thomas Townsed c. John Hales*, OUA, Hyp/B/5, fo. 222^{v}.

[26] *Peter Yate c. William Taylore*, OUA, Hyp/B/6, fos 128–30.

[27] *Thomas Knights c. John Nashe*, CUA, V.C.Ct.I.30, fo. 157.

[28] A witness remembered the defendant promising *three or four* barrels of beer to the couple; *Roger Hylls c. Richard Stevenson*, CUA, Comm.Ct.II.4, fo. 22.

pre-emptively conferred such a gesture upon Elizabeth Hylls suggests she was to make the final decision in the hiring of this aspiring tapster. The central roles women played in shops and public houses—in selling goods, providing services, and supervising servants and employees—obliged many husbands to give their wives a say in how the household business was to be run.

Indeed, some women were just as involved in bargaining for supplies which were necessary for the household business, and managing the credit arrangements which accompanied such deals, as they were in assisting in household production and vending goods in the shop or tap room.[29] For instance, William Golbrand of Liverpool and his wife ran afoul of town regulations by bargaining for and purchasing wool before it could be offered to the mayor and his deputies, who were supposed to have the first opportunity to make purchases.[30] In 1596, Alice Leader, the wife of a victualer, admitted that even though she still owed John Sherman, a prominent Cambridge brewer, money for beer she had bought from him, she nevertheless accepted beer from Francis Bird; Bird's sale of beer on credit to Alice Leader violated an agreement among Cambridge brewers that no brewer should sell beer to a victualer who was still in debt to another brewer.[31] The extent to which some wives could exercise control over the household business is indicated by the testimony of Richard Yorke in a debt case brought against his mother and stepfather in the Chancellor's court of Oxford in 1630. In describing his mother's commercial responsibilities while she was married to Yorke's stepfather, a tavern keeper, Yorke noted that his mother "by and with [Thomas, her husband's] allowance and approbation [did] com[m]onlie and usualie deale for … Thomas in buyeinge sellinge bargaineninge and borrowinge … and [his mother] was com[m]onlie knowen to be her saide husbands agent in all or most of his affaires."[32] That Richard Yorke would give a deposition damaging to his stepfather and mother's case perhaps hints at familial tensions; nevertheless, his testimony suggests that it was not beyond the realm of the court's imagination to envision the household mistress to be very much in charge of the commercial activities of the household.

We have thus far focused on the commercial activities women engaged in within the space of the household itself. But women were too crucial to the running of the household business to confine their commercial activities to the house alone. Sales of small amounts of goods could be dispatched at the shop counter, but vendors who dealt in bulky goods such as beer and ale or catered

---

[29] Confer with McIntosh, *Working Women in English Society*, p. 239.

[30] J.A. Twemlow (ed.), *Liverpool Town Books 1550–1862* (2 vols, London: University of Liverpool, 1918), vol. 2, p. 643.

[31] Thus, Sherman brought suit against Bird in the University Vice-Chancellor's court: *John Sherman c. Francis Bird*, CUA, V.C.Ct.I.3, fos 7, 10. See also, for instance, *Richard Bradley c. Thomas Hayes*, CUA, Comm.Ct.II.2, fo. 46; *Robert Oliver c. John Sherman*, CUA, V.C.Ct.II.22*, fos 1–4.

[32] *Humphrey Jones c. Thomas Pink*, OUA, Hyp/B/6, fo. 52.

to wholesale buyers found it necessary to deliver their goods. Husbands busy with manual labor or overseeing household production often entrusted deliveries and transactions conducted outside the household to their wives. For instance, the Cambridge brewer Michael Holmes in 1588 sued Christopher Grimes for beer delivered by Holmes's wife; and Thomas Hayes sued John Richardson to obtain payment for victuals delivered by Hayes's wife.[33] The centrality of wives' involvement in household commerce is underscored by the business done between the universities, which were voracious consumers of food and drink, and local suppliers. Mary Mase, the wife of a Cambridge brewer, acted as her husband's seller of beer to Queen's College.[34] Susanna Wheeler, the wife of a cook of Jesus College, Oxford, regularly collected payments from the college for the food supplied to the college by her husband.[35]

As these cases suggest, there must have been a great deal of cooperation between many couples regarding the business dealings of the household. Husbands had to inform their wives of the intricacies of the household business if wives were to collect debts, and wives had to inform their husbands as to how the household business was doing. In Oxford, male brewers often trusted their wives and servants with commercial dealings with the University and other buyers. Roger Jones, a bachelor of theology, testified in a debt case heard before the Chancellor's court in 1614 that he had "verie often seene … alebrewers wives or servants [deliver] warninge to customers houses … with a booke wherein all the brewers customers names are sett with such ale as hath bin delivered for redie monie or uppon credit to them."[36] Ipswich brewers also relied on their wives to collect payments from customers.[37] Poorer couples too worked together for the common good of the household. Richard Metcalfe, an inn-holder prosecuted for allowing his tenants to sell food and drink without license, admitted before the Cambridge Vice-Chancellor's court that for the last four years "one davyes and hys wyef haue sold and doe sell beere bread & other vittell in his … howse … aswell … as forthe the doares."[38] Joan Lenton, the wife of a Southampton laborer, examined before the JPs on suspicion of accepting stolen goods, "confessed" that "both shee and her husband have for the space of eight yeares bought of seafaring

33 *Michael Homes c. Christopher Grimes*, CUA, Comm.Ct.I.2, fo. 215v; *Thomas Hayes c. John Richardson*, CUA, Comm.Ct.I.1, fo. 182. See also *Robert Bales c. John Rogers*, CUA, Comm.Ct.III.8, no. 127; *John Durante c. Francis Sawnders*, CUA, V.C.Ct.I.4, fo. 271; *John Hunte c. William Stevens*, OUA, Hyp/B/3, fo. 92.

34 *Mary Mase c. Martin Rust,* CUA, V.C.Ct.III.16, nos. 54, 55; as evidenced by the fact that she brought a defamation suit against Rust, a cook of the college, for an insult he hurled at her while she was in the college kitchen. For a fuller analysis of this case, see below, Chapter 6.

35 *Thomas Price c. William Tomson*, OUA, Hyp/B/6, fo. 53v.

36 *William Dewye c. Thomas Brooke*, OUA, Hyp/B/4, fo. 230v.

37 ESRO, C/2/3/8/1, pp. 101–2.

38 *Office c. Richard Metcalfe senior*, CUA, V.C.Ct.I.5, fo. 148; see also *Office c. Jeremy Tibb*, fo. 87v.

[men] and Fishermen … cordage old netts and raggs by which they have made a benefitt by sale to paper mills."[39] Such humble common commercial endeavors necessitated communication and cooperation between spouses.

It is hard to measure quantitatively the percentage of women who occupied the booths of public markets, for such booths were often held in the name of the male householder. But there is compelling incidental evidence that wives often operated as traders for their husbands, and were prominent participants in England's public marketplaces and fairs. Dairy farming and cheese making had long been considered a traditional female occupation,[40] but by the early modern period, women had taken to vending their produce in local marketplaces. Southampton's court leet in 1615 made mention of the "Butter woemen" and other market women, both from the town and the countryside, who sold provisions such as poultry, eggs, and cheese in the public marketplace. Although it is likely that, for many of these women, the booths were legally held by male householders, the leet's presentment leaves no doubt that women did the selling.[41] Among the traders who witnessed Agnes Shaw in Cambridge's fish and meat market accuse a journeyman, Robert Simpson, of a sexual relationship with her daughter-in-law were several wives of fishermen and butchers who were tending market stands.[42] Wives' attendance of market booths left husbands, such as the fishermen and butchers of Cambridge, free to pursue their trades.

Because the care and preparation of household provisions was a central duty of "good housewifery," it is unsurprising that wives were particularly active in vending the food and drink produced by the household. But wives were not confined to selling victuals in the marketplace and fair. Artisans' wives sometimes sold their husband's manufactured goods in public markets. For instance, in describing the occasion upon which she witnessed the criminal activities of a female pickpocket, Elizabeth West, the wife of a Southampton mariner, recalled that she had visited Southampton's fair in order to buy cloth from a booth operated by one "Lymburner[']s wife," who was married to a linen maker.[43] Similarly, "mistres mosse," the wife of a Cambridge draper, in 1590 operated her husband's

---

39 R.C. Anderson (ed.), *The Book of Examinations and Depositions, 1622–1644*, Southampton Record Society Publications (4 vols, Southampton: Cox and Sharland, 1929–1936), vol. 4, pp. 15–16.

40 Deborah Valenze, "The Art of Women and the Business of Men," pp. 144–7.

41 F.J.C. Hearnshaw and D.M. Hearnshaw (eds), *Court Leet Records [of Southampton]*, Southampton Record Society Publications, 1, 2, 4, 6 (4 vols, Southampton: H.M. Gilbert & Son, 1905–1908), vol. 3, p. 489.

42 Including Agnes Burff, wife of Richard Burff, a fisher, Joan Frenche, wife of Roger Frenche, a "pikemonger," Thomasina, wife of Andrew Cocklye, Joan Atkin, and Margaret Wilkenson, wife of Thomas Wilkenson, a butcher; *Robert Simpson c. Agnes Shawe*, CUA, Comm.Ct.II.6, fos 88–9, 93^{v}, 101–4. See also *John Smith c. Roger Wylson*, CUA, V.C.Ct. II.2, fo. 116 regarding the stall of Mrs. Cawthorne in the fishmarket (1598).

43 Thomson (ed.), *Examinations and Depositions Before … the Justices of Southampton*, p. 64.

booth in Stourbridge Fair.[44] Leet court presentments against wives for using "short yards" also indicate that women were involved in the sale of manufactured goods such as cloth.[45] The commercial activities of wives were therefore not confined to the site of the house itself. Rather, women were integral traders in the commercial networks of their environs.

There were, however, social and cultural constraints upon the ways in which women participated in commerce. Men dominated long-distance trade—from the profitable sectors of trade in high-priced manufactured goods and wholesales to the sale of cheap print and used clothes. There were powerful prejudices against women who traveled long distances alone. An account of the arrangements of Ann Kirke of Cambridge, who was planning a trip to Bedfordshire, is revealing. According to a widow who made money by hiring horses, Ann Kirke hired two horses, one for herself and one for her husband, for "it was noe creditt" for a woman "to ryde alone."[46] In the face of such attitudes, held by both men and women, many independent female traders would have found it difficult to raise the capital necessary to engage in long-distance trade in wholesales. The University court leet of Elizabethan Cambridge prosecuted 14 men, but no women, for exporting corn and other staples outside of the jurisdiction of the university—which extended a mere three miles from the boundaries of the town.[47] Although women dominated the production of cheese and butter in rural Suffolk, the traders who brought the dairy goods from the country to Cambridge's Stourbridge and Midsummer Fairs were usually men.[48]

There were exceptions. Some poor women found it necessary to travel across the countryside, from town to town, to make a living. Usually such itinerant traders found it necessary to be accompanied by male chapmen, either for protection or to allay the suspicions of local authorities who wanted to prevent vagrant single women from entering their towns and villages.[49] Wealthier women had more opportunities than humble women to engage in long-distance trade without male oversight. Some husbands evidently prized the commercial canniness of their wives more than the tenets of patriarchal convention. The wife of one Francis Empereur, a merchant of Norwich, operated as a factor for her husband, buying in 1643 £106 14s. 5d. worth of linen and other draper's wares in London, which

---

44 *John Powre c. Robert Wood*, CUA, Comm.Ct.II.4, fo. 48.

45 For example, see J.P. Earwaker (ed.), *The Court Leet Records of the Manor of Manchester* (12 vols, Manchester: H. Blacklock and Co., 1884–1890), vol. 4, p. 15.

46 *Mary Offield c. Roger Kirke*, CUA, V.C.Ct.II.14, fo. 36^{v}.

47 CUR 17, fos 15–49; usually such goods were destined for the sea port of King's Lynn.

48 CUA, Comm.Ct.V.5–11, passim.

49 For example, see B. Howard Cunnington (ed.), *Some Annals of the Borough of Devizes: Being a Series of Extracts from the Corporation Records, 1555–1791*, 2 parts (Devizes: George Simpson & Co., 1925), part 2, pp. 21–2: examinations of Hugh Clyffe and Elizabeth Browne.

she had loaded for shipment by sea to her husband in Norwich.[50] Similarly, Margery Elwood, the wife of a coal merchant, visited King's Lynn, sometimes with and sometimes without her husband, to buy sea coals for transport and sale in Cambridge.[51] As these examples illustrate, wives were not excluded from the profitable sectors of long-distance trade, but their activities were probably contingent upon arrangements they made with their husbands.

It was more common for husbands than wives to travel long distances to buy and sell. But this elevated, rather than diminished, the commercial importance of many wives, for they had to act as agents in selling household goods and managing their husbands' credit arrangements in their husbands' absence. As one witness recalled before the Commissary's court of Cambridge University in 1585, Margery Elwood, when she did not accompany her husband on his trips to King's Lynn, often "sould sea coales to divers persones in her husbands absence [and] hath received monye for them."[52] Simon Talbye, a cheesemonger of London, left for the continent for more than a year in 1589, leaving the conduct of his business to his wife. As John Grimpston, Talybe's apprentice, recalled in a debt suit brought before Ipswich's petty court, Talbye's wife directed the business, and regularly ordered him to borrow whatever money necessary to purchase cheese in Suffolk for sale in London.[53] Just as crucial to her husband's business was Jane Elwood, the wife of a Cambridge waterman who imported malt. Upon arriving in King's Lynn in 1597, Henry Elwood found himself without enough coin to buy the malt he was under contract to deliver to Michael Holmes, the Cambridge brewer. Elwood thus borrowed 20s. from a "woman passynger" of his boat who was on her way back to Cambridge before he was. He hurriedly sent a letter back to his wife directing her to borrow 20s. from Michael Holmes and pay the money to his creditor once she arrived. Jane borrowed the necessary money from Holmes's wife, and repaid the passenger on her arrival in Cambridge.[54] That these wives found little difficulty in obtaining goods, selling merchandise, and securing loans in their husbands' absences demonstrates a wide acceptance among many traders that wives had the legitimate responsibility to deal on behalf of their absent husbands.

What therefore made the household a durable economic institution throughout the early modern commercial revolution was not its deep roots in patriarchal teachings—which had been preached with as much fervor in the medieval as the early modern period—but its adaptability to economic circumstance. Historians have long noted that many households departed from the patriarchal ideal, in which the husband assumed responsibility for public matters and the wife confined herself to the domestic duties of the household. But this argument does not go far enough. Economic survival took precedence over concerns that proper female

50 CLRO, MCD, 1/89.

51 *Henry Mays c. Richard Ellwood*, CUA, Comm.Ct.II.2, fo. 100^{v}.

52 *Henry Mays c. Richard Ellwood*, CUA, Comm.Ct.II.2, fo. 100.

53 *John Carnaby v. Simon Talbye*, ESRO., C/2/3/8/2, pp. 176–7.

54 *Michael Homes c. Henry Elwood*, CUA, V.C.Ct.II.2, fos 33–8.

decorum be maintained. The extent of the flexibility of the early modern household economy can be glimpsed in Darlene Abreu-Ferreira's studies of the commercial activities of women in Portuguese coastal towns. With much of the male population away on fishing and trading expeditions, wives and widows dominated not just the retail trade in fish in the marketplace, but also the wholesale trades in fish and imported goods. As Abreu-Ferreira admits, such outright female dominance over the marketplace was probably unique to Portuguese seaside towns, if only because other western European ports such as London and Bristol did not see such a large proportion of their men as these Portuguese towns engaged solely in seafaring.[55] Nevertheless, those urban English male householders engaged in long-distance trade were just as willing as their Portuguese counterparts to cede the running of the commercial affairs to their wives.

However necessary cooperation was between husbands and wives for the survival of many households, we should avoid idealizing domestic relations. As historians have long recognized, conflict as well as cooperation marked domestic relations.[56] Although husbands and wives who brought cases to court often had an interest in presenting a common front—confirming each others' testimony regarding what they owed or what was owed to them—there are tantalizing hints in depositions from several debt cases that conflict between husbands and wives on commercial matters colored relationships between husbands and wives. Sara Mendelson and Patricia Crawford have argued that wives had the most to lose in spousal conflicts, for they often depended on their husbands for material support. Margaret Hunt has emphasized the legal and social advantages husbands had over wives in domestic disputes over how to run the household business.[57] Indeed, wives whose marriages had broken down could find themselves in an unenviable position. In cruelly turning his wife and daughter out of the house in 1578, John Beale, an Ipswich blacksmith, recommended that they make their living by "begging." Beale's wife was forced to reside with friends, and had to bring suit to recover some of the property she brought to the marriage.[58] The plight of Margaret Beale and other wives whose marriages had failed give us, however, a misleadingly dire impression of the nature of conflict and authority in early modern English households. Legal separation was rare; and bad husbands, who failed to support their wives, abused them, or turned them out of doors, risked the scorn and derision of neighbors. Indeed, the blacksmith John Jay, his occupational

---

55 Darlene Abreu-Ferreira, "Fishmongers and Shipowners: Women in Maritime Communities of Early Modern Portugal," *The Sixteenth Century Journal* 31 (Spring 2000): 7–23; and see also her article "From Mere Survival to Near Success: Women's Economic Strategies in Early Modern Portugal," *Journal of Women's History* 12 (Summer, 2001): 58–79.

56 See Keith Wrightson, *English Society*, ch. 4.

57 Mendelson and Crawford, *Women in Early Modern England*, p. 142.

58 ESRO, C/2/3/8/1, p. 265; probably in the form of dowry, though this is not specified in the depositional evidence.

affinity with John Beale notwithstanding, seems to have had few qualms about testifying against Beale on Margaret Beale's behalf before Ipswich's petty court.[59] The dependence of many husbands on the commercial services provided by their wives ensured that power relations between husbands and wives were more complex than historians have supposed. Depositions from debt cases suggest not just that some wives had the temerity to disobey their husbands, but that the central role wives played in the management of household economy allowed them to sometimes get their way even when their husbands disagreed with their wives' conduct of the business.

Conflicts between husbands and wives could be especially intense if the wife was a remarried widow. As Barbara Todd argued, many of those widows fortunate enough to be able to practice a craft or trade in their own right prized their independence enough not to remarry.[60] Some of those widows who found it economically advantageous to remarry sought to preserve a measure of the economic independence they had enjoyed. Here it is worth examining in detail a complex debt case brought in December 1592 by John and Agnes Shaw of Cambridge against Edward Upcher, a gentleman of Sutton. The Shaws brought suit for £100 worth of damages for corn they claimed Upcher failed to deliver to them; Upcher countered that the Shaws overstated the amount of corn he was to deliver to them, and that, in any case, they failed to pick up the corn, waiting so long that it became moldy.[61] Agnes had been married to John Vepen, a corn merchant, and she continued her late husband's business. During the months of December and January, 1588–1589, while she was still a widow, Agnes Vepen purchased 40 or 60 quarters of barley,[62] 20 quarters of wheat, and one quarter of peas for shipment back to and sale in Cambridge. But just after these deals were made, the price of barley dropped sharply. According to Upcher, Agnes, at this point married to John Shaw, failed to pick up the corn and desired instead to have her money back. However, her new husband, a maltster, wanted to receive the barley at the original price. Perhaps he was worried for his new household's reputation for plain dealing, or he may have simply coveted the profits he could earn by malting corn he had not paid for. After John Shaw succeeded in collecting 10 of the bushels of barley, Agnes Shaw attempted to re-establish her control over the household's commerce by paying a visit to Upcher. According to Upcher's account, Agnes, "weepeinge and cryeinge," requested "that he … not deliver the … barlye wheat & peaze,

---

[59] For expectations of husbands, see Shepard, "Manhood, Credit and Patriarchy;" Elizabeth Foyster, "Male Honour, Social Control and Wife Beating."

[60] Barbara Todd, "The Remarrying Widow: A Stereotype Reconsidered," in *Women in English Society* (ed.) Mary Prior (London and New York: Methuen, 1985), pp. 54–92.

[61] For depositions and allegations in this case, see *John and Agnes Shaw c. John Upcher*, CUA, Comm.Ct.II.4, fos 228–31, 240, Comm.Ct.II.6, fos 8^v, 13–15, Comm. Ct.III.6, nos. 13, 92.

[62] The amount of barley bargained for was in dispute: the Shaws claimed Agnes had bought and paid for 60 quarters, Upcher claimed she had bought 40 quarters.

unto … John Shawe … sayeinge that he [John Shaw] & she were fallen out & were at a iarre." She added that her "husband should not have that which was hirs, but that which he had gotten alredy," and that she would be willing to deliver a bond to Upcher, saving him "harmlesse from hir … husband" for the corn.[63] Clearly remarried widow-traders such as Agnes Shaw felt that, despite the husband's legal rights over the household property, they should retain some independence and stake in the businesses they had built; indeed, her point to Upcher that the delivery should be delayed because she and her husband had "fallen out" regarding the deal suggests that, the doctrine of coverture notwithstanding, wives expected to have a say in the commercial dealings of the household. Unfortunately for the Shaws, the claims of Upcher and his witnesses that Agnes Shaw had failed to accept the corn for self-interested reasons, and that she had in fact taken measures to prevent the delivery of the corn to her husband, proved convincing enough for the court to decide the case in his favor.[64]

But why did Upcher agree to Agnes Shaw's request that he not deliver the corn to her husband if he had it on hand? No definitive answer can be deduced from the depositional evidence, but the possibilities are suggestive of the tensions and ambiguities which could mark the joint commercial efforts of husbands and wives. It is of course possible that Upcher anticipated the legal difficulties that the Shaws would face if they sued him for debt. But, in referring to Agnes Shaw's "weepinge and cryeinge," Upcher seems to have wanted to make clear to the court that he was moved by her consternation over losing control of the business she had worked hard to build and operate. Sympathy alone, however, can hardly account for his acceptance of her promise of a bond to save him from efforts by her husband to collect the disputed corn: in most cases, only heads of the household could make bonds regarding the debts owed by, and to, the household. Thus, Upcher's deposition underscores the legal ambiguities surrounding the activities of some women traders. Cambridge's borough court did allow some married women to trade and bring suits as *femes sole*. Agnes Shaw, who had established herself as an independent and prominent fishmonger during her first marriage, seems to have enjoyed *feme sole* status, with the power to make commercial deals without the consent of her husband; perhaps Upcher was attempting to play upon her anomalous legal status as a trader in constructing his case.

But whatever Agnes Shaw's precise legal status, Upcher's claims before the court reflected the very active and independent roles wives such as Agnes Shaw could play in building the wealth of the household. Her loss of control over her household was, in fact, temporary. As depositions in a case brought by John Atkin

---

63 *John and Agnes Shaw c. Edward Upcher*, CUA, Comm.Ct.II.4, fos 215^{v}–16.

64 An appellate case to be heard by the Vice-Chancellor's court did not get past the initial stage. The clerk recorded the case heading, but did not get so far as to record the complaint. Either the Shaws got cold feet, or they came to some private agreement with Upcher before pursuing the suit. *John and Agnes Shaw c. Edward Upcher*, CUA, V.C.Ct.I.30, fo. 22^{v}.

against John and Agnes Shaw for debt in 1597 revealed, John Shaw had moved to London permanently in 1595, and rarely visited his wife since the move. To support his claim that he could not repay the debt if the plaintiff won the case, Shaw admitted to having no say over the commercial activities of his Cambridge household. According to John Shaw, although Agnes made a good deal of money selling fish and other commodities, she also "hath dealt verie dissolutelye and not so carefullye & providently as she might & ought to have done" in managing the household; particularly galling to John Shaw was that his wife had "procured … manie Comodies (of right belonging unto herself & to … her poore husband [i.e. himself])" in order to give them over to John Vepen the younger, her son by her first marriage.[65] But remarried widows were scarcely the only women who had the confidence and acuity to challenge their husbands. The intense involvement of wives in the commercial affairs of the household gave them some room to deal as they saw fit.

Because they regularly bought daily necessities, such as food and fuel, wives often had a more immediate appreciation than their husbands of the damage caused by failure to pay debts to neighbors on time. Harried by creditors, the wife of Richard Warren in 1581 took advantage of her husband's "absence" to sell one of his horses—a mare—for 13s. She used the much-needed money to pay some of the debts owed by the household. Richard Warren claimed before Cambridge University's Commissary court that because his wife had sold the mare "without his consent," John Orgar, the buyer, should return the horse. The court, mindful of the doctrine of coverture, required Orgar to return the horse, but it also ordered Warren repay the 13 shillings Orgar paid for the horse.[66]

At first glance, it appears that this case reaffirms the impression that male householders alone had control over the household economy. And yet, Warren's wife did accomplish her goal. After all, the debts had been paid. If the creditors refused to return to Warren the money paid by his wife for acknowledged debts, Warren would have had to embark on a number of legal cases—which he may well have lost—to retrieve relatively small sums of money; and it must always be remembered that litigation could be expensive, both in terms of legal fees and strained relationships with neighbors. Richard Warren was thus probably left with the options of working harder, calling in debts from neighbors, or obtaining loans from neighbors to repay Orgar for the horse in dispute. But it is also possible that Warren's wife sold the horse with her husband's secret blessing as a crafty legal strategy to buy some time in repaying debts, though they would give a different impression to the court.[67] In either case, Warren's wife succeeded in her attempt to sell a piece of her household's property in order to re-establish the household's credit, at least temporarily.

---

65 *John Atkin c. John and Agnes Shawe*, CUA, Comm.Ct.II.8, fo. 30^{v}.

66 CUA, Comm.Ct.I.1., fo. 76.

67 I thank Prof. Dan Bornstein for alerting me to this possibility.

It would be mistaken to see wives as the sole provocateurs of domestic disputes. The kind of conflicts described in the popular literature analyzed above, in which spendthrift, drunken husbands provoked marital conflicts—not least because the excessive consumption of alcohol by husbands drained the household of resources and rendered husbands incapable of working—had real world analogues. Cuthbert Johnson, a Cambridge innkeeper, and—according to a household servant—a "common drunkard," frequently tested his wife's patience. On one occasion, she reportedly punished him by striking his shins and face. On two other occasions Cuthbert went so far as to threaten to commit suicide if she continued to "chastise" him for his drinking: on the first occasion, he climbed up to the beams of his roof with a rope to hang himself; later he waded into the River Cam as if to drown himself. In both instances, his wife was able to talk him out of suicide.[68] Wives had to assume positions of responsibility over commercial affairs in households headed by husbands who proved unable to perform their duties.

Women worked as individuals as well as members of family units. As Wrigley and Schofield have estimated, from 1560 to 1720, between five and 27 percent of women never married.[69] While domestic service to an established householder was the commonest occupation of never married women, these workers sometimes practiced occupations independently of masters and mistresses. Wives too often worked independently of men. Married women were prominent in the buying and selling of second-hand goods, huckstering, trading in market provisions as local middlemen, money lending, and pawn brokering. The activities and status of women who operated as traders in their own right is the subject of the next chapter. Nevertheless, the household economy remains an important unit of analysis through which to explore female commercial activities and economic agency. The fact that the husband held legal authority over household property and enjoyed public recognition as the head of house should not blind us to the cooperative aspects of the household economy. The occupational and economic status of many husbands depended on the productive and commercial work provided by their wives. Thus, the household economy was shaped as much by cooperation, negotiation, and conflict as it was by patriarchal authority.

---

[68] *Cuthbert and Joan Johnson c. James Jurdeine*, CUA, Comm.Ct.I.2, fo. 93^{v}; *Joan Johnson c. Thomas Wilkenson*, CUA, Comm.Ct.II.3, fo. 64.

[69] E.A. Wrigley and R.S. Schofield, *The Population History of England, 1541–1871: a Reconstruction* (Cambridge, Mass.: Harvard University Press, 1981), 260–63.

Chapter 4

Traders, Hucksters, and Creditors: Independent Tradeswomen and the Commerce of Early Modern Towns

In 1630, the mayor's court of Norwich prosecuted Mary Uttinge, the wife of Robert Uttinge, for regrating, and found that she "usually buyeth Corne & grindeth the same at Trowse Mill and selleth meale in this Markett." She escaped a fine, but the court did forbid her to buy corn in the marketplace.[1] The efforts of petty traders such as Mary Uttinge—retailers who hawked provisions or trucked in second-hand durable goods—may seem marginal to the story of England's transition toward a commercial society; until recently, historians have been interested in them more for what their careers can tell us about the place of women in the early modern labor force than their economic impact. And yet, at the local level, they helped satisfy ever-increasing consumer demands. Such demands, and their satisfaction, may not constitute a "consumer revolution." [2] But they do suggest that England in the sixteenth and seventeenth centuries prospered despite inflation and economic uncertainty. Although dearth remained a threat, England avoided the subsistence crises seen elsewhere in Europe. And, as Carole Shammas's careful investigations have shown, on the whole English households in the mid-seventeenth century possessed more, and a wider range of, durable consumer goods than their mid-

---

[1] William Sachese (ed.), *Minutes of the Norwich Court of Mayoralty 1630–1631* (Norwich: Norfolk Record Society, 25, 1942), p. 91.

[2] Some efforts have been made to make the case for the rise of a consumer society before the eighteenth century: Thirsk's *Economic Policy and Projects* focuses on new rural industries. Margaret Spufford focuses on seventeenth-century itinerant traders in *The Great Reclothing of Rural England: Petty Chapmen and Their Wares in the Seventeenth Century* (London: Hambledon Press, 1986). More recently, Lisa Jardine has reframed the history of the Renaissance as a period of novel conspicuous consumption: *Worldly Goods: A New History of the Renaissance* (London: Macmillan, 1996). Nevertheless, most historians of England have seen the eighteenth century as the period in which goods once considered luxuries became everyday necessities. See Neil McKendrick, John Brewer, and J.H. Plumb, *The Birth of a Consumer Society: The Commercialization of Eighteenth-Century England* (Bloomington: Indiana University Press, 1982); Peter Stearns, "Stages of Consumerism: Recent Work on the Issues of Periodization," *The Journal of Modern History* 69 (Mar., 1997): 102–17, especially p. 104; and various essays in John Brewer and Roy Porter (eds), *Consumption and the World of Goods* (London and New York: Routledge, 1993).

sixteenth-century counterparts.[3] Petty trading women, often operating outside of markets and in defiance of urban regulations, played a crucial role in satisfying everyday wants.

Scholars of women's work have long seen female involvement in local trading as emblematic of the nature of women's work within early modern towns. Historians working within the narrative framework established long ago by Alice Clark have envisioned huckstering, pawnbroking, and trading in second-hand goods as important, female-dominated trades which allowed women to contribute to the household economy before the rise of industrial capitalism displaced the household and town marketplace as the loci of economic activity.[4] More recently, historians skeptical of the notion that the pre-industrial period constituted a "golden age" for women workers have drawn pessimistic conclusions regarding the place of women who traded by their own names. According to this "pessimistic-critical" paradigm, the involvement of women in petty trades was indicative of the low economic status women enjoyed in the early modern commercial economy. Unlike craftsmen and merchants, townswomen tended to practice petty trading not full time but on a casual basis, to allow them to attend to household duties. Furthermore, huckstering and petty lending offered fewer opportunities for profits than the practice of skilled crafts or wholesale, long-distance trading.[5] Women, so the current consensus holds, pursued the types of commercial activities men found to be too little paying to pursue.

And yet, as scholars such as Heather Swanson and Peter Earle have shown, late medieval and early modern households commonly considered it advantageous to pursue a variety of moneymaking ventures at once.[6] Many male householders who practiced a guild craft found it hard to make ends meet, and wives who worked as independent traders played a crucial role in supplementing household earnings. Skilled craftsmen who might seem economically independent had an interest in allowing their wives to pursue a wide variety of commercial ventures. For instance, in addition to selling her husband's candles, the wife of Thomas Harker of Carlisle

---

3 Carole Shammas, *The Pre-Industrial Consumer in England and America* (Oxford: Clarendon Press, 1990), ch. 4. See also Craig Muldrew, *The Economy of Obligation: The Culture of Credit and Social Relations in Early Modern England* (London: Macmillan, 1998), pp. 21–36.

4 Clark, *Working Life of Women*; Louise A. Tilly and Joan W. Scott, *Women, Work, and Family* (New York: Holt, Rinehart and Winston, 1978); Merry Wiesner Wood argues for the economic importance of such traders in Nuremberg: "Paltry Peddlers or Essential Merchants? Women in the Distributive Trades in Early Modern Nuremberg," *The Sixteenth Century Journal* 12, no. 2 (1981): 3–13.

5 McIntosh, *Working Women in English Society*, pp. 130–32; Mendelson and Crawford, *Women in Early Modern England*, p. 278.

6 Heather Swanson, "The Illusion of Structure: Craft Guilds in Late Medieval English Towns," *P&P* 121 (1988): 29–48; Peter, Earle, "The Female Labour Market in London in the Late Seventeenth and Early Eighteenth Centuries," *EcHR* new series, 42 (Aug., 1989): 328–53.

was fined for keeping an illicit bowling green and unlawfully selling butter and eggs.[7] For widows excluded from regulated crafts and wives married to laborers, trading in provisions and used goods assumed even greater importance for the survival of the household. Certainly women trading in their own names could expect to reap fewer profits from their efforts than the types of work pursued by freemen and burgesses; but the earnings they could make were hardly insignificant in buttressing the household economy. As we shall see, contrary to the common assumption, many men believed it worth their time to hawk food and fuel on the streets alongside female competitors.

Thus, women's presence in the trades of huckstering, pawnbroking, and trading in second-hand goods does not mean that these trades must have been among the worst occupations open to denizens of early modern towns. It is misleading to lump, as some have done, petty retail trades with very low paid, female-specific occupations such as spinning, house cleaning (performed by "charmaids"), and prostitution. Rising commodity prices eroded the value of laborers' wages, but they also opened commercial opportunities for traders.[8] Population growth made demand for consumer goods increasingly inelastic, presenting opportunities for those who had the money or credit to accumulate a cache of daily necessities. Hucksters took advantage of rising food prices and the limited hours kept by public markets by selling food on the streets, in parcels small enough that even the poorest could afford them. Middlemen such as Mary Uttinge were able to reap profits by transporting food to where it was most in demand. Humble consumers who could not afford craftsmen's prices for newly produced wares often bought used goods, to the profit of traders, female and male, who bought and sold clothes, cooking utensils, and other durable household goods.

The inflation that occurred in the midst of a cash-poor economy is a powerful indication of the flexibility and strength of the early modern "culture of credit," in which money was treated primarily as a unit of account instead of as a unit of exchange, and purchases made on credit and cash loans were an everyday feature of local commerce.[9] The price revolution opened opportunities for lenders of all

---

7 R.S. Ferguson and W. Nanson (eds), *Some Municipal Records of the City of Carlisle* (Carlisle: Cumb. And West. Ant. and Arch. Soc., e.s. IV, 1887), pp. 302, 333, 603, 605.

8 Paul Slack argues that while poverty became less severe, it became more widespread in the sixteenth and seventeenth centuries; see *Poverty and Policy in Tudor and Stuart England* (London: Longman, 1988). For price indices, see E.H. Phelps-Brown and Sheila V. Hopkins, "Seven Centuries of the Prices of Consumables, Compared with Builders' Wage-Rates," and "Seven Centuries of Building Wages," both in *Essays in Economic History*, (ed.) E.M. Carus-Wilson (2 vols, London: Edward Arnold, 1962), vol. 2, pp. 194–6; 170, Figure 1. J.R. Wordie demonstrates the role inflation played in spurring production of food and manufactured goods: "Deflationary Factors in the Tudor Price Rise," *P&P* 154 (1997): 32–70.

9 For the use and cultural meanings of credit, see Craig Muldrew, "Credit and the Courts: Debt Litigation in a Seventeenth-Century Urban Community," *EcHR*, new series, 46 (Feb., 1993): 23–38, and his *Economy of Obligation*.

kinds and of both genders: financial services provided by money lenders and pawnbrokers were increasingly in demand, for consumers needed some cash if they were to make a reckoning with traders; those who defaulted on debts risked lawsuits and, just as troubling, their economic reputations among their neighbors. As Marjorie McIntosh and Amy Froide have shown, unmarried women who earned wages had to lend their money at interest if they hoped to retain the value of their earnings in the midst of inflation.[10] But for women of any marital status with access to cash, lending or pawnbroking could be a moneymaking venture, and not merely a survival tactic.[11] Some unmarried women could make their livings by providing financial services, and wives could easily practice occasional pawnbroking and lending along with other commercial and domestic activities.

There was thus a plethora of informal commercial activities which women could practice outside of the household. In this chapter, we shall examine the participation of townswomen in three types of commerce. Women were active in the provisioning trades; they not only sold their own, homegrown produce in the marketplace but also traded in and around the marketplace as middlemen. Records from courts leet, which retained jurisdiction over the marketplaces of Cambridge, Liverpool, Manchester, and Southampton, indicate that the profits which could be made from such trading were large enough to attract men as well as women to trading locally in provisions. Secondly, women were central agents in the trade in second-hand manufactured goods. The extensive depositions taken by Southampton's quarter sessions are a rare and particularly valuable source for assessing the commercial activities of such traders. Many of these depositions related to theft cases and the circulation of stolen goods within the commercial networks of the town. They therefore provide us with an unusually rich source for analyzing how married women earned profits by pursuing part-time occupations as traders in second-hand goods. Finally, depositions from debt cases heard before the university courts give insight into the practices of female moneylenders and pawnbrokers.

The Provisioning Trades

Women as well as men took advantage of the commercial opportunities offered by town marketplaces. Usually located at the center of town, the marketplace served as the central point in which consumers could obtain trade commodities such as corn and malt, and household necessities, such as bread, meat, produce,

---

10 Amy M. Froide, *Never Married: Singlewomen in Early Modern England* (Oxford: Oxford University Press, 2005), p. 89; McIntosh, *Working Women in English Society*, pp. 103–5.

11 Froide in particular has demonstrated that single women, provided that they had substantial capital, were able to build highly profitable careers as moneylenders: *Never Married*, pp. 128–41.

and fuel. The market provided a convenient place to sell goods for women from the nearby countryside who operated dairies and tended gardens.[12] Townswomen too produced provisions for sale in the marketplace, including produce grown in gardens, and meats and pies, as is indicated by the frequency with which women were fined for allowing their pigs and other animals to pollute the streets. In Manchester women commonly baked and sold spiced bread in the marketplace, to the consternation of the local leet jurors, who believed that such superfluous treats raised the price of bread.[13]

The town marketplace remained a vital economic institution throughout the early modern period.[14] And yet the public function of the regulated marketplace was always under threat from "engrossers," "forestallers," and "regraters"—those traders who, in the view of officials, preyed upon the marketplace and its consumers by buying up provisions before or after they reached the market in the hopes of selling them again at an artificially high price. But, these traders served an important economic function in transporting and selling food whenever and wherever there was demand, unlike local producers tied to the public markets. Certainly, such commercial practices had medieval antecedents.[15] But the rise in food prices during the late sixteenth and seventeenth centuries undoubtedly made trading in provisions an ever more attractive alternative to wage labor, especially for women, who on average earned less than men. To what extent were women as well as men able to take advantage of this lively, often profitable, extra-legal trade in provisions? We have already seen that women were rarely in a position to operate as long-distance corn merchants, but were they at least able to take advantage of the commercial opportunities in and around their local marketplaces?

The presentments of courts leet of Cambridge University, Liverpool, and Manchester confirm the impression that women regularly traded in provisions as middlemen. And yet women did not dominate such trades. What emerges from the leet records is a complex picture of participation in the provisioning trades. Lists of presentments against forestallers, engrossers, and regraters by Cambridge University's leet which survive from 21 years from the reign of Elizabeth give the names of 104 men (76 percent) and 33 women (24 percent) who were prosecuted at least once for engrossing, forestalling, regrating the food, fuels, and sedge sold in the market. In Elizabethan Liverpool, women were more prominent (76 percent of presentments), but men too engaged in side dealing which skirted the regulations of the marketplace (see Table 4.1).

[12] For the presence of "women's markets" in some towns, see below, Chapter 5.

[13] Earwaker (ed.) *Court Leet Records ... of Manchester*, vols 1–5, passim.

[14] W. Thwaites, "The Corn Market and Economic Change: Oxford in the Eighteenth Century," *Midland History* 16 (1991): 103–25.

[15] R.H. Hilton, "Lords, Burgesses and Hucksters," *P&P* 97 (1982): 15, and his article "Small Town Society in England before the Black Death," *P&P* 105 (1984): 65–8.

Table 4.1 Traders prosecuted at least once for forestalling, engrossing, or regrating in Elizabethan Cambridge and Liverpool, by gender and marital status

Gender/Marital Status	Cambridge		Liverpool	
Men, listed by name alone	104	76%	61	34%
Widows	15	11%	17	10%
Wives	13	10%	51	29%
Women, never-married or listed by name alone	3	2%	49	28%
Women presented as wives and later as widows	2	1%	0	0%
Total	137	100%	178	101%

Note: Those prosecuted for exporting goods outside the town jurisdiction not counted. The percentage totaling more than 100% is the result of rounding.
Sources: Cambridge: CUA, CUR 17, fos 15–49. Liverpool: Twemlow (ed.), *Liverpool Town Books*, vol. 2.

It is possible that the proportion of traders who were women is under-represented in Elizabethan Cambridge leet records. In cases in which wives were offenders, the husband was held accountable and was legally responsible for paying the fine. Although the clerks usually seemed to be concerned with identifying the actual trader who violated marketplace regulations, it is possible that they sometimes named husbands alone for offences committed by their wives. In Liverpool, the clerks were particularly scrupulous in identifying the gender of the offender and, if the offender was female, noting her relations. The involvement of women in skirting the marketplace in early modern Manchester was also more pronounced than in Cambridge. Of the 50 traders prosecuted at least once for forestalling, engrossing, or regrating provisions and goods such as leather and hides during the particularly well recorded years of 1648 to 1662, 28 were men (56 percent) and 22 were women (44 percent). Although women commonly traded as middlemen on behalf of their households, men too found it advantageous to deal in provisions. In Liverpool, while many men ran afoul of commercial regulations by dealing in hemp (a crucial commodity in a port town), others, including at least one skilled artisan—a slater—retailed fruits, butter, and meats, the very same goods sold by his female colleagues. In 1597, the Carlisle court leet attempted to fine three related men (all had the surname Crockbaine) £5 each for regrating and forestalling salmon, trout, and other fish. The heftiness of the fine perhaps suggests that surprisingly high profits could be made from such "petty" dealing.[16]

Trading in provisions was an attractive work option for both wives and widows. As Table 4.1 indicates, both widows and wives were prosecuted in

[16] Ferguson and Nanson (eds), *Records of ... Carlisle*, p. 273. The mayor, perhaps balking at the high amount of the fines, vetoed them.

Table 4.2 Frequency of prosecutions in Elizabethan Cambridge and Liverpool of regraters, forestallers, engrossers, and exporters, by gender

Number of Times Prosecuted	Cambridge Male Traders	Cambridge Female Traders	Liverpool Male Traders	Liverpool Female Traders
1	71	23	32	75
2	17	4	7	12
3	2	2	3	5
4	6	1	0	1
5	5	0	1	0
6+	3	3	0	0

Note: Those prosecuted for exporting goods outside the town jurisdiction not counted.
Sources: Cambridge: CUA, CUR 17, fos 15–49. Liverpool: Twemlow (ed.), *Liverpool Town Books*, vol. 2.

Cambridge and Liverpool for forestalling, regrating, and engrossing. Most of the never-married women, as daughters or servants, were trading as servants on behalf of householders. Marital statuses among female traders in Manchester were also mixed, although we have less evidence that widows were regularly active in provision-trading: at least nine of the women presented were married; at least three were widows; the ten women listed by name alone may have been never-married.[17] With the exception of those women who could continue operating the shop of their late husbands, work options for widows were limited. Trading in provisions as a middleman was a way widows could support themselves and their children. For wives, trading in provisions brought a welcome supplement to the earnings of their husbands.

Historians have argued that women's work, as opposed to the work of men, was often of an intermittent, casual nature; rarely did women devote their full working day to one occupation.[18] Certainly, the occasional trading in and around the marketplace constituted for many women a by-employment which could be conveniently combined with domestic work and assisting the household business. And yet, as indicated by the number of times traders were prosecuted before

[17] Earwaker (ed.) *Court Leet Records ... of Manchester*, vols 4–5.

[18] Mary Prior, "Women and the Urban Economy: Oxford 1500–1800," in *Women and English Society*, (ed.) Prior, pp. 95–6; Sue Wright, "'Charmaids, Huswyfes and Hucksters:' The Employment of Women in Tudor and Stuart Salisbury," in *Women and Work in Pre-Industrial England*, (ed.) Lindsey Charles and Lorna Duffin (London: Croom Helm, 1985); Maryanne Kowaleski, "Women's Work in a Market Town: Exeter in the Late Fourteenth Century," *Women and Work in Preindustrial Europe*, (ed.) Barbara Hanawalt (Bloomington: Indiana University Press, 1986), p. 157.

Cambridge University's and Liverpool's courts leet, men were little more likely than their female counterparts to engage in trading as middlemen full time. Table 4.2 presents the number of times each male and female trader was prosecuted in a period of contiguous, or, in the case of Cambridge, nearly contiguous records.

These numbers must be treated with caution. For Cambridge, leet records in the years immediately before and after the periods in question have not survived, and thus we do not know whether some of these traders were prosecuted before or after the period. Furthermore, it is impossible to tell from the leet evidence how successful middlemen were in evading market authorities. Nevertheless, the fact that the large majority of all traders, both men and women, were fined only once or twice in the 18-year period suggests that most men and women traded as middlemen on an occasional basis. Downturns in the craft trades, or particularly promising commercial opportunities in the provisions trades, probably prompted both women and men to periodically trade in provisions as middlemen.

Both men and women profited from the limited hours and heavy regulations of the marketplace. Such restrictions evidently inhibited market traders from satisfying the full demand of consumers and public house keepers who sought food. Men were more likely to trade in wholesale provisions. Twenty-three of 104 male traders prosecuted at least once for forestalling, regrating and engrossing by Cambridge University's leet were involved in the corn trade, while only two of 33 female traders traded in corn; male traders were more likely to command the resources and credit necessary to trade wholesale in corn and malt. Nevertheless, a substantial number of men as well as women found it worth their time to trade in victuals such as bread, fruit, and butter. Particularly illustrative is the business of huckstering—the selling of victuals, ale, and fuel on the streets. Huckstering has been seen as one of the lowest, least profitable trades of the early modern town: the lugging of goods through the streets was taxing work, and, as Marjorie McIntosh has pointed out, hucksters could expect "only a tiny profit" for each of the items that they sold.[19] Thus, most historians of working women have seen huckstering as the work predominantly of poor women who lacked other economic opportunities. But if it can be shown that huckstering was attractive to men (who would have had more opportunities than women to engage in wage labor), then we should rethink the commercial opportunities open to even the humblest of female traders. Because neither Cambridge nor Manchester authorities designated which middlemen sold goods as street traders, we shall turn to the court leet of Southampton, which in the late sixteenth and seventeenth centuries made a concerted effort to control the numbers and more rapacious commercial activities of hucksters, and has thus left revealing records.

The evidence from Southampton belies the notion that huckstering was predominantly an occupation of poor women. Although women made up a large segment of hucksters, they did not dominate the ranks of street traders. Of the 149 persons designated as "hucksters" by the court leet between 1550 and 1652, just

19 McIntosh, *Women and Work in English Society*, p. 132.

55 were women (37 percent), of whom 43 were widows.[20] For women, huckstering could easily be combined with other trades in order to support the household economy. While it is difficult to recover the other types of work done by female hucksters, we know that at least six of the 55 women designated as hucksters also ran victualing houses. The overlap in the personnel of the two trades reflects the fact that successful public house keeping and huckstering required a common set of contacts and commercial skills. Both tipplers and hucksters had to have contacts with bakers, butchers, costermongers, dairy producers, and other suppliers of victuals; and both had to have the bargaining skills necessary to "cheapen" and then sell their provisions for profit. Huckstering provided victualers a way to recoup the losses of provisions left unsold from the night before. Victualers were not the only traders tempted to trade part-time as hucksters; among other traders listed as hucksters were a sawyer, a joiner, and the town musician.[21]

That even skilled workers found it worth their time to sell goods on the street suggests that historians have had too gloomy a view of huckstering. Hucksters exploited commercial openings which could not be fulfilled by traders tied to shops or market booths. After all, they sold everyday necessities whenever and wherever there was demand in parcels small enough that even most of the poor could afford them. Indeed, as the Southampton leet jurors noted in 1605, the "comon poore people of this towne" most often bought goods such as eggs, bread, and faggots not at the marketplace or shop, but rather "by the penny at the second hand."[22] The marketplace, as both a venue *and* source of goods, thus offered women commercial opportunities.

Just as important for some provision traders as their skirting of the marketplace, for at least part of the year, were the opportunities for profit presented by the fairs held in many towns.[23] While men dominated the trades in wholesale and manufactured goods in fairs, fairs offered an opportunity for women to vend victuals and drink to hungry, thirsty visitors. We know this because fair officials regularly prosecuted women for breaking the rules which governed the selling of food and drink in Stourbridge and Midsummer fairs.[24] Some wives trading in the Cambridge fairs had obtained *feme sole* status from the town. For example, Stourbridge court officials specified the wife of John Edwards, prosecuted in 1642 for selling beer and wine over the statutory price and using un-inspected vessels,

[20] SCA, SC 6/1/2–56. The marital status of men is not given in the leet court records.

[21] SCA, SC 6/1/12, unfoliated; SC 6/1/32, fos 23^v, 33. Each of these three traders were men; the occupations of hucksters was rarely noted.

[22] Hearnshaw and Hearnshaw (eds), *Court Leet Records [Southampton]*, vol. 3, p. 425; see also Earwaker (ed.) *Court Leet Records ... of Manchester*, vol. 3, p. 289.

[23] For the growing number of fairs as a sign of commercial expansion in the late-medieval period, see S.R. Epstein, "Regional Fairs, Institutional Innovation and Economic Growth in Late Medieval Europe," *EcHR*, new series, 47 (Aug. 1994): 459–82.

[24] CUA, Comm.Ct.V.2–11, passim.

as a "sole trader."[25] But wives did not need to obtain *feme sole* status in order to trade in the fair. Husbands, no doubt aware of the profits which could be made by selling food and drink at the crowded fair grounds, were often willing to allow their wives to set up stalls. The Stourbridge Fair court, for instance, noted in 1641 that Martin Cowledge's wife "affirmeth" that she was "intrusted [by her husband] in this bysiness to drawe the beer." Similarly, Henry Clarke's wife recounted that she was "intrusted in this fayr" by her husband "to sell & retayle ale."[26] But though these women used the word "intrust" and claimed to defer to their husbands' authority, we should not underestimate the degree of control wives exercised in running their drinking and victualing booths. Some of these traders were not merely taking orders from their husbands. Ann Webster was very much in charge of the victualing booths she opened in Cambridge's Midsummer and Stourbridge Fairs in the 1640s. Deponents in a 1651 debt case against her testified that they often heard Richard Webster, her husband, say that "he did never intermedle with the wine, beere, or victuals which came into the boothes, but that his wife Ann Webster tooke all, and paid all." As these witnesses recalled, Richard Webster played very much the role of a servant within the booth: he would immediately deliver any money he collected from a customer to his wife.[27]

Female victualers could expect to make considerable profits at large fairs such as Stourbridge Fair. Women's booths at Stourbridge Fair were substantial undertakings. Some women's victualing booths were large enough to require hired help. For instance, both "widow Ledham" and John Robinson, her servant, were fined in 1641 for selling wine in Stourbridge Fair without first obtaining a license.[28] The booths of Ann Webster were particularly large. She sold a wide variety of food and drink, including wine, beer, meats, and bread, and thus needed to hire several servants. Her cook, William Lambe testified in 1651 that Webster had hired him for the last three Stourbridge Fairs; Thomas More, a tailor, fetched drink purchased by Webster to supplement the earnings he made by his trade.[29] Stourbridge Fair was large enough to lure substantial female victualers from well outside Cambridge and its environs. In 1615, the Stourbridge Fair court prosecuted two women, "widow" Gawen of Newmarket and Margaret Couper of King's Lynn, for selling overpriced beer in un-inspected pots.[30] The court also amerced Alice Payne, married to Thomas Payne of Lincoln, for selling unwholesome victuals in 1611.[31] Elizabeth Foxgrave, a victualer from London, opened two stalls in the fair

25 CUA, Comm.Ct.V.10, fo. 33^{v}.

26 CUA, Comm.Ct.V.10, fo. 23.

27 *Edward Harley c. Ann Webster*, CUA, V.C.Ct.II.38, fos 33^{v}–4.

28 CUA, Comm.Ct.V.10, fo. 25.

29 *Edward Harley c. Ann Webster*, CUA, V.C.Ct.II.38, fos 33^{v}, 35A; as her servants testified, Ann Webster herself, and not her husband, hired servants for the booth.

30 CUA, Comm.Ct.V.8, pp. 97, 119.

31 CUA, Comm.Ct.V.7, p. 513.

of 1574.[32] That such traders saw it as worthwhile to transport food and drink over long distances for sale in the fair is suggestive of the high profits which tempted fair victualers and drink peddlers. The fairs and marketplaces of early modern towns thus offered commercial opportunities to women as well as men.

Trading in Second-Hand Wares

The regulated marketplace was famously at the center of the provisioning trades as both a venue for sellers and as a source of provisions for middlemen. Less visible to historians, but no less important to many townswomen, was the trade in second-hand manufactured goods. Traders dealing in durable used goods, often operating outside the purview of guilds and markets, had plenty of room to maneuver. These traders supplied the many consumers who could not always afford to buy new clothing and other wares. Because much of this trading was done in homes, alehouses, and the streets—outside the regulated marketplace—much of the evidence we have of this "informal economy" involved the circulation of goods which were suspected to have been stolen. Such evidence suggests that townswomen were especially well positioned to profit from the trade in second-hand goods.

At first glance, we might suspect that the restrictions on female property ownership enshrined in the common law doctrine of coverture would curtail the ability of women to trade in durable goods. But, as Garthine Walker has convincingly argued, "popular perceptions of ownership did not strictly adhere to legal definitions."[33] Moveable property constituted the most common type of property reserved for marriage portions, and wives considered themselves the owners of these goods during their marriages.[34] Furthermore, wives, charged with the buying and care of clothes, utensils, and other household wares, probably had a sense of informal proprietorship over these possessions; they also had an especially immediate appreciation, and keen knowledge, of the value of used goods. Indeed, some women were prized for their ability to appraise household goods when the values of such items were in dispute.[35] When one Nicholson, a bookbinder of Cambridge, sought to collect a debt from Rachel James (a remarried widow) and

---

32 CUA, Comm.Ct.V.5, fo. 77.

33 Garthine Walker, "Women, Theft and the World of Stolen Goods," in *Women, Crime and the Courts in Early Modern England*, (ed.) Jenny Kermode and Garthine Walker (London: University of London Press, 1994), p. 83.

34 Amy Louise Erickson, *Women and Property in Early Modern England* (London and New York: Routledge, 1993), ch. 6. Widows almost always regained ownership of their portions after the death of the husband.

35 In early modern Germany, some women earned livings as professional appraisers; see Merry E. Wiesner, *Working Women in Renaissance Germany* (New Brunswick: Rutgers University Press, 1986), pp. 143–7.

her husband, he called Jane Walker to testify to the worth of Rachel James's goods after the death of her first husband.[36] In a probate case brought by Edward Carpenter, heir of Andrew Carpenter of Oxford, Ursula Webb of Reading, Edward's mother, contended that the value of the estate had been grossly underestimated. Altogether, she re-valued 144 items, and in some instances buttressed her appraisals with reference to the quality and level of wear-and-tear of the items.[37] Many men, their legal prerogatives notwithstanding, had an interest in allowing their skilled wives leeway in buying and selling second-hand goods for profit.

As the Southampton quarter sessions depositions indicate, used, durable goods often circulated within female-dominated commercial networks. For instance, in 1587, the justices of Southampton suspected the wife of William Whithorne of Southampton of vending stolen goods after she sold the wife of one Gratian four yards of bone lace and a pair of white fustian sheets.[38] Mary Evans, married to Richard, admitted to delivering several items which were suspected to have been stolen to female intermediaries for sale, including a cloak and a black hat. She also sold a cloak to Stephan Legg, a tailor, who initially denied buying the cloak from Evans, but later admitted to buying it for 5s.[39] Suspected thieves sometimes claimed to have bought goods from female hawkers; that they hoped that such explanations would be believable to the justices suggests that women commonly trucked in used wares. Arrested in 1630 while in possession of the merchant William Cheeke's cloak, Frances Chapman, the wife of a weaver, claimed that she had bought the cloak from a woman "straunger" who had visited her house.[40] When asked in 1627 by the justices of Southampton how he came into possession of a ruff, a napkin, and an apron which belonged to one Mr. Pryaulx, Thomas Sager, an upholsterer of Newbury, claimed that he had bought all of the goods from a woman hawker whom he had never met before. When confronted with the fact that he had been seen in Pryaulx's garden, Sager admitted to having entered the garden and stolen the goods. But when asked about yet another item on his person, a cypress hatband, he fell back on the familiar story: he claimed that he had bought the hatband from "a woman of this Towne whom hee knoweth not" for 6d.[41] Thieves and fences would have been under pressure to sell hot goods for whatever prices they could get; the deals they offered must have been tempting to many women who traded in second-hand goods.

---

36 *Nicholson c. Rubin and Rachel James*, CUA, V.C.Ct.II.36, fo. 35^{v}.

37 OUA, Hyp/B/2, fo. 92^{v}; two male witnesses supported her contention that the estate had been under-valued: fo. 101; see also, for instance, the interrogation of Alice Deye, in ESRO, C/2/3/8/1, p. 30

38 SCA, SC 9/3/7, unfoliated.

39 Anderson (ed.), *Examinations and Depositions [of Southampton]*, vol. 1, pp. 52–3. See also vol. 4, p. 59, and Thomson (ed.), *Examinations and Depositions Before the ... Justices of Southampton*, pp. 78–9.

40 Anderson (ed.), *Examinations and Depositions [of Southampton]*, vol. 2, p. 59.

41 Anderson (ed.), *Examinations and Depositions [of Southampton]*, vol. 1, p. 102.

Southampton justices uncovered an extensive network of female fences in the course of their investigation in 1584 of Thomas Clyford, who was suspected of having stolen a number of linen wares.[42] The depositions from the case reveal what must have been a common strategy, in which goods would be passed along through one or more middlemen removed from the thief so as to disguise the true origins of the goods. Thus, unable to sell the goods openly, Clyford delivered them surreptitiously to a number of female dealers for them to sell on his behalf. To Chrystian Howell, the wife of a tankard bearer, he paid a fee of 6d. and 2d. worth of coal for her to sell a smock on his behalf. Clyford also delivered a number of wares, including two tablecloths, a pair of sheets, two aprons, a shirt, and four table napkins, to Joan Allice, the wife of a wool-comber, for her to sell for him; he later rewarded her with an apron for her efforts. Among Allice's customers for these goods was Jane Ricart, who had been suspected the previous July of being in possession of a stolen neckerchief.[43] Allice's desire to be rid of the goods quickly, and thus disguise her culpability in receiving stolen goods, is indicated by her refusal to allow Jane Ricart to dry the wet linen goods in her house. Ricart then made a mistake in offering the smocks to Margaret Smyth while admitting "I ame afrayd they have byn stollen"; Smyth later provided a damaging deposition. In addition, Allice was suspected of having sold smocks and sheets to one Alice Goodwin, the wife of John, though Alice Goodwin denied receiving any such goods. Joan Allice's husband, Michael, played a secondary role in the dealings, delivering some goods by order of his wife to Jane Ricart, and delivering the money Ricart paid for them to his wife. Though the suspected thief was male, women dominated the network of distribution, for these traders could assess the value of the goods and could easily find customers.

We should not conclude from such investigations that traders in second-hand wares dealt exclusively in stolen goods. Knowing receivers of stolen goods risked punishment along with thieves.[44] As the records of the Southampton quarter sessions themselves indicate, some traders took measures to protect themselves against the risks which came with buying suspect goods. Elizabeth Fashin, a married woman and victualer of Southampton, accepted a kettle as payment for beer she had sold a sailor, but, as she recounted to the justices, she refrained from selling the kettle for a day, in order to hear first if it had been cried for as stolen.[45] When presented with a proposed sale of a suspect silver spoon which had been cried for in the town, the wife of one Mr. Thringe of Southampton reported the matter to the justices, who

---

42 The below account is from SCA, SC 9/3/6, unfoliated (examinations from 8 and 10 November, 1584). Clyford claims to have inherited the suspect goods from his deceased mother.

43 SCA, SC 9/3/5, unfoliated (examination of Jane Rickat, 22 July 1584).

44 For example, see SCA, SC 9/3/2, unfoliated (examination on 13 January, 1576 of Elin Clarke, who was ordered to be put in the stocks by the mayor with "a sign on her for those who steal or buy or receave stolen goods").

45 Anderson (ed.), *Examinations and Depositions [of Southampton]*, 2, p. 8–10.

called the seller, Anne Greaterex, and the suspected thief, Margaret Symes, for examination.[46] That buyers would take such precautions suggests that, however common trading in second-hand wares was, fences and sellers of stolen goods engaged in a perilous business.[47] But traders did not have to buy stolen goods in order to turn a profit, for they were in an advantageous position in dealing with any seller in need of ready money. Parnell Merrill, a married woman of Cambridge who kept a shop, spotted a commercial opportunity in 1618 when Anthony Clifford, an impecunious scholar of Magdalene College, offered to sell her his cloak. She bought the cloak for 8s., but as subsequent testimony revealed, the value of the cloak was in fact between 13s. 4d. and 20s. If she resold it, she would have made a handsome profit indeed.[48] Women thus played central roles in the commerce of their neighborhoods as middlemen, trading in provisions and used wares. Just as important to their communities were the financial services they offered to their neighbors, for these activities made local commerce possible within the context of a cash-poor economy.

Financial Services

Townswomen employed the knowledge and skills associated with "housewifery"—including a familiarity of local buyers and sellers, a sense of the value of household wares, and an ability to bargain for the best price—to work as agents between producers and consumers. In 1615, William Blyth of Cambridge gave "certayne goods & houshold stuffe" worth £3 14s. to Elizabeth Hodson for her to sell for him, "w[i]th the privitye of her … husband," John Hodson. A subsequent suit brought by Blyth against Elizabeth and John Hodson in Cambridge University's Vice-Chancellor's court resulted in a judgment that the Hodsons should pay Blyth £3 10s. (4s. less than the stated value of the goods), which suggests that at the center of the dispute was the compensation Elizabeth was to receive for selling Blythe's goods.[49] In other cases, women who acted as commercial intermediaries sued to obtain payment for their services. Joan Johnson, a widow of Cambridge, in 1599 sued Thomas Gardiner of Waterbeach for payment for performing unspecified work for him, and also for "things bought" by her on

---

46 Thomson (ed.), *Examinations and Depositions Before the … Justices of Southampton*, pp. 88–9.

47 For more examples of women identifying stolen goods, see Walker, "Women and the World of Stolen Goods."

48 *Adrian Scrope, BA c. John Merrill*, CUA, Comm.Ct.II.18, fos 25, 26–7. Scholars were forbidden to sell their goods to local traders, and thus Parnell Merrill found herself sued by Scrope, a fellow of the college. Parnell Merrill claimed that she thought the young man was a "Country youth."

49 *William Blyth c. John and Elizabeth Hodson*, CUA, V.C.Ct.I.8, fos 201^{v}–2.

behalf of Gardiner.[50] Occasionally, women traded for others as payment for goods or services. This appears to have been the situation when in 1581 George Ingram and his wife requested Hellen Arrant, who along with her husband was staying in the Ingrams' house at the time, to sell a cassock for him at the highest price Arrant could fetch for it. Though the Ingrams wanted no less than 16s. for the cassock, Arrant could only get 11s. for the item, but with the agreement of the buyer that if he was given 12s. in half a year or a year's time, he would give the cassock back to the Ingrams.[51] If residents sometimes felt it necessary to employ trading women to deal on their behalf, outsiders looking to procure or sell goods had an even greater need to find local brokers. Judith Newarke of Bristol was one such intermediary. In 1652 she helped provision a Dutch ship driven to the port by winds and a lack of supplies. She put the sailors in contact with sellers of provisions, and bought beer for the ship, for which she was to be reimbursed.[52] It seems likely that she received a commission for her services. Tradeswomen knew how to leverage their position as trusted local traders to extract profits from long-distance traders.

Indeed, female pawnbrokers did much business with outsiders whose credit was unknown, and who thus found it necessary to pledge goods in order to obtain necessary loans. These traders could expect profits either from interest or, if the borrower defaulted, by selling the pawned goods, and thus generated profits from those in desperate need of ready cash. Detained in 1652 by the JPs of Southampton as a vagrant, Robert Gant was a tallow chandler of Kent who took to the road after, as he claimed, his shop and home had been consumed by a fire. When asked what brought him to the town, he answered that he was there to redeem a coat from "Goody Knights," which he had pawned for 6s. 6d. The money, he perhaps sheepishly admitted, was spent two weeks ago on a two-day drinking binge with his "companyons."[53] Women who ran victualing houses and alehouses commonly accepted pawns, not the least because their establishments attracted travelers who were in need of ready money. When authorities of Reading interrogated Thomas and Elizabeth Skynner in 1624 on suspicion of possession of stolen goods, Elizabeth admitted that she accepted from two men in lieu of payment for

---

50 *Joan Johnson c. Thomas Gardiner*, CUA, Comm.Ct.I.6, fo. 54. See also *Edward Parker c. Lawrence Johnson*, CUA, Comm.Ct.I.2, fo. 116^v, Comm.Ct.II.3, fos 46–62, Comm.Ct.III.4, no. 58, for "certeyne worcke" Agnes Parker, wife of Edward Parker, did for John Johnson, MA (whose executor was Lawrence Johnson), including her procurement of meat and "certayne wares" for him.

51 *George Ingram c. Henry Mase*, CUA, Comm.Ct.II.1, fo. 8; for another example, see *George Dawson c. Arthur Grenoppe*, CUA, Comm.Ct.I.1, fo. 20^v.

52 H.E. Nott and Elizabeth Ralph (eds), *The Deposition Books of Bristol*, (2 vols, Bristol: Bristol Record Society, 6, 13, 1935–1948), vol. 2, p. 111.

53 Thomson (ed.), *Examinations and Depositions Before the ... Justices of Southampton*, p. 135. Gant was accompanied by a woman whom he claimed was his wife, though he later admitted that he had not been married "by any lawfull Minister; but that he tooke her to be his wife & soe he sayth that he will live & dye with her."

drink a red velvet girdle, several knives, and a few gold rings as pawns.[54] In other instances, alewives and female victualers found it advantageous to accept pawns from regular, local customers as a way to increase sales.[55]

Coverture could complicate, but did not preclude, married women from working as pawnbrokers. To be sure, husbands particularly wary of legal entanglements may have forbidden their wives to act as pawnbrokers, for disagreements over the terms of transactions—most commonly regarding the amount of time the borrower had to redeem the pawn—often led to lawsuits. Wives who pawnbrokered without their husband's permission would have been in a tenuous legal position if called to court.[56] But many husbands evidently appreciated the profits their wives could earn by pawnbroking enough to risk legal entanglements. Although her husband, Richard, earned a good living as a draper, Joan Filoe of Cambridge operated as a pawnbroker. In 1600, she deposed to the University's Commissary court that she was in possession of three beds, two blankets, and two bolsters, all of which were goods pawned to her by one customer, Thomas Gill, a prominent Cambridge draper.[57] As this case suggests, female pawnbrokers occasionally catered to respectable clients in immediate need of ready money, and not just impecunious travelers or local spendthrifts. In 1598, William Howlsworthe, a fellow of Emmanuel College, Cambridge University, sued Thomas Thomlinson after Thomlinson's wife refused to let Howlsworthe redeem a satin doublet worth 14s.[58] In other households, both husbands and wives acted as pawnbrokers; they lent money for pawns in hopes of selling unredeemed goods, or accepted pawns from customers as sureties for debts.[59]

Women were also involved in the early modern money market, if only out of necessity. Those who kept cash in hand over the long term would see the value of their money eroded by the steady inflation which afflicted England in the late sixteenth and seventeenth centuries.[60] Women seeking to preserve the value of their coin commonly lent money at interest. Records of debt litigation give some indication of their activities. A sample of the debt cases heard by Oxford University's Chancellor's court shows that women plaintiffs outnumbered women defendants by about three to one.[61] This pattern of female involvement in debt litigation was not unique to Oxford: Craig Muldrew has found similar proportions

[54] J.M. Guilding (ed.), *Reading Records. Diary of the Corporation* (4 vols, London: James Parker and Co., 1892–1896), vol. 2, p. 176.

[55] For example, see SCA, SC 9/4/6, unfoliated; examination of Edward Cox.

[56] McIntosh, *Working Women in English Society*, p. 105.

[57] *Thomas Gill c. Richard and Joan Filoe*, CUA, Comm.Ct.I.6, fo. 146.

[58] *William Howlsworthe, BA c. Thomas Thomlinson*, CUA, V.C.Ct.I.4, fo. 110v; the court found in Howlsworthe's favor, and ordered Thomas Thomlinson to give back the doublet.

[59] For example, see *Roger Johnson c. John Dorrinton*, CUA, Comm.Ct.I.1, fo. 80v.

[60] McIntosh, *Working Women in English Society*, p. 100; Phelps-Brown and Hopkins, "Prices of Consumables."

[61] See below, Chapter 5.

of female plaintiffs and female defendants in the borough court of early modern Great Yarmouth.[62]

Never-married women in particular would have found it necessary to lend money. Some of these women intended cash savings to be part of their future dowries, and many of them earned wages as domestic servants. As Amy Froide has found in her work on the wills of never-married women, around 40 to 45 percent of never-married women had debts owed to them at the time of their death.[63] Never-married women resorted to local courts to collect from debtors when the loans were large. Joan Lyveinge, a single woman of Cambridge, in 1583 brought suit against Daniel Tytterington, the chaplain of St. Benedict's College to collect the sum of 40s., "which she lent to him at divers tymes, to bye & provide him of such necessaries as he wanted & stode in nede of."[64] Similarly, Agnes Sowter in 1586 sued one Henry Briggam of Cambridge for the recovery of a loan of 21s.[65]

While most female moneylenders operated on a small scale, lending modest amounts of money to their neighbors, some especially well-positioned female moneylenders succeeded in establishing substantial businesses. As Robert Tittler has shown in his study of the career of Joyce Jefferies, a money lender residing in Hereford in the first half of the seventeenth century, it was possible for never-married women to earn large profits from money-lending.[66] The relative of a family of local gentry, Jefferies inherited a substantial amount of money, which she put to good use. In the 1630s and 1640s, the years for which her account book survives, she earned several hundred pounds annually, most of which came from lending money at interest, though she also rented property and sold the provisions grown in her garden. Her family certainly appreciated her acumen; her half brother, Humphrey Coningsby, a scholar and travel writer who became "reasonably wealthy," named her as his executrix, as did her cousin Sir Thomas Coningsby. As Tittler shows, Jefferies lent money to a diverse group of borrowers, including family members, local gentry and merchants, and friends and neighbors of more humble status. Certainly most women would have had less opportunity than Jefferies to demonstrate their commercial skills. Nevertheless, her case is suggestive of the central roles women played as commercial agents in their communities.

---

62 Craig Muldrew, "'A Mutual Assent of her Mind?' Women, Debt, Litigation and Contract in Early Modern England," *History Workshop Journal* 55 (2003): 54–5.

63 Froide, *Never Married*, p. 130.

64 *Joan Lyveinge v. Daniel Tytterington*, CUA, Comm.Ct.I.1, fo. 117^{v}.

65 *Agnes Sowter v. Henry Briggam*, CUA, Comm.Ct.I.2, fo. 111^{v}.

66 See Robert Tittler, *Townspeople and Nation* (Stanford: Stanford University Press, 2001), ch. 8.

Historians interested in the involvement of women in credit markets have naturally enough focused on never-married and widowed women.[67] Unmarried women often had limited occupational options, and they also possessed the right to sue in their own names to reclaim lent money. They therefore had powerful incentives and the legal agency necessary to put their money out at interest. And yet money-lending was a fundamental practice of household economy practiced by married women as well as unmarried women. Because they could not bring debt suits to common law and university courts, married creditors are less visible in legal records than unmarried creditors. Nevertheless, married women could establish themselves as substantial creditors. Suzanna Averill, married to Thomas, explained in her testimony as a witness in a 1620 suit brought before the Vice-Chancellor's court that she made her living by persuading "divers" men and women in Cambridge to entrust their money to her, which she in turn loaned out at interest. In one deal, she accepted £100 from Mary Whitfield, a remarried widow, with the agreement that Averill would lend the money out at interest, to their mutual profit. The size and scope of Averill's transactions indicate that she was a substantial broker indeed, and must have had contacts with numerous, economically reliable borrowers.[68] It is likely that single women continued to lend money after marriage, and that many widow creditors were building upon credit operations they had previously established. Women's involvement in money-lending was a firmly established aspect of the early modern household economy.

This chapter has argued for the importance of women's independent commercial activities in the organization of the household economy. But if we reconsider Mary Uttinge, the corn regrator banned from buying corn in the marketplace, we encounter a conundrum. The rules which governed the marketplace would seem to foreclose the very types of commercial activities practiced by female middlemen. Furthermore, male householders and guilds were always protective of their particular privileges, and resented the competition offered by women brokers and traders. But, as we shall see when we explore the extent to which legal systems and town government regulations limited townswomen's commercial roles, membership in, or affiliation with, a respectable household was an asset for women traders. The enforcement of marketplace rules and male privilege was tempered by a good deal of pragmatism.

---

67 See B.A. Holderness, "Widows in Pre-Industrial Society: An Essay Upon their Economic Functions," in *Land, Kinship and Life-Cycle*, (ed.) Richard M. Smith (New York: Cambridge University Press, 1984); see also Holderness, "Credit in English Rural Society Before the Nineteenth Century, with Special Reference to the Period 1650–1720," *Agricultural History Review* 24, no. 2 (1976): 97–109; Froide, *Never Married*, pp. 128–41.

68 *John Sherman c. Richard Ashby*, CUA, V.C.Ct.II.22, fos 35^v–6.

Chapter 5

Conflicting Interests, Common Interests: Female Traders, Marital Status, and Town Authorities

Well-off male householders held a near monopoly of power over the institutions which regulated the commerce of early modern English towns. Guilds almost never admitted female apprentices, and although they often allowed widows to carry on the trades of their husbands, they did not allow them to become guild officers. Only male burgesses could serve as mayors and aldermen, and the vast majority of officers in charge of overseeing the markets were men. Men alone were judges in the courts which handled debt cases. And yet authorities allowed many women surprising latitude to pursue commercial ventures.

This claim seems at first glance to be counter-intuitive, for established male householders dominated the institutions charged with regulating economic affairs and were hardly shy about complaining against female competitors. This chapter addresses the question of whether the public, male-dominated institutions which governed the commerce of towns were decisive in constraining the commercial activities of tradeswomen. In order to do so, it draws upon the especially extensive published records of several towns, especially those of Southampton, Nottingham, Carlisle, Northampton, Reading, Liverpool, and Manchester. In addition, I use the archival records of a variety of local courts charged with regulating fairs and markets.

Such an exploration is long overdue. Historians of women's work have sometimes fallen into the trap of selecting isolated examples of municipal decisions which cut against the interests of a particular woman, or a particular group of women, to infer the existence of a sweeping hostility toward women traders in general.[1] While town authorities never went so far as to enthusiastically defend women's liberties to trade (given the cultural and political assumptions of the period, it would have been surprising if they had done so), the fact that they overwhelmingly targeted never-married female traders, and not married women or widows, for exclusion from the commercial economy suggests that something

---

[1] For example, see Clark, *Working Life of Women*, p. 207; McIntosh, *Working Women in English Society*, p. 132; David Underdown, "The Taming of the Scold: Enforcement of Patriarchal Authority in Early Modern England," in *Order and Disorder in Early Modern England*, (ed.) A. Fletcher and J. Stevenson (Cambridge: Cambridge University Press, 1985).

more than mere misogyny was at play. Paradoxically, women could best protect their commercial agency by working within—or in cooperation with—the patriarchal household.

After all, early modern political thinkers, guilds, and town governments alike did not conceive of towns as communities comprised of competing male and female constituencies any more than they saw them as amalgams of individuals. Instead, they upheld, above all, the ideal of the economically self-sufficient household as the foundation of the corporate community. Such households, to the early modern urban mind, formed the basis of the social and political order. Aristotle's contention that the purpose of the household was to fulfill "men's everyday wants," leaving them free to pursue the higher good of building political communities, looms large in early modern conceptions of urban community. But some of the "citizens and burgesses" would not have enjoyed their status as men "of some substance," capable of bearing the "charges" of public service, had it not been for their wives' careful tending of household business.[2] The patriarchs who governed courts and towns were under no illusion that women should be prevented from conducting business in the public and quasi-public places of the marketplace, fair, or shop front.

The need to protect the economic interests of established householders was an over-riding imperative that molded urban authorities' regulation of public markets. While authorities seldom sought to hinder the wives and widows of burgesses and masters, they did target unmarried individuals who operated outside established households. Never-married tradeswomen faced considerable restrictions. But town governments targeted bachelor traders as well. Town governments and guilds showed no more sympathy toward young men who had not served an apprenticeship or who did not have the means to pay an entrance fee than they did toward never-married women who declined to enter household service. Townswomen married to established craftsmen and traders therefore enjoyed more freedom in pursuing their businesses than both single women and those men who lacked the financial resources and "social capital" necessary to achieve the rank of citizen.

Women trading on behalf of "respectable" households would have found it very difficult to conduct business if they lacked recourse to the local courts which adjudicated debt cases. Almost all urban households were enmeshed in a web of credit arrangements; if women could not resort to courts to collect debts or contest claims made against them, their commercial activities would have been severely curtailed. Historians have long argued that a married woman's need to gain the consent of her husband to go to court is emblematic of the severe social and legal constraints women faced in the late medieval and early modern period. And yet such constraints were always mitigated by the recognition that the household economy was necessarily a cooperative enterprise. Wives, at least in practice, were hardly helpless before common law courts. Their husbands often found it to their advantage to support their wives' claims of debt, and thus routinely brought

[2] The quotes are from Smith, *De Republica Anglorum*, p. 73.

suits, in their own names or jointly with their wives, in order to obtain payment for their wives' sales and loans. Despite the legal ambiguities which could accompany wives' trades made without the explicit consent of their husbands, many husbands were comfortable in granting their wives wide discretion in their commercial dealings. The institutions which governed the commerce of towns and resolved commercial disputes thus left room for at least married women and widows to support their households and defend themselves in economic disputes.

Economic Restrictions and Never-Married Women

In 1634, Norwich's Court of Mayoralty ordered that Anne Allen, a young, never-married woman "livinge by her owne hand" be committed to Bridewell until she could be "reteyned in service."[3] Such actions against single women who lived and worked outside the confines of a respectable household were common. A consideration of the restrictions placed upon the economic and social activities of never-married women brings into sharp relief town governments' commitment to protecting the self-sufficient household economy. Town governments often complained that "spinsters" who were "out of service," and traded to support themselves "at their own hand," harmed the businesses of respectable householders. Never-married tradeswomen thus faced considerably more challenges than married and widowed women who worked within the context of the household economy. Nevertheless, as we shall see, at least a few never-married women were able to find accommodation with established householders and local authorities.

One of the most significant obstacles never-married women faced was the unwillingness of town authorities to grant them citizenship, and thus the right to participate fully in the commercial life of their towns. In the two centuries after the great plague, towns occasionally allowed never-married women to inherit their fathers' citizen status or to purchase the freedom of the town, but these avenues closed in the sixteenth and seventeenth centuries as population growth led to rising rates of unemployment.[4] A desire to protect privileged shopkeepers and market traders from competition informed the policies of urban authorities. For instance, the new corporation of Kirbie Kendall, desirous to advance the interests of its newly enfranchised freemen, in 1583 shut down the shop of Elizabeth Pyckeringe, a never-married woman, for her business impinged on the rights of the town's salters.[5] In another case, in 1607 the mayor of Southampton and his assembly

[3] William Sachese (ed.), *Minutes of the Norwich Court of Mayoralty 1632–1635*, (Norfolk Record Society, 36, 1967), p. 185. For more instances, see Paul Griffiths, *Youth and Authority: Formative Experiences in England, 1560–1640* (Oxford: Clarendon Press, 1996), ch. 7.

[4] Goldberg, *Women, Work, and Life Cycle*, pp. 338–9.

[5] R.S. Ferguson (ed.), *A Boke off Recorde of Kirbie Kendall* (Cumb. And Westm. Ant. And Arch. Soc., e.s. VII, 1892), p. 122.

refused to consider the petition of one Acton's wife that her never-married stepdaughter be allowed to open a shop to sell "smale wares by retailer."[6] Never-married women found licenses which allowed non-citizen town residents to trade almost as hard to obtain as citizenship. Amy Froide has found in her study of Southampton's "stall and art" lists, which registered the fees paid to the town government by the hundreds of traders who did not have the freedom of the town, that there was only one never-married woman recorded during our time period as a licensed huckster—Eleanor Beeston in 1611. Beeston also worked as a charmaid and, allegedly, a prostitute. Only two other never-married women before 1680 appear in the town's stall and art lists: a woman whose trade is unknown, and a daughter who inherited her mother's shop.[7] Froide has suggested that these three individuals may have had particularly strong connections with members of the town government. But most never-married women would have found it difficult, if not impossible, to trade by their own names without fear of prosecution.

Work restrictions fell particularly hard on adolescent women. Authorities expected young, unmarried women living outside their parents' household to work exclusively as domestic servants or apprentices in "housewifery." Coupled with a fear of competition was an intense concern that never-married women who lived and worked independently of a respectable householder would invariably succumb to immoral temptations. Town governments feared that single women's economic independence led to incontinence. Even those never-married women who made their livings primarily by cleaning households—and thus did not compete with household businesses—faced restrictions designed to ensure that they work and live under the moral supervision of a respectable householder. Southampton's town assembly regularly punished charmaids who worked for more than one employer for cash wages, rather than for one household under contract.[8] A similar situation obtained in Norwich. In his study of Norwich's Mayor's court, Paul Griffiths found that between 1560 and 1645, the mayor's court prosecuted 273 young women—as opposed to just 52 young men—for being "out of service" or living "at their own hand."[9] Towns were certainly concerned with the independence and misbehavior of young men, but the pattern of prosecution suggests that young, independent never-married women were the most mistrusted group in urban communities.

The sixteenth-century Manchester court leet explicitly linked the economic activities of independent, single women with threats to the moral order. According

---

[6] W.J. Connor (ed.), *The Southampton Mayor's Book of 1606–1608*, Southampton Record Series, 21 (Southampton: Southampton University Press, 1978), p. 107. For similar instances, Earwaker (ed.), *Court Leet Records ... of Manchester*, vol. 1, p. 241; vol. 2, p. 37.

[7] Froide, *Never Married*, p. 95.

[8] J.W. Horrocks (ed.), *The Assembly Books of Southampton [1602–1616]*, Southampton Record Society, 19, 21, 24, 25 (4 vols, Southampton: Cox & Sharland, 1917–1925), vols 1–4, passim. This was not unique to Southampton; see, for instance J.A. Twemlow (ed.), *Liverpool Town Books* vol. 1. p. 717.

[9] Griffiths, *Youth and Authority*, p. 358.

to a 1584 presentment, many "se[ngle] women … doe backe & brewe & vse other tr[ades] to the great hurte of the poore Inhabitants havinge wieffe & children." Just as distressing to the jurors was that these women supposedly took readily to "abu[sing] them selves w[i]th yonge men & others havinge not anny man to controle them to the gret Dishonor of god and Evell ensample of [*sic*: to] others," presumably because their trades allowed them to keep their own quarters independently of a respectable householder and thus receive male visitors in private.[10] The leet declared that any never-married woman who kept her own quarters was to be fined six shillings, eight pence, and imprisoned at the discretion of the steward, borough reeves, and constables of the town. Never-married women who illicitly produced commodities for sale would face the same penalty; in addition, they would be forced to forfeit the goods they meant for sale. It is difficult to assess how effective such orders were; but the frequency with which the leet jury felt the need to remind the town of restrictions against independent, single women is probably indicative of the difficulty local authorities had in enforcing the rules.[11] Nevertheless, as the actions of Manchester's leet illustrates, town authorities saw the moral and economic order which protected respectable households as inextricably linked.

The closing of never-married women's' ale-breweries and alehouses is one of the clearest examples of how contemporary prejudices, coupled with a desire to maintain established householders, constrained economic opportunities enjoyed by previous generations of "spinsters." In the aftermath of the Black Death, labor shortages and greater per capita consumption of ale opened new opportunities for aspiring brewsters of all marital statuses. But, as Judith Bennett has argued, the economic reorganization of the brewing trade in the fifteenth and sixteenth centuries—including the formation of male-dominated brewers' guilds, and the rise of a capital-intensive beer industry—pushed "spinsters" out of brewing. Just as importantly, moralists became more vociferous in their attacks on the supposed vices of female alehouse-keepers.[12] Such attacks, coupled with the 1552 licensing act which required alehouse-keepers to obtain licenses from JPs, prompted authorities to take action against never-married brewsters. Sixteenth and seventeenth-century town authorities were especially concerned with those drinking establishments which they believed encouraged vice by catering to vagrants and drunkards. Evidence of alehouse licensing in sixteenth and seventeenth-century Cambridge illustrates the challenges faced by never-married alehouse-keepers. By the mid-sixteenth century, the exclusion of "spinsters" from the ranks of licensed alehouse-

10 Earwaker (ed.), *Court Leet Records … of Manchester*, vol. 1, p. 241. Similar concerns were present in late sixteenth-century Kirbie Kendall, whose corporation forbid residents to take in never-married mothers as tenants and any single woman "w[ch] cannot be intended to be ffree of this Bourghe." Ferguson (ed.), *Recorde of Kirbie Kendall*, p. 136.

11 Earwaker (ed.), *Court Leet Records … of Manchester*, vol. 2, pp. 23 (1588), 27 (1588), 37 (1589), 51 (1590), 178 (1602).

12 On these points, see Bennett, *Ale, Beer and Brewsters*, esp. ch. 7.

keepers had already begun. Only two of the 54 alehouse-keepers licensed by the University were "spinsters."[13] None of the subsequent lists of alehouse-keepers in Cambridge list "spinsters" as licensed operators.[14] Never-married women had little hope of gaining alehouse licenses in a society which saw the rise of a competitive labor market *and* a growing sense that female economic independence in the drink trade led to social disorder and sexual immorality.

Although town corporations showed particular interest in controlling the economic (and thus social) activities of never-married women, they did not grant unmarried men who were not citizens of the town a free hand to conduct business. Single men who had not served an apprenticeship had more opportunities than never-married women to find remunerative work as laborers, but they, like their female counterparts, encountered obstacles when they entered the marketplace or fair. Towns were quick to quash the aspirations of male interlopers who sought to sell their manufactured wares. The city of Carlisle banned unmarried men from hiring apprentices.[15] Stourbridge Fair officials barred bachelors from trading for themselves. The youthful appearance of some male traders attracted the unwelcome attentions of fair officials searching for bachelors who were not likely to hold licenses as dairy traders, commonly called "badgers." University proctors closed down the booths of John Catchpoll and Edward Lawe because both of these young men were selling dairy goods without license. Similarly, the same year, the proctors turned away two other men, William Turner and Robert Webster, because they were unmarried and thus did not enjoy the status of being "a sole housekeeper."[16] Age alone, therefore, was not the only factor in this court's deliberations. Though John Dod was 30 years old, his status as a bachelor prompted the court to investigate his claim that he had the right to sell cheese as a factor for another man.[17] Furthermore, town authorities usually declined to grant never-married men alehouse and victualing licenses.[18] Only male householders who possessed town citizenship or a license to trade could be certain that they could trade freely in marketplaces and fairs.

Although many householders would have supported the actions town authorities took against "spinsters," the alliance between householders and town governments against never-married women traders was not as tight as it might appear at first glance. As Amy Froide has argued, never-married women were hardly pariahs within their neighborhoods; they often enjoyed extensive contacts with family,

---

13 CUA, T.I.10.

14 CUA, T.IX.1, T.I.11, T.I.12, T.I.1, V.C.Ct.III.38, no. 28.

15 Ferguson and Nanson (eds), *Records of ... Carlisle*, p. 156.

16 CUA, Comm.Ct.V.5, fos 89, 88^{v}, 89^{v}, 88^{v} respectively.

17 *Office v. John Dod*, CUA, Comm.Ct.V.5, fo. 105^{v}.

18 The Southampton leet jurors in 1603 went so far as to designate the mayor's own undertenant as being "unfit" to keep an alehouse: SCA, SC 6/1/27, unfoliated, under the list for Holy Rood parish. See also Ferguson and Nanson (eds), *Records of the City of Carlisle*, p. 66.

kin, and neighbors.[19] Some never-married women were capable of establishing business relationships with respectable householders, thus undermining authorities' attempts to confine them to the occupation of household service. The threat of prosecution evidently did not discourage unlicensed alehouse-keepers from selling drink, or householders from renting spare rooms to these vendors. Many brewers were willing to risk the occasional fine in the course of selling their drink to these establishments.[20] Some town governments lacked either the will or the means to eliminate unlicensed public houses. In 1619, a petitioner to the quarter sessions of Nottingham complained that "ther[e] is noe reformacion" of the great number of unlicensed alehouses established by "straungers" in "euery nooke of ye back side" of the houses in the town. The fact that the petitioner chose to remain anonymous is suggestive of the resentments faced by those who were too eager to meddle in their neighbors' affairs.[21] Keith Wrightson has persuasively argued that there was a gap between the rhetoric of moralists and authorities on the one hand, and on the other the willingness of constables to enforce the letter of the law. Local officers often moderated enforcement efforts to placate their neighbors' demands that the tenets of "neighborliness" and "good fellowship" be observed. As Wrightson demonstrates, "busy" officials who pried too aggressively into their neighbors' businesses were commonly targets of insults and assaults.[22] We cannot, therefore, assume that town orders against never-married women were effectively enforced.

The possibilities of symbiotic commercial relationships between householders and never-married women were recognized by at least one local authority: the University officers charged with overseeing Cambridge's Midsummer and Stourbridge Fairs. Officials knew that the crowds which visited these large fairs had to be satiated somehow if business was to be done. While it is impossible to obtain exact numbers of never-married women who sold food and drink in Stourbridge Fair, it was a common, and legitimate, practice for householders to rent out their kitchens and rooms to victualing women—including wives, widows, and "spinsters"—for the duration of the fair.[23] Fair officials allowed householders to rent out kitchens and rooms to "spinsters" if the householder agreed to enter into a bond which held the householder liable for any moral infractions which resulted from the arrangement—including prostitution and the entertainment of "idle scholars." In 1587, Richard Scotte entered into a bond which held him liable to pay an amercement of 40s. to the fair court if Rachel Stowe, a never-married

---

19 Froide, *Never Married*, ch.3.

20 E.g. SCA, SC 6/1/31; CUA, V.C.Ct.I.9, fo. 252v; V.C.Ct.III.36, no. 120a.

21 W.H. Stevenson et al. (eds), *Records of ... Nottingham*, vol. 4, p. 361.

22 Keith Wrightson, "Two Concepts of Order: Justices, Constables and Jurymen in Seventeenth-Century England," in *An Ungovernable People. The English and their Law in the Seventeenth and Eighteenth Centuries*, (ed.) John Brewer and John Styles (New Brunswick: Rutgers University Press, 1980), pp. 21–46.

23 E.g. *Francis Gibbinson c. Hellen Cutbert*, CUA, Comm.Ct.I.6, fo. 58v.

woman who had hired rooms in his house to sell victuals during Stourbridge Fair, misbehaved. During the course of the fair, the court judged that Scotte had to surrender the sum after Stowe was found to be "a lighte and inco[n]tinent woman" who had "receive[d] scholars" in the house.[24] During the Midsummer Fair of 1615, officials prosecuted Christina Nashe, who hired a house from one "morton" to sell beer, on suspicion of fornication.[25] But for those never-married women who maintained their reputations for moral uprightness, Stourbridge and Midsummer fairs offered commercial opportunities. Early modern urban communities were flexible enough to accommodate the commercial ambitions of at least some independent, never-married women.

Wives, Widows, and Commercial Regulations

Wives and widows had considerably more allowance to trade than their never-married counterparts. It was against the interests of the institutions which governed town commerce to impose heavy-handed restrictions on wives and widows whose economic activities helped sustain their households. Towns and guilds recognized that banishing wives and widows from shops or marketplaces would cripple the town's households, and the social stability of the community. Thus, what is most striking is the consistency with which towns and guilds sought to reconcile on the one hand the interests of established householders, and on the other the commercial roles played by wives and widows. Restrictions on the commercial activities of wives and widows considered by early modern English towns were notable above all for their mildness.

Wives of burgesses, guild members, and market stallholders shared their husbands' right to trade in markets and shops. The city of Carlisle made the rights of wives explicit in 1561 by upholding the right of bakers and brewers' wives to sell their husbands' products. In the late seventeenth century, the same town government granted a "poor" woman long abandoned by her shoemaker-husband and who evidently lacked the skills of the craft the right to sell the shoes produced by his apprentices.[26] Such disputes as did arise over the rights of wives to trade on behalf of their households tended to confirm this status quo. In 1561, the town government of Northampton considered the claims of some butchers that their competitors' wives were selling meat in the shambles on days and times other than those of official market days and fairs. The town responded by ordering that butchers' wives only be allowed to sell meat on butcher's row on fair and market

---

24 *Office v. Richard Scotte*, CUA, Comm.Ct.V.7, p. 33. See also *Office v. Margery Blandon*, CUA, Comm.Ct.V.3, fo. 12; *Office v. Brugesse*, CUA, Comm.Ct.V.3, fo. 90^{v}. Never-married women were also hired to help work fair booths; for example, see *Office v. Dickinson*, CUA, Comm.Ct.V.9, fo. 194^{V}.

25 *Office v. Christina Nashe*, CUA, Comm.Ct.V.3, fo. 8.

26 Ferguson and Nanson (eds), *Records of the City of Carlisle*, pp. 69–70, 187.

days, and specified a fine of 8s. 6d. for those women who violated the order.[27] The power of butchers' wives to conduct business on behalf of their households during specified hours, however, remained intact. While coverture might in theory have limited married women's ability to sell their husbands' provisions, it appears that courts and town governments were satisfied that a married woman could legally buy and sell as long as her husband granted her a general permission to trade on behalf of the household.[28] The later position was upheld in 1573 by the town government of Rye when questions were raised regarding the legality of merchants' wives' transactions. The mayor and his assembly concluded that the wives of overseas merchants had the right to trade while their husbands were at sea.[29] In some towns, wives of freemen enjoyed advantages over "foreigners" and never-married men and women. In 1561, the city government of Carlisle declared that after the mayor, aldermen, and town council had been served by market traders, the "honest" freemen of the town *and their wives* would have the chance to make purchases before the market was opened to outsiders and never-married residents.[30] Towns recognized that if households were to flourish, coverture could not be interpreted too strictly.

Traveling merchants and craftsmen busy in their workshops relied on their wives to vend the goods, and so could hardly have supported restrictions on their spouses' commercial activities. But a consideration of the rights of widows suggests that there was something more than narrow self-interest at work in the allowances towns made for married or widowed tradeswomen. The willingness of towns and guilds to allow widows of burgesses and guild members to continue their husbands' businesses demonstrates the respect accorded to widows as heads of house, and a desire to maintain a stable community buttressed by economically independent households.[31] When a citizen or guild member died, his status passed to his widow rather than his sons.[32]

The claim that women shared in the economic status of their husbands has been contested by Marjorie McIntosh, who has argued that "for contemporaries, a key question was whether women's work in production and sales threatened the livelihood or social position of male household heads."[33] McIntosh goes on

---

27 Christopher A. Markham and J. Charles Cox (eds), *The Records of the Borough of Northampton* (2 vols Northampton and London: Northampton, 1898), vol. 2, p. 273.

28 Muldrew, "'A Mutual Assent of her Mind?,'" p. 48.

29 *HMC* Rye and Hereford Corporations (1892), p. 27.

30 R.S. Ferguson and W. Nanson (eds), *Records of ... Carlisle*, p. 6.

31 Indeed, poor, "honest" widows were the primary recipients of poor relief.

32 Mendelson and Crawford, *Women in Early Modern England*, pp. 52, 330–31; Goldberg, *Women, Work, and Life Cycle*, pp. 127–8, 131–2, 333. See also, for example, Ferguson and Nanson (eds), *Records of ... Carlisle*, pp. 112, 146.

33 McIntosh, *Working Women in English Society*, p. 121. McIntosh's contention is more appropriate to the German cities studied by Merry Wiesner—which seem to have been especially hostile toward female-headed households—than English towns. Economic factors were more important than town policies in explaining why many widows were

to claim that those towns most beset by economic troubles were the least tolerant of female artisans and shopkeepers. Early seventeenth-century Southampton provides a good case for testing the validity of McIntosh's hypothesis. Once a major port for the export of cloth, Southampton had been displaced by London and had entered into a period of economic stagnation and demographic decline. The town's economic troubles did in fact prompt the companies of the town to attempt to tighten their control over "mysteries" in order to control competition. In 1616, four companies—the tailors, shoemakers, serge makers, and clothiers—requested that the town reaffirm the companies' right to bar interlopers from trading in their respective wares. But only the clothiers—who must have felt the town's decline most heavily—attempted to add new restrictions on the widows of company members: they requested that widows who married men who "were not free of the … Companie" be prohibited from continuation to operate their shops, which for the time was a rather mild restriction.[34] This prohibition did not affect those widows who decided to remain unmarried, such as the wealthy Southampton clothier Judith Delamotte, whom we met above. Though masters rarely accepted women as apprentices,[35] they showed little desire to prevent masters' widows from continuing their husbands' businesses; because wives were expected to assist their husbands in the workshop and counter, their marriage served as a kind of apprenticeship which qualified them to trade independently as widows. It is likely that many male masters wanted to ensure the economic position of their families if their wives survived them.[36]

Some town governments so valued the skill and experience of particular female traders that they appointed these tradeswomen to marketplace offices. Male householders certainly made up the large majority of the inspectors, gaugers, fee farmers, and other officials charged with enforcing marketplace and fair regulations, but there is evidence from Liverpool, Reading, and Manchester that women occasionally assumed market offices. In Liverpool, women served in a

---

unable to assume their husbands' occupation roles. Young widows were hampered by a lack of training in the craft; a pressing need to sell off the shop's equipment to pay off the late husband's creditors could deprive experienced widows of the tools of the trade.

34 Horrocks (ed.), *Assembly Books of Southamtpon*, vol. 4, pp. 53–9, 68–72, 74–9, 79–84; for the clothier's request, see p. 83.

35 For rare exceptions, Ilana Krausman Ben-Amos, *Adolescence and Youth in Early Modern England* (New Haven and London: Yale University Press, 1994), pp. 135–7. See also the 1631 deposition of Thomas Egleston, a draper of Cambridge: CUA, V.C.Ct., II. 27, fo. 5^{v}; according to Egleston, one Jane Gomell, later the wife of the defendant in the case, served him for eight years as an "apprentise in his … trade." The purpose of her training was not to qualify her to set up her own draper's shop, but to make her an especially attractive wife for an aspiring draper, as is indicated by the fact that she later married a draper, James Sadler.

36 Similar considerations were at work in the use of jointure contracts; see Erickson, *Women and Property*.

minor capacity as setters of market booths and the "fleshboards" of butchers.[37] In 1625, one "Widowe Moore," a fee collector of Reading's butchers' shambles, complained to the town assembly that Phillip Tomee refused to pay the fees he owed for his stall. Similarly, one "mistress Stevens," who was appointed to weigh wool sold in the market, claimed that William Elkyns and his sons had refused to allow her to weigh his wool or to pay her fee "as hath byn accustomed."[38] Manchester's court leet in 1639 appointed Anne Thorpe, the widow of a merchant who had traded in Irish imports, the town's weigher of "Ireish yarn."[39] At least a few widows were able to leverage their positions as householders and traders to gain remunerative marketplace offices.

Wives and widows of freemen and guild members therefore shared in or inherited their husbands' social and economic status. But town governments and guilds drew a line when confronted by female artisans and shopkeepers who did not enjoy the freedom of the town or guild privileges, for these artisans and shopkeepers competed with established householders. In 1617, Southampton's court leet amerced Widow James 2s. 6d. for keeping a shop in which she sold pepper and starch, "to the great hindrance of other shopkeepers of this Towne;" she was to be fined £5 for any subsequent offence.[40] In 1686, the town government of Nottingham closed down four women's shops—including two groceries, a linen draper's shop, and a brewery—for none of these women, according to the town, had served apprenticeships.[41] Such actions against female interlopers, it must be noted, benefited widows who carried on their husbands' businesses as well as privileged male householders.

Company members took matters into their own hands when they believed that town authorities had failed to move quickly enough to close down the operations of female interlopers. When Bristol's Common Council, in an effort to alleviate the food shortage during the dearth of 1621, decided to allow "foreign" bakers from outside the city to sell bread in the city's markets, the city's bakers took strong action. Five Bristol bakers, with the help of the town sergeant, intercepted three "foreigners," including one Joan Flower, and forcibly seized the outsiders' bread, which they claimed as a fine for violation of their privileges. In response, the mayor and his council, who were eager to protect the food supply of the town, brought a suit in Star Chamber against the bakers' company.[42] The conflict between the town and company occurred under unusual circumstances. More commonly, town authorities were sympathetic to the interests of companies. In 1636, the sons

37 Twemlow (ed.), *Liverpool Town Books*, vol. 2, passim.

38 Guilding (ed.), *Reading Records*, vol. 2, p. 258; vol. 3, p. 400.

39 Earwaker (ed.), *Court Leet Records ... of Manchester*, vol. 3, pp. 55, 321.

40 Hearnshaw and Hearnshaw (eds), *Court Leet Records [Southampton]*, vol. 3, p. 527.

41 Stevenson et al. (eds), *Records of the Borough of Nottingham*, vol. 5, pp. 329, 331–2.

42 PRO, STAC 8/54/3.

and apprentices of Leicester's butchers attacked Ann Birch, whom they believed was illicitly selling meat in the market shambles. They drove Birch from the market by pelting her with "snow balls," some of which concealed stones. One of the stones struck Birch in the head, causing a severe injury. After the incident, the town's JPs, in response to the petition of Birch's husband, amerced one of the youths 10s., to be paid to Ann Birch's surgeon. But the JPs also took the occasion to uphold the principle that the company had the right to exclude interlopers from the market, and declared that Ann "shall not offer any of her commodities to sell in the Shambles."[43] Female traders unconnected by marriage to a company member, such as Ann Birch, would have found it difficult, if not impossible, to break into a company trade.

There was something more at work than misogynistic prejudice in such actions. Companies and town governments were just as vigilant in shutting down the operations of unprivileged men. Apprenticeship to a skilled craft or trade was an avenue of advancement open only to young men,[44] but not *all* young men. Laborers and humble husbandmen would have had difficulty paying even modest apprenticeship fees for one son, not to mention several sons. Many of those young men who were apprenticed were unable to complete their terms of service for a variety of reasons.[45] Young men who had not completed an apprenticeship or who failed to earn enough money to gain entrance to a company enjoyed little sympathy. Southampton's town assembly, at the behest of the companies, regularly expelled from the town immigrant craftsmen, along with their wives and children, who had not served an apprenticeship or lacked the money to pay an entrance fee to the companies.[46] Even in towns which lacked guilds and companies, such as Cambridge, town governments barred untrained or impecunious men who could not afford to buy the freedom of the town from practicing skilled crafts and trades. Alexandra Shepard has demonstrated how young male craftsmen were particularly protective of their newly won status, and vociferously defended their claims to be self-sufficient patriarchs; they were quick to resort to fisticuffs or litigation in response to attacks against their status as masters and patriarchs.[47] The stakes were high for men whose status as masters was in doubt. Between 1562 and 1650, Stourbridge Fair officials brought 33 prosecutions against men for selling goods (including fish, meat, bread, tools, leather, barrels, and saddles) without having served the appropriate apprenticeship; they brought no prosecutions against

[43] Helen Stocks (ed.), *Records of the Borough of Leicester* (Cambridge: Cambridge University Press, 1923), 285.

[44] Regarding female apprentices and servants, see Ben-Amos, *Adolescence and Youth*, ch. 6.

[45] Wrightson, *Earthly Necessities*, p. 59.

[46] Connor (ed.), *The Southampton Mayor's Book 1606–1698*, passim; Horrocks (ed.), *Assembly Books of Southampton*, passim.

[47] Shepard, "Manhood, Credit and Patriarchy."

women.[48] Despite this, it is unlikely that female booth holders faced less scrutiny than their male counterparts.[49] Never-apprenticed men who sought to trade in Stourbridge Fair were probably more optimistic than women that they could play the part of a trader who had served an apprenticeship, but they did face scrutiny. Widows who inherited their trades from their husbands were in a far stronger position to claim the right to trade in fairs and marketplaces.

A 1579 case brought by the University's proctors against Thomas Isard, a tanner of Harwich, for selling fish in the fair without license is particularly illustrative of the suspicion many male traders faced when setting up their booths in the fair (given the use of urine in early modern tanning, perhaps Isard was attempting to break into a somewhat less odoriferous trade). The proctors argued that Isard's fish stand in Stourbridge Fair should be closed because he was "not free of the fishmongers, neither having bene Apprentise in that facultie." In his defense, Isard claimed that he had renounced the trade of tanner after he married a widowed "fyshmong[e]rs wyef" and that he had traded in fish for seven years (which, perhaps not coincidentally, was a typical length of service for apprentices).[50] Whatever the truth of his statement, Isard was clearly trying to emphasize not just that he had gained the right by marriage to engage in fish mongering, but also that he had traded in fish for a long period of time under the tutorship of his wife. Unfortunately, the allegation accompanied by Isard's brief statement is the sole entry in the Stourbridge Fair court book regarding this case. We therefore do not know the decision in the case, but the lack of any further entries suggests that the court found Isard's explanation convincing enough. Isard's case highlights the fact that women aligned by marriage to a respectable craft or trade or who operated as widow-masters enjoyed considerably more commercial opportunities than young, un-apprenticed male interlopers.

We have focused so far on the participation of wives and widows in those trades that towns and guilds reserved for qualified heads of households. But as we have seen, women commonly traded as middlemen in victuals and second-hand durable goods. Officials often, of course, accused such traders of fleecing customers by selling goods at artificially high prices; there is, however, little evidence to suggest that regulations against regraters, forestallers, and brokers were effective.[51] More surprising is that at least some towns were willing to provide hucksters and female brokers with licenses and space in the marketplace to carry out their trades.

Women who traded outside the regulated marketplace risked running afoul of local authorities determined to protect citizen shopkeepers and consumers. For instance, Leicester's town government in 1573 prohibited the town's

48 CUA, Comm.Ct.V.5–10. Women were most commonly charged with selling beer, victuals, and especially wine without having license from the authorities.

49 Female visitors, whether traders or customers, indeed faced intense scrutiny by fair officials who were especially concerned to keep prostitutes out of the fair.

50 *Office v. Thomas Isard*, CUA, Comm.Ct.V.6, fo. 5[v].

51 See also Goldberg, *Women, Work and Life Cycle*, p. 118.

"Brogers" and "pledge women" who worked on Leicester's streets from selling townspeople's clothes and other household goods for commissions. Town officials accused these traders of shortchanging their clients. But, rather than eliminate brokering altogether, the corporation sought to control and regulate the trade by granting two men, Richard Raynsford and William Shippon, exclusive licenses to sell goods as brokers. These two men were forbidden to collect fees greater than 1d. per one shilling's worth of goods they sold on behalf of townspeople. The town government, in characterizing the town's pledge women as "evill" and "disorderly," drew upon contemporary, gendered anxieties surrounding independent female traders in justifying its order.[52] But the result of Leicester's prohibition of female street brokers may have been merely to push them indoors, where the trade would have been harder to regulate.

Leicester's prohibition against all *women* brokers seems to be an isolated example. Authorities in other towns were willing to tolerate widows and married women who traded in the streets. The mere presence of regulations against hucksters and regraters cannot be taken as evidence of misogynistic prejudice, for, as we saw in the last chapter, many men as well as women hawked victuals and fuel on the streets in the sixteenth and seventeenth centuries. The pattern of enforcement of commercial regulations does not give us much reason to believe that authorities singled out female traders. The case of late sixteenth and early seventeenth-century Southampton, which has left extensive records, is illustrative. The mayor, town assembly, and the JPs consistently ignored the pleas of the court leet—whose jurors may have resented the marketplace shortages and competition offered by hucksters—to prosecute unlicensed hucksters and those hucksters who "forestalled" the market by buying food and fuel in the market before 11 a.m., when the market opened to non-retail trade.[53] In the absence of the town government's support, the court leet tried to control huckstering by fining forestallers and those hucksters they deemed unfit for huckstering licenses. As the 1603 list of "fit" and "unfit" hucksters underscores, the leet was especially permissive in allowing wives and widows to trade on the streets. Out of eight women presented in 1603, seven women, including five widows and two married women, were deemed "fit" for licenses. Only widow Hamm, who also ran a victualing house, was deemed "unfit" for a huckstering license. By contrast, only nine out of 20 male hucksters were granted licenses in 1603.[54] The leet showed no greater hostility to female than male hucksters in deciding how much to amerce offending traders. Between 1604 and 1640, the leet levied 124 fines against hucksters. The median fine levied against female hucksters was 3.5d.; the median fine levied against male hucksters

---

[52] Mary Bateson (ed.), *Records of the Borough of Leicester* (7 vols, London: C.J. Clay, and Cambridge: Cambridge University Press, 1905), vol. 3, p. 147.

[53] For the complaints of the leet against the mayor and the JPs' unwillingness to enforce market regulations, see Pennington, "Taking it to the Streets," pp. 669–72.

[54] SCA, SC 6/1/27, unfoliated.

was 4.5d.[55] However hostile the Southampton leet jurors were to huckstering in general, they were loath to deprive wives and widows of one of the few trades they could practice to support themselves and their families.[56]

Some towns recognized the important commercial roles of women by reserving specific sections of the market for female traders. The towns of Northampton, Southampton, Nottingham, and Leicester all had "huswyves'" or "women's" markets.[57] The women who worked in these markets sold the produce of their gardens and dairies, such as fruits and vegetables, butter, poultry, eggs, and cheese. In addition, traders in women's markets trucked in second-hand manufactured goods, a business which occasionally brought them into conflict with craftsmen. For instance, the Leicester town government ordered that no linen or wool draperies be sold in the "husyfes market, but onlye in" the drapers' market "accordinge to the auncient custome."[58] Despite the tensions that could arise between male householders and their female competitors in the women's markets, these markets, in Leicester and other towns, survived through the seventeenth century. The endurance of women's markets is clear testimony to the importance at least some town governments placed on the commercial activities of wives and widows.[59]

Women and Debt Litigation

Tradeswomen would have been severely hindered in their businesses if they had no recourse to the local courts which heard and decided debt cases. Concomitant

---

55 SCA, SC 6/1/28, unfoliated; SC 6/1/32, fos 23–4; SC 6/1/33, unfoliated; SC 6/1/35, fo. 27^{v}; SC 6/1/36, unfoliated; SC 6/1/37, fo. 24; SC 6/1/51, fo. 23^{v}. The average inflation-adjusted fine is a less appropriate measure of central tendency than the median, for the average fine of the female huckster is skewed by three atypically large amercements of female hucksters in 1616 (Allice James [5s], Joane Baker [2s] and widow Groundye [2s]). Nevertheless, the average inflation-adjusted fine levied against female hucksters (6d) versus male hucksters (4.5d) again indicates a near parity between the amounts of fines against women vis-à-vis men. The leet jury had the right to determine the amount of the fine, but the mayor had the power to veto the jury's recommended fine. This may have made leet juries hesitant to levy extraordinarily large fines.

56 Similar consideration was given to poor widows who ran alehouses; Horrocks (ed.), *Assembly Books of Southampton* vol. 4, p. 1; see also Peter Clark, *The English Alehouse. A Social History 1200–1830* (New York: Longman, 1983), p. 79.

57 Bateson (ed.), *Records of the Borough of Leicester*, vol. 3, pp. 240, 243; Markham and Cox (eds), *Records of the Borough of Northampton*, 2: 86; Stevenson et al. (eds), *Records of Nottingham*, vol. 4, p. 334; vol. 5, p. 135; Hearnshaw and Hearnshaw (eds), *Court Leet Records [Southampton]*, vol. 3: 489.

58 Bateson (ed.), *Records of the Borough of Leicester*, vol. 3, p. 243.

59 While not all towns had specific spaces for independent female traders, women probably sold victuals and second-hand wares in every town; in those towns which did not have women's markets, female traders could sell their goods in their homes or door-to-door.

with population growth and commercial expansion was an explosion in rates of litigation. Craig Muldrew estimates that by the 1580s, there was, on average, one debt suit per household per year.[60] Because sixteenth and seventeenth-century England was a cash poor economy, neighbors most commonly sold goods to each other on credit. Informal credit arrangements, in which money was treated as a unit of account rather than a unit of exchange, allowed the multitude of households with a paucity of coin to exchange goods, with the differences being paid in cash after periodic "reckonings" between households. These arrangements between households could be incredibly complex; debt cases often resulted from conflicting tallies and recollections of oral agreements.[61] Borough courts (and, in the case of Oxford and Cambridge, university courts which were empowered to hear debt cases brought by "privileged" persons who did business with the university) thus played an indispensable role in resolving economic disputes. Most cases never proceeded to final judgment, in part because long court cases were costly; plaintiffs most commonly settled their cases through private negotiations rather than by pursuit of a verdict. Nevertheless, as Muldrew has argued, vendors and creditors found the threat of litigation to be an effective tactic in prompting customers to pay their debts. We must therefore ask whether the early modern legal system was flexible enough to accommodate the needs of tradeswomen, vendors who surely had their share of debtors.

Married women, at first glance, would seem to have had a particularly hard time going to law to collect debts. While widows and those single women who had reached majority were free to bring debt suits in their own name, a married woman, even if she practiced a trade independently of her husband, in almost all instances would have been required to gain her husband's consent to bring a case against a debtor. Wives were not entirely absent as debt case litigants in the borough and University courts, but coverture seems to have played some role in depressing their numbers, for they were certainly under-represented. Table 5.1 illustrates the numbers of debt cases which had female litigants brought to the Chancellor's Court of Oxford University.

The evidence from Oxford University's Chancellor's court is not atypical. Female litigants were involved in about seven to eight percent of debt cases heard by Cambridge University's Vice-Chancellor's court in the early seventeenth century. In the late sixteenth and early seventeenth century, female litigants were involved in 10 to 13 percent of cases heard by the borough court of Great Yarmouth.[62] Most of these female litigants were widows or never-married women. Husbands sometimes brought debt suits jointly with their wives, but this practice was uncommon. In only 12 (1 percent) of the sampled 1,057 Oxford University Chancellor's court cases did married women stand jointly with their husbands

60 Muldrew, *Economy of Obligation*, p. 236.

61 Muldrew, *Economy of Obligation*, pp. 107–9.

62 For Cambridge, see Shepard, "Litigation and Locality," p. 17; Muldrew, "'Mutual Assent of her Mind?,'" p. 54.

Table 5.1 Female debt case litigants in Oxford University's Chancellor's Court, 1585–1641

Year	Suits with Female Plaintiffs		Suits with Female Defendants		Total Suits with Female Litigants		Total Number of Suits
1555–56	13	9%	4	3%	15	11%	142
1600–01	4	3%	4	3%	8	6%	136
1615–16	22	10%	5	2%	27	12%	228
1630–31	8	5%	2	1%	10	6%	172
1640–41	13	3%	11	3%	24	6%	379
Total:	60	6%	26	2%	84	8%	1,057

Note: I have taken two-year samples at 15-year intervals, except in the case of the last sample (1640–41), because litigation rates dropped sharply during the civil war. For the period 1585–86, two cases had both female plaintiffs and female defendants.
Source: Catalogue of Chancellor's court cases held at OUA.

as litigants in debt cases. This may be because, as Timothy Stretton has shown, there were powerful, gendered prejudices against female litigants.[63] The cases in which husbands and wives sued as joint litigants usually involved the property of remarried widows or property over which women retained ownership even after marriage, cases in which married women were on firmer legal ground than in other types of cases.[64] Unless there were solid legal grounds to do so, many husbands were probably wary of unnecessarily suing jointly with their wives. But an examination of the gender of litigants alone is hardly a good measure of women's involvement in debt litigation.

Indeed, as allegations and depositions from the university courts indicate, many debt suits ostensibly involving only men centered on wives' commercial transactions. Husbands regularly sought to collect payment for goods their wives sold on credit. Thomas Vaughan sued John Newman after Newman failed to pay for feathers Vaughan's wife sold on credit to Newman's first wife.[65] Thomas Gyll sued Richard and Joan Fyloe for goods delivered by Gyll's wife to the Fyloes.[66] Although William Cotton delivered part of the money he owed for a horse to the wife of James Hintson, Hintson and his wife grew impatient and sued Cotton for

[63] Timothy Stretton, *Women Waging Law in Elizabethan England* (Cambridge: Cambridge University Press, 1998), ch. 3.

[64] E.g. *Juliana (?and Albert) Eden c. Edmund Alexander*, CUA, Comm.Ct.I.3, fo. 143^{v}; *John Benson c. William and Hellen Bemont*, CUA, Comm.Ct.II.3, fo. 142^{v}. As Shepard has shown, husbands and wives were more likely to act as joint litigants in injury cases, particularly those which involved accusations of defamation: Shepard, "Litigation and Locality."

[65] *Thomas Vaughan c. John Newman*, CUA, Comm.Ct.I.4, fo. 203.

[66] *Thomas Gyll c. Richard and Joan Fyloe*, CUA, Comm.Ct.II.10, fo. 38.

the rest of the money.[67] Husbands were also prompted to sue to recover their wives' cash loans. For instance, Richard Gryffin sued Henry Holland for repayment of money lent by his wife.[68] Similarly, Robert Britton sued Richard Willyams after both he had his wife were rebuffed in their attempts to reclaim loaned money.[69] In a particularly complex case, John Longworthe sued John Richardson after his wife gave money to the defendant to deliver to one Ball for a debt she owed. When Ball later arrived to claim his money, Vaughan and his wife suspected that Richardson had pocketed their money.[70] Even in cases involving male litigants alone, married women played the part of de facto litigants: they furnished oral testimony and depositions to support their husbands' attempts to recover their debts.

Coverture was thus not as significant a disadvantage to married women, including those who practiced a trade independently of a husband, as has been assumed. In a recent study of litigation involving married *femes sole*, Marjorie McIntosh persuasively argues that married women in the sixteenth and seventeenth centuries rarely found it to their advantage to apply to town authorities for independent legal status. Married *femes sole*—those women registered as practicing a trade or craft independently of their husbands—could take apprentices, bring debt suits on their own behalf, and obtain loans in their own names—an advantage for wives married to men of poor reputation and credit. However, *femes sole* faced significant legal disadvantages: if they were to retain their independent legal status, they were barred from drawing upon the assistance or resources of their husbands, and were alone responsible for paying their creditors.[71] Because male householders retained control of the household's common property, it was easy for them to claim that they were owed debts for the transactions performed by their wives or other household "assigns;" that they were not necessarily privy to the details of every transaction does not appear to have disqualified them from bringing suits to recover their wives' debts.[72] Patriarchal prejudices notwithstanding, common law and university courts were flexible enough to accommodate the many couples that were able to work together to pursue litigation in the interests of their households.

Urban authorities and courts were careful not to foreclose women's participation in commerce. Wives and widows of freemen and licensed male traders shared in their husbands' privileges. They were also given latitude to pursue trades

67 *James Hinston c. William Cotton*, CUA, Comm.Ct.II.3, fo. 142^{v}.

68 *Richard Gryffin c. Henry Holldan*, CUA, Comm.Ct.I.6, fo. 37^{v}.

69 *Robert Britton c. Richard Willyams*, CUA, V.C.Ct.II.39, fo. 21.

70 *John Longworthe v. John Richardson*, CUA, Comm.Ct.I.4, fo. 377^{v}.

71 McIntosh, "*Feme sole* status," p. 427. McIntosh also points out that married *femes sole* litigants may have faced legal officials unsympathetic toward female litigants. Furthermore, a claim to *feme sole* status may have been taken by creditors as a "statement of no confidence" in the husband's abilities to repay his debts.

72 E.g. *Michael Holmes c. John Jones*, CUA, V.C.Ct.III.3, no. 14; *Michael Holmes c. Thomas Crowfoot*, V.C.Ct.III.4, no. 203; *Edward Parker c. Lawrence Johnson*, CUA, Comm.Ct.III.3, no. 58; *Robert Bales c. John Rogers*, CUA, Comm.Ct.III.8, no. 127; *Edward Spencer c. John and Elizabeth Dod*, CUA, Comm.Ct.III., no. 18.

independently of their husbands. There was a strong element of male self-interest at work here: husbands and town authorities alike relied on the commercial acumen and earnings of women to ensure the economic viability of households, and thus a socially stable urban community. Patriarchal privilege and female commercial agency were not mutually exclusive prospects for early modern townspeople. Nevertheless, such agency would hardly seem possible if women were judged by their friends, neighbors, and authorities only in terms of how well they lived up to the ideal of the submissive, home-bound, thrifty housewife. The next chapter makes the case that, in everyday life, the way in which a woman's reputation was constructed embraced a wider range of behaviors and issues than domestic moralists would have been comfortable with.

Chapter 6
Women, Commerce, and Female Reputation

Mary Mase, the wife of a Cambridge brewer who sold her husband's ale and beer, was doing business in the kitchen of Queen's College when she was accosted by Martin Rust, a cook of the college. According to allegations in a defamation suit Mary Mase brought in 1611 against Rust, he declared to the kitchen staff that Mase was "an … ould skuruive coseninge Jade." Rust then turned directly to Mase and wished on her "a plauge of god," for "thou art an ould skurvie cosening Quean and thou workest with the diuell."[1] At first glance, the way in which Rust framed his accusations seems to confirm the claims of scholars who argue that early modern notions of female and male propriety were divergent, and indeed incommensurable. While contemporaries expected male householders, as rulers and the public representatives of their households, to assume a commanding bearing, they often characterized assertive female traders such as Mary Mase as lascivious, combative scolds—the very opposite of the idealized docile, chaste, modest housewife. And yet what seems to have fired Rust's anger was his belief that Mase was a "cozener"—a trader who cheated her customers. His claim that Mase's deceptive business practices left her parish "the worse … by 1000li [£1000] and god knoweth what the towne is the worse" would have worried any trader, male or female. Because townswomen were active as consumers, retailers, and creditors, contemporaries rarely gauged their reputations solely in terms of sexual behavior and conformity to patriarchal prescriptions. Cultivating and defending a reputation for honesty and plain-dealing was as important for trading women as it was for male householders. Mase herself found vindication. Although the Vice-Chancellor's court refused to levy the £100 demanded by Mase as recompense for the damage Rust did to her good name (such inflated sums, and their reduction or dismissal by the court, were common in defamation cases), they did require Rust to don the white cloak of the penitent and make a public apology to Mase before the congregation of her parish church. Restoring her reputation as both a clean living *and* an honest trader was clearly important to traders such as Mary Mase.

Mase's defamation case calls into question studies which argue for the centrality of chastity and obedience to early modern conceptions of female respectability and "honor."[2] This is not to suggest that historians of gender relations lack good reasons to focus on contemporary conceptions of the gendered order and sexual

[1] *Mary Mase c. Martin Rust*, CUA, V.C.Ct.III.16, nos. 54, 55.

[2] Because contemporaries most often applied the term "honor" to elite women, this chapter uses the contemporary terms "credit" and "repute" in its discussion of poor and middling women's reputations.

morality. Fidelity to the male householder was of course the central patriarchal value upheld by preachers and courts; and moralists highlighted the difference between female "honor"—rooted in the passive virtue of chastity—and the active and public virtues that characterized male "honor."[3] As both Keith Thomas and Lawrence Stone argued some time ago, female infidelity inspired far more concern amongst men than male infidelity because adulteresses endangered their patriarchs' ability to maintain legitimate lines of succession and inheritance.[4] More recently, Laura Gowing has drawn upon the rich depositional evidence of London's ecclesiastical courts to contend that there was in fact no "double standard," but rather two distinct, "incommensurable" standards of male and female propriety.[5] Age, deportment, industriousness, occupational status, and ability to control his wife and other household subordinates all influenced a male householder's status within his community. Unlike this multifaceted conception of male "honor," female "honor," according to Gowing, was defined *solely* in terms of chastity and sexual purity. Because sexual reputation was the chief benchmark by which a woman's reputation was assessed, contemporaries commonly claimed that unchaste women were prone to engage in a host of other sins, including scolding, drinking, and frittering away of household resources. Gowing's analysis of the different ways in which the language of sexual insult was deployed against women and men is incisive, but it does little to reveal how women traders were able to build and maintain the kind of reputation necessary to succeed in commerce. Townspeople were hardly so preoccupied with sexual mores that they failed to note whether or not a female trader dealt honestly with her neighbors, honored commercial agreements, and paid her debts on time. Recent research has suggested that judgment of women's reputations were more complex than has previously been suspected, and that women's work ethic was an important part of such judgments. As Garthine Walker has persuasively argued, the language of sexual insult provided men and women with a powerful "linguistic repertoire" with which to assail a woman's reputation, but that did not preclude women from defining and framing their own reputations in more positive ways.[6] The ways in

---

[3] Amussen, *An Ordered Society*, chs. 2, 4; Gowing, *Domestic Dangers*, pp. 1–2, 112; Stretton, *Women Waging Law*, ch. 8. Scholars of early modern Germany have argued in a similar vein: Lyndal Roper, *The Holy Household: Women and Morals in Reformation Augsburg* (Oxford: Clarendon Press, 1989), pp. 36–40; Ulinka Rublack, *The Crimes of Women in Early Modern Germany* (Oxford: Clarendon Press, 1999), pp. 255–7.

[4] Keith Thomas, "The Double Standard," *Journal of the History of Ideas* 20 (April, 1959): 195–216; see also Lawrence Stone, *Family, Sex and Marriage in England 1500–1800* 2nd edn (New York: Harper, 1979).

[5] Gowing, *Domestic Dangers*, pp. 2, 52, 59–60, 107, 110, 112.

[6] Garthine Walker, "Expanding the Boundaries of Female Honour," *Transactions of the Royal Historical Society*, 6th series, 6 (1996): 236, 239. See also Hubbard, *City Women*, pp. 191–4. Historians who have examined evidence other than ecclesiastical court records have noted the importance of economic credit to early modern notions of female reputation: see Stretton's study of women litigants in the Elizabethan Court of Requests, *Women*

which ordinary townswomen maintained their reputations as honest and provident buyers, borrowers, and vendors is the subject of this chapter.

The importance contemporaries attached to female sexual passivity did not entail an insistence on economic passivity. If women were to be extended credit to provision the household, they needed to build and maintain a level of trust amongst their neighbors. In running the household shop, women had to cultivate reputations as honest dealers who would not shortchange or "cozen" regular customers. Notions of male reputation may have been more closely related to occupational status than notions of female reputation because women tended to operate at the lower rungs of the commercial and manufacturing sectors, selling goods in the local market and earning money in by-employments. Nevertheless, wives too, as consumers and traders, had to protect their credit. Economic reputation could be just as important to laundresses, alewives, pawnbrokers, and hucksters as it was to male merchants, artisans, and laborers. The credit of a household within early modern towns was thus not just a measure of how trustworthy the male breadwinner was and how sexually honest his wife was. Female economic reputation mattered to the survival of many humble households.

The records of the Cambridge and Oxford University courts are particularly helpful in reconstructing the multiple ways in which female economic reputation was constructed, defended, and undermined in early modern provincial towns. The unusually detailed depositions of these courts in cases involving a wide range of debt and slander accusations suggest that contemporaries hardly judged women in terms of sexual honesty alone. While sexual insult made up a great deal of cases involving female litigants, women sued to the university courts for many other reasons as well. According to Alexandra Shepard, between 1581 and 1640, 50 percent of Cambridge University slander cases brought by female plaintiffs for which depositions survive involved assertions of sexual impropriety; 30 percent of insults against townsmen involved accusations of sexual dishonesty.[7] By far the second largest category of insult which brought female plaintiffs to Cambridge's university courts (23 percent) involved accusations of theft or receipt of stolen goods, a finding that confirms the impression that women were particularly active in the buying and selling of second-hand goods. Cambridge women also sued those who accused them of scolding, cozening, and heavy drinking. The broad range of reasons for which women brought defamation suits to the university courts, along with the fact that cases of sexual slander often arose out of economic disputes, indicates that popular conceptions of female "honor" were more nuanced and complex than has usually been recognized.

***

Waging Law, pp. 192–3; and Maria Lynn Cionci, "Women and Law in Elizabethan England with Particular Reference to the Court of Chancery" (PhD diss., Cambridge University, 1974), pp. 222, 278, 288.

[7] Shepard, *Meanings of Manhood*, pp. 165–6.

Chastity was clearly a more important aspect of a woman's reputation than a man's reputation, but not only because fornication violated the precepts of obedience to the male householder. The language of sexual slander was often inflected by aspersions on the victim's commercial credit. Litigants commonly linked fornication and prostitution with indolence, drunkenness, and other vices which endangered the household economy. For instance, John Jollie of Cambridge accused Joan Millesent not just of adultery, but also of being a "Base raskally queane," a "drunken queane," and a "base beggarlie quean [and] stincking durtie rascall."[8] Contemporaries often associated prostitution with thievery. Katherine Sparks, for instance, accused Brian Swindall of claiming that Sparks went to London to earn money as a prostitute in order to pay for a ruff she was found to have stolen from a Cambridge seamstress.[9] Poor women were in a particularly vulnerable position, for neighbors with an axe to grind could claim that such women made ends meet by engaging in prostitution. William Ellery and his wife Tabitha sued two men after these two men allegedly claimed that Tabitha was a "spittle howse whoore" who fornicated with scholars in exchange for the coal and hay she sold.[10]

Because calling a woman "whore," "flirt," or "lewd woman" was a potent way to undermine her commercial reputation, many sexual slander suits brought by women arose out of disputes that had little or nothing to do with sexual behavior. Men and women were quick to resort to sexual insults when they had an economic dispute with a female trader. For instance, on the very same day that Dionisia Goodbody, a widow of London, brought a debt suit against Lawrence Barker of Cambridge for money owed to her for room and board, Barker, allegedly in open court, declared that Goodbody was a "notable whoare & a common whoare as enye ys in England," a slander that provoked yet another suit.[11] Women who had a reputation for adultery were particularly vulnerable to sexual put-downs when they became entangled in economic disputes. John Sherman, a Cambridge brewer visiting Midsummer Fair in 1597, suspected that Elizabeth Vepen and her husband, a wealthy merchant, were trying to buy all the nails in the fair in order to sell them later for a higher price. When Elizabeth Vepen refuted his accusation and claimed that there were plenty nails remaining in the fair to buy, Sherman, evidently aware that Elizabeth's mother-in-law had beaten her in the street for committing adultery,

---

8 *Joan Millesent c. John Jollie*, CUA, Comm.Ct.III.15, no. 154.

9 *Katherine Sparks c. Brian Swindall*, CUA, Comm.Ct.III.16, no. 24; see also *Alice Farnham c. John and Helen Rolfe*, CUA, V.C.Ct.II.36, fo. 91, V.C.Ct.III.38, no. 3; *Margaret Wylliams c. Hugh Joanes*, CUA, V.C.Ct.I.30, fo. 89; ESRO, C/2/3/8/1, p. 16.

10 *William and Tabitha Ellery c. Samuel and George Mase*, CUA, V.C.Ct.I.7, fo. 38.

11 *Dionisia Goodbody c. Lawrence Barker*, CUA, Comm.Ct.I.1, fo. 177[v]; and *Dionisia Goodbody c. Lawrence Barker*, CUA, Comm.Ct.I.1, fos 177[v]–8; see also *Elizabeth Martin c. Adam Underwood*, CUA, Comm.Ct.II.2, fos 47, 48, 51; *Edmund Bennet c. William Ells*, OUA, Hyp/B/1, fo. 1; *Alice Flexney c. John Wayt*, OUA, Hyp/B/1, fo. 226[v]; *Anne Ashlea c. Thomas Wood*, OUA, Hyp/B/4, fos 60[v]–61; ESRO, C/2/3/8/2, p. 116.

declared that "yf I should stand talking from morninge untyll nighte, I would not speake evell enough of you … goe toe [for] … thowe arte an arrante whoare."[12] In such cases, sexual insult was employed as a tactic to undermine female traders, but the disputes themselves had little to do with sexual behavior.

It is not the argument here that sexual defamation cases brought by women were merely a function of the economic tensions which existed in urban communities; the frequency with which men and women attacked the sexual reputations of female neighbors is indicative of real anxieties regarding the boundaries of proper sexual behavior, and female sexual conduct in particular. Nevertheless, the cases of sexual slander brought to the university courts which intersected with judgments of economic honesty and creditworthiness underscore the multiple ways in which neighbors assessed the moral reputations of the female traders and consumers.

The diverse economic roles women played in supporting the household economy had important implications for the ways in which women—as litigants and witnesses—described their own economic statuses. Nevertheless, gendered assumptions do inflect the written record; when university court clerks asked wives the standard question of what their economic worth would be if they paid all of their debts, most married women responded that they were under covert baron, and were therefore by themselves worth nothing. For wives in economically secure households, to answer the question regarding their economic worth that they lived by their husbands was enough to vindicate their credit.[13] But the fact that litigants and their legal representatives asked the question at all suggests that the answer a married woman would give could not be taken for granted. Indeed, there are occasional glimpses of married women crafting responses that highlighted their own individual economic credit. Testifying twice in a 1590 debt case on behalf of her husband, Elizabeth Hylls, the wife of an inn-holder who helped run her husband's business, answered the interrogatory regarding her worth that she got her living "by & under hir husband," but she added that she "getteth hir lyveinge honestly."[14] In poor households, wives as well as husbands were expected to work as petty traders or as wage laborers. Margaret Woodward made no reference to her husband at all when she answered the interrogatory regarding her worth; conceding that she was worth little if her debts were paid, she added that "she

12 *John Sherman c. Elizabeth Vepen*, CUA, Comm.Ct.II.6, fos 191^{v}–2; response of Vepen to allegations. She was accused of calling Sherman a whoremaster after he allegedly called her a whore. Interestingly, John Vepen, Elizabeth's husband, seems to have stood aside as a spectator of the altercation. Elizabeth Vepen also brought suit against John Sherman: see CUA, Comm.Ct.III.8, nos. 71, 72.

13 Despite the fact that she was a fishmonger in her own right, Agnes Burff responded that "she is a marryed woman, & is worthe nothinge of hir self, but as she hathe at of hir husband." *Robert Simpson c. Agnes Shawe*, CUA, Comm.Ct.II.6, fo. 88^{v}. See also the interrogation of Mary Bust, fo. 92^{v}; *Robert Prance c. John Carowe*, CUA, V.C.Ct.I.1, fo. 38, testimony of Joan Towers; Shepherd, *Meanings of Manhood*, pp. 200–201.

14 *Roger Hylls c. Richard Stevenson*, CUA, Comm.Ct.II.4, fos 10^{v}, 23.

getteth hir lyveinge honestlye, as a poore woman."[15] It was not only in the context of court testimony that women asserted their worth as individual workers. While complaining of having to surrender a calf worth 14 or 15 "good shillings" to pay for tithes, Elizabeth Smith told a group of women outside the parish church that "wee may well be master" of Nicholas Plummer, the rector of All Saints parish of Southampton, "for I am sure wee pay him, hee gets more by his tongue then wee by our labour."[16] Widows and single women also emphasized their honesty and industriousness. Agnes Barlye of Cambridge, for instance, testified in a 1584 debt case that "she getteth hir lyveinge honestlye & that she ys a lawndresse;" she noted, with unusual precision and perhaps some pride, that her worth would be 40 shillings even if she paid all her debts.[17] Both men and women, and particularly women from humble households, felt the need to maintain their reputations as honest, industrious workers and traders.

Women made protestations of their economic honesty and industriousness in order to protect their economic reputations, and thus their ability to buy goods on credit or borrow money from their neighbors. Because many purchases had to be based on informal credit, honesty, industriousness, and conscientiousness in repaying debts were crucial values that all but the wealthiest households had to abide by if they were to maintain their economic agency within urban communities.[18] Creditors often sued when the ability of women to repay household debts came into question. For instance, the wife of Simon Collton of Oxford provoked a debt suit against her husband and herself when she bragged to too many neighbors that she had succeeded in borrowing 20 pounds from a kinsman, and that he had "nothing to shewe for it nether script nor scrowle [i.e. scroll]" (though she did add that she did plan to repay him eventually, and that she would give him one of her cheeses as a gift for lending her such a large sum).[19] When a creditor accosted Ann Ellis in the Mitre, an inn in Cambridge, she took care not just to assuage his fears, but those of any eavesdroppers; she declared that if he would but "give her a littel tyme," she would "see everybody satisfied & noebody should lose a penny by her."[20] The webs of credit which linked households together, allowing neighbors to buy and sell in an economy short of hard currency, were fragile; women, whether

---

15 *Robert Prance c. John Carowe*, CUA, V.C.Ct.I.1, fo. 42^{v}. See also *Agnes Grime c. William Warde*, CUA, Comm.Ct.II.18, fo. 81–3^{v}, Comm.Ct.III.13, no. 41.

16 Anderson (ed.), *Examinations and Depositions*, 1: 76.

17 *Richard Elwood c. Henry Mase*, CUA, Comm.Ct.II.2, fo. 55; see also, for instance, the testimony of Hellen French, servant, in *Robert Prance c. John Carowe*, CUA, V.C.Ct. II.1, fo. 36; testimony of Margaret Rook, widow, in *John Bonye c. Thomas Hodilowe*, CUA, V.C.Ct.II.1, fo. 1.

18 Muldrew, *Economy of Obligation*, pp. 123–95; Margaret Hunt, *The Middling Sort: Commerce, Gender, and the Family in England, 1680–1780* (Berkeley: University of California Press, 1996), chs. 1–2.

19 *Edward Sandwich c. Simon Collton and his wife*, OUA, Hyp/B/3, fos 35^{v}–7.

20 *Mr Chester c. Ann Ellis*, CUA, V.C.Ct.II.37, fo. 4^{v}.

they were widows or wives charged with buying household provisions, necessarily had to guard their credit with neighbors.

Coverture probably made it more rather than less important for married women to maintain their reputations for repaying debts on time. If a male defendant in a debt case could show that his wife had made a purchase without his consent, then the transaction could be rendered null. Traders regarded married women who did not repay their debts, or who passed those debts off as the responsibility of their husbands as a way of buying time or avoiding payment, with especial suspicion. John Mosse, a draper of Cambridge, was one such trader. When in 1587 John Hudson, a tailor, came to Mosse's shop on behalf of Mrs Langham to ask why he had refused to sell her goods on credit, Mosse complained that "I have often tymes ben disceyved & have not bene payd for such war[e]s as I have delivered to other mens wifes." Despite Hudson's protest that Mrs Langham was "a very honest ge[n]til woman and one who doth vsually paye and will paye for such things as she receyve of eny manns," it was only after Hudson agreed to act as surety for the repayment of the debt that Mosse consented to sell her goods on credit. When she did not repay him on time, Mosse sued Hudson.[21] As this case suggests, even women of high social and economic status could have difficulty in obtaining credit if the particular trader did not know them. But in communities in which most economic transactions were conducted between neighbors who knew each other well, female consumers who had a reputation for repaying debts on time and not resorting to the legal defense of coverture to delay or avoid payment had an easier time in receiving credit from traders.

Women had to maintain a reputation for repaying their debts not just to borrow money and purchase necessary household provisions but also to buy the supplies necessary for running household businesses. Widows who sought to continue running their husbands' shops were under especial pressure to prove their creditworthiness, for the death of a householder could provoke creditors to call in debts. Following the death of her husband, Katherine Davis of Oxford was sued no less than eight times for debt in the Chancellor's university court. In 1581, Thomas Walker, a witness for Davis, supported her claim before the Chancellor's court that Richard Hill had "hindred" her "Lyving" by claiming that she had fled the county to escape paying those debts.[22] The importance of economic credit to female business owners is underscored by the case of Rachel Tierry, a Frenchwoman living in Southampton who owned a cloth press and had been abandoned by her husband. When in 1599 Tierry took the bold step of requesting the Privy Council award her a royal patent for pressing cloth, the mayor and aldermen, worried that a patent would put other cloth pressers out of business and poor laborers on the streets, drew upon familiar, misogynistic stereotypes in opposing her plea. In a

---

21 *John Mosse c. John Hudson*, CUA, Comm.Ct.III.3, no. 101.

22 Unfortunately, what Davis did for a living is not recorded in the depositions, for it was common practice to note only the marital status of women; *Katherine Davis c. Richard Hill*, OUA, Hyp/B/2, fo. 174.

letter to Sir Julius Caesar, they noted that Tierry's request for *feme sole* status was unusual because she was married, and they caustically concluded that she was a "A prattlinge Gossipp, vnfitt to vndertake a matter of so great a Charge." And yet, significantly, they also attacked her industriousness and economic credit. She was, according to the town government, "verie poore & beggerlie" and "verie vntrustie;" any clothier who would entrust cloth to her was "worsse then madd," for she could not offer "anie good Caution" that she could pay them back if she ruined their cloth while pressing it.[23] But economic credit was not just important for widows who inherited their husbands' shops and the few wives who operated as *femes sole*. Many wives, while technically under the provision of their husbands, were nevertheless intimately involved in their husbands' businesses or operated independently of their husbands, as, for instance, hucksters, victualers, and managers of alehouses. They too would have had to maintain good credit with their suppliers if they were to continue to run their businesses.[24]

It therefore makes more sense to think in terms of household credit rather than distinct, "incommensurable" notions of female and male reputation. Husbands too were injured when neighbors attacked the economic reputations of their wives, for such slanders cast doubt on the honesty of the whole household. When Joan Creare accused Elizabeth Blandfield of theft in 1539, Elizabeth's husband claimed that not only was Elizabeth "in numerous ways injured and worsened in the good name, fame and reputation … by which she was known before then," but also that he himself "has lost much gain and profit which he, William, would have had … by virtue of buying, selling and exchanging which the same William and Elizabeth would have performed."[25] Although wives had the right to bring slander cases in their own right to the university courts, it is suggestive that husbands sometimes brought cases in their own name in order to defend their wives; husbands too were harmed when their wives' honesty was called into question. For instance, Robert Gaskin provoked a suit brought by both William Elsden, a coal merchant, and his wife Mary when he accused Mary of being "A Cutthroate Jade" because "for [a debt of] 2^{d} thou [Mary] wilt take 4^{d}."[26] In 1637, John Barnes caused unintentional offence when he claimed that he had been pickpocketed in the alehouse of John Hankes of Trumpington. In arguing that his comment did not harm Hankes's business, he noted that "John Hankes and his wife … att the time of the uttering of the … words and since att the present are people of honest life, and so comonly

---

23 BL, Lansdowne MSS 161, fo. 127.

24 For example, *Edward Harley c. Ann Webster*, CUA, V.C.Ct.II.38, fos 33–5A.

25 R.H. Helmholz (ed.), *Select Cases on Defamation to 1600* (London: Selden Society, 1985), p. 38.

26 *William and Mary Elsden c. Robert Gaskin alias Wing*, CUA, Comm.Ct.III.12, no. 2. The dispute was over damages Gaskin owed to Elsden for beasts which had trespassed on Elsden's land; see also for example *James Davies c. Elizabeth Mathhewe*, CUA, Comm. Ct.I.4, fo. 265^{v}; *John Scott c. Thomas Gregory*, CUA, Comm.Ct.8.I, fo. 45^{v}.

accompted."[27] Catherine Bowdell, testifying on behalf of Anthony Nicholson in a debt case he brought against Henry Dickinson in 1679, took care to note that both Nicholson and his wife Margarett were "reputed" to be "honest persons, and gett their livelihood honestly and by taking great paines."[28] Though the diligence and honesty of the male householder was probably the most important factor in his neighbors' assessments of his household's creditworthiness, the honesty of his wife was nevertheless a significant factor in many such judgments.

Indeed, when the male householder wasn't trusted by his neighbors, the wife could keep the household economy afloat if she was considered an honest trader and careful in repaying debts. Traders who doubted the trustworthiness of the male householder sometimes preferred to deal with his wife instead. When Thomas Hayes told Richard Bradley that he would not accept any more beer from Bradley, Bradley responded curtly "Be youe quiet, & let your wief take in beare & I will aske *you* noe monye for yt."[29] As we have seen, wives often bargained and purchased the supplies necessary for producing goods for sale; if their husbands were not trusted, then their responsibilities were all the greater. Because the maltster Robert Oliver was a reputed drunkard who, according to his father-in-law, spent any money he could get his hands on in the alehouse, his suppliers of barley clearly preferred to deal with his wife, who was more trusted to pay for the corn she received.[30] As this case suggests, women married to "idle" men or spendthrifts could gain a great deal of influence over the operation of the household business if suppliers were reluctant to deal with the husband.

However important women were in maintaining their households' reputations as conscientious consumers and borrowers, to view popular notions of female economic reputation solely in terms of consumption is to examine only one side of the coin. Wives of tradesmen and artisans and widows who inherited their husbands' shops made their livings by vending goods. And, as we have seen, many women often traded independently of their husbands as hucksters, pawnbrokers, and traders in second-hand goods. These women traders had to do more than repay their debts on time; they also needed to cultivate their reputations as honest plain-dealers if they were to contribute to the household economy.

The ways neighbors assessed the honesty of female dealers were inflected by the particular commercial roles women played in urban communities. This is indicated by the pattern of insult in the Cambridge University court depositions. Between 1581 and 1640, female litigants were almost twice as likely as male plaintiffs to bring suits for slanders involving accusations of theft or knowingly receiving stolen goods, a trend which reflects the prominent role women played

---

27 *John Hankes c. John Barnes*, CUA, V.C.Ct.II.32, fo. 75^{v}.

28 *Anthony Nicholson c. Henry Dickinson*, CUA, V.C.Ct.II.40, fo. 54^{v}.

29 Emphasis is mine. That Bradley expected to collect money for the beer, and that the beer was not a gift, is indicated by subsequent testimony; *Richard Bradley c. Thomas Hayes*, CUA, Comm.Ct.II.2, fo. 46.

30 *Robert Oliver c. John Sherman*, CUA, V.C.Ct.II.22*, fos 1–4.

in the informal trade in second-hand goods. As we have seen, women commonly engaged in pawnbrokering and opportunistic buying and selling of second-hand goods to supplement household earnings. But such trading could create resentments if neighbors suspected that the goods being bought and sold were stolen from within the community. According to one witness in 1584, Agnes Bradley, the wife of a brewer, was "very much hindered" in her business "& payned amongst her neighboures" after Thomas Barker reported that she commonly received stolen goods from a Cambridge University servant.[31] Traders sometimes accused female vendors in markets and fairs of pilfering other traders' goods. For instance, Ann Hilles, the wife of a cordwainer who sold dairy products in Garlick Fair outside of Cambridge, in 1621 sued Thomas Sandcroft, a chapman from Norfolk, after Sandcroft accused Ann and her son of stealing butter and cheese from his tent; according to Hilles's servant, Hilles would have been better off if she had lost a hundred pounds "then [to] have bine soe iniured & wronged as she was."[32] In 1625, the wife of Alexander Addle, a smith of Carlisle, won 6s. 8d. from a glover, James Blaklocke, who the court found had falsely accused her of being a thief and receiver of stolen sheets.[33] Accusations of theft or reception of stolen goods were especially damaging to women, because they directly called into question a woman's adherence to the ideals of good neighborliness. Women who were reputed to be thieves or knowing receivers of stolen goods risked being ostracized by their neighbors, limiting their ability to buy and sell in their communities.[34]

Thus, accusations of theft or reception of stolen goods often arose out of disputes which on their face had little to do with actual thefts. Theft was of course a crime, and this undoubtedly drove many women accused of theft to defend their good names in court. But early modern townspeople often linked theft with covetousness, a willingness to shortchange or cheat one's neighbors; in other words, the lines between theft and cozening were blurred in the popular imagination, for both acts endangered bonds of trust which held neighborhoods together. Henry Iveson made the link between theft and covetousness explicit when he encountered Agnes Vepen, a notable fishmonger, who was trying to buy up supplies of fish outside Trinity College in 1585. He provoked an argument with her when he demanded that she stand aside and let the poor have the first chance to buy the fish; when

---

31 *Agnes Bradley c. Thomas Barker*, CUA, Comm.Ct.II.2, fo. 89.

32 *Ann Hilles c. Thomas Sandcroft*, CUA, Comm.Ct.III.13, nos. 83, 84; Comm. Ct.II.20, fos 7–9. Women, as we shall see, were hardly too polite to accuse each other of similar crimes. For instance, see Ferguson and Nanson (eds), *Records of ... Carlisle*, pp. 280–81, 287.

33 Ferguson and Nanson (eds), *Records of ... Carlisle*, p. 280.

34 Because Isabell Dale, a servant, was of "light and lewd behauior" and a known thief, she was reported to have been banned from many Cambridge shops; CUA, Comm. Ct.III.13, no. 84. ESRO, C/2/3/8/1, p. 327: according to one witness, around the time in which Elizabeth Estowe had sued John Dicklie in an action of detention of property, Dicklie tried to undermine Estowe's good name by accusing her of purloining fish and corn.

Vepen called him "arrant knave," he allegedly responded "goe home to thye house & looke to thye herringes thowe didest steale."[35] Henry Blythe accused Agnes Bradley of being an "arrant theefe" after she, Blythe contended, took 10 barrels of "Grudgeons" from a college when she only had paid for "Breme," a cheaper fish.[36] Accusations of theft also arose out of misunderstandings resulting from informal borrowing and lending amongst women. Traders who did not repay loans or return borrowed goods risked having their names sullied by angry neighbors. John Swetson provoked a suit when he supported his claim that Margaret Cotton was a thief by claiming that "my wyefe lent to [Cotton] mye hipocrasse bagge, and a pewter fruit dishe, which I could never have … backe againe."[37] No actual act of purloining had to be committed for a woman to be labeled a "thief" or "receiver of stolen goods" by her neighbors.

Women selling goods in markets, household shops, or the streets had to maintain their reputations as honest traders if they were to keep their customers. Dishonest traders had many opportunities to shortchange their customers, either by selling goods by false weights or measures, or by overcharging, for as Keith Thomas has shown, most early modern consumers and traders had only rudimentary skills in numeracy.[38] Accusations of "cozening" could provoke women to bring suits to the university courts.[39] Because assessments of debts between households often depended on the records of shopkeepers' books, many wives had to have not just the ability to help keep the books but also a reputation for honestly recording debts and payments, particularly if the shopbook was to be used as evidence in debt suits. This would most evidently have been the case in instances in which widows sought to collect debts owed to their late husbands. When Jane Goldsborough brought a debt suit in 1595 against John Hamond for £3 7s. worth of meat she and her late husband, a butcher, sold to Hamond, the two witnesses for Hamond claimed that the debt might be smaller than it appeared in the shopbook, for Jane's husband refused to cross off entries in his book until they were fully repaid. Nevertheless, when interrogated, they admitted that *both* Jane and John Goldsborough "were & be accompted of good & honest reporte or dealeinge, & such as wold not falsefye

---

35 *Agnes Vepen als. Fypennie c. Henry Iveson*, CUA, Comm.Ct.I.2, fos 65r, 133^{v}; Comm.Ct.II.3, fo. 11^{v}; Iveson was sentenced to pay Vepen £3 6s. 8d. in damages and court costs; for a similar equation between cozening and theft, see *Richard Elwood c. Henry Mase*, CUA, Comm.Ct.II.2, fo. 49

36 *Agnes Bradley c. Henry Blythe*, CUA, Comm.Ct.III.2, no. 39

37 *Margaret Cotton c. John Swetson*, CUA, Comm.Ct.II.11, fo. 26, Comm.Ct.III.9, no. 106. On another occasion, Swetson accused all of the Cotton family of being thieves: *Richard Cotton c. John Swetson*, CUA, Comm.Ct.11, fos 7^{v}–9, Comm.Ct.III.9, no. 103.

38 Keith Thomas, "Numeracy in Early Modern England," *Transactions of the Royal Historical Society* 5th series, 37 (1987): 103–32.

39 For example, *Joan Johnson c. Ralph Dunthorne*, CUA, Comm.Ct.III.3, no. 38; *Hayes c. the wife of William Dickinson*, CUA, Comm.Ct.III.12, no. 53; *Mary Mase c. Pepys*, CUA, Comm.Ct.V.7, p. 484; *Agnes Beeton c. Lucy Wenham*, CUA, V.C.Ct.III.23, nos. 29, 30, 32.

theire shoppe booke."[40] Widows had to maintain their reputation for honest bookkeeping if they were to carry on their husbands' businesses and, if need be, sue customers who failed to repay debts. In another instance, in 1676, Ann Linsey, a Cambridge widow and proprietor of a linen shop, brought a debt case to the Vice-Chancellor's court against Thomas Head for linen she had sold him, as recorded in her shopbook. According to Richard Linsey, a fishmonger who used to help run his mother's shop, his mother "doeth keepe a shop booke which he believeth is true and that he never heard any of the Customers … ever find fault with any thing that was writt into it but alwayes allowed of it."[41]

We have little evidence regarding the ways in which the credit and reputations of hucksters and traveling chapwomen were assessed, but we should not therefore conclude that the values of honesty and plain-dealing were unimportant to these humble traders. While the Cambridge University courts heard cases brought by litigants engaged in a very broad range of occupations, laborers and street traders were severely under-represented, perhaps because of the costs involved in bringing suits to court.[42] While hucksters made frequent appearances before the University court leet and Vice-Chancellor's court for various economic infractions, the scale of their transactions—for instance, sales of bread loaves or firewood bundles for a penny each—were too small to be the cause of a debt suit. It made more sense for customers who felt cheated to buy provisions from other traders or inform authorities. But hucksters who traded honestly and provided much needed supplies to their neighbors were valued by their customers. Sarah Young, the wife of a cooper and a chapwoman who served Epping, Essex, gained the appreciation of her neighbors by supplying them with "small wares and wallnuts." When she was arrested in 1684 at Sabridgworth Fair in Hertfordshire on suspicion of theft, her neighbors sent a certificate to the justices declaring that Young followed an "honest imploy[ment]" in buying goods at the fair for sale in Epping, and that she was "a very honest and well-behaved woman, not given to pilfer or steale."[43] Because hucksters bought goods in large quantities to sell on the streets, they would have also had to maintain their personal credit amongst bakers and other suppliers.

Women who ran or owned victualing houses and alehouses needed to guard their reputations amongst their neighbors and customers as well. Disorderliness and dishonesty could provoke neighbors to complain to local authorities. For instance, several residents of Nottingham in 1633 complained that one Caulton, a widow, kept several "disguysed Persons" in her alehouse, "to scare certayne

40 *Jane Goldsborough c. John Hamond*, CUA, V.C.Ct.I.1, fos 86–7^{v}.

41 *Ann Linsey c. Thomas Head*, CUA, V.C.Ct.II.40, fo. 7^{v}.

42 Of all Cambridge University court cases between 1581 and 1640 for which depositions survive, less than one percent of cases involved litigants who were laborers, and no hucksters are recorded as litigants (there may have been a few, but women were almost always identified only by their marital status). See Shepard, "Litigation and Locality," p. 21.

43 W.J. Hardy (ed.), *Notes and Extracts from the Sessions Rolls 1581 to 1698 [Hertfordshire],* (3 vols, Hertford: C.E. Longmore, 1905–1910), vol. 1, p. 347.

women [th]at come thither for their husbands."[44] Such alehouse keeps risked fines or closure of their businesses.[45] Thus Edward Staunton's alehouse in Southampton was closed down in 1596 by the town government because, as the court leet was informed, Staunton's wife was "a verie lewd woeman and of bade fame & name."[46] Communal concerns were not limited to suspicions of illicit sexual conduct. In 1613, the court leet warned the town government of Christopher Ubley's alehouse: not only was it "a verie disorderlye howse entertayninge … Lewd & vitious persons," but also Ubley's wife "lewdly entertayneth by waye of brocaridge [i.e. as a pawnbroker]" in the house. In this case, it seems that the leet jurors were concerned that Ubley's wife, in pursuing this line of work, was cheating customers or attracting thieves to the town who needed a fence.[47]

Because they were so often central in running drinking and victualing houses, wives sometimes took it upon themselves to defend their good names to local authorities. Lamenting the "false asspersion which Ill neighbours hathe laid upon me," Goodwife Confye of St Michael's parish, Cambridge petitioned the Vice-Chancellor in 1645 to restore her husband's alehouse license; crucial in gaining the Vice-Chancellor's consent was the support she enjoyed from the churchwardens, the overseers for the poor, and the constables of the parish.[48] Keeping neighbors and customers happy was central to many women who sold food and drink. Mary, a widow and alehouse owner of Standon, Hertfordshire who lost her license in 1678 because she married John Briggs, a recusant, garnered the support of her neighbors in petitioning the county justices to reinstate her license. According to her fellow parishioners, Mary Briggs "hath always kept very good order in her house and from her trade hath always mayneteyned herselfe and her children [from her previous marriage] very well, and wee doe conceive her a very fitt woman to continue in [her] calling."[49]

Just as important for many women traders as their sexual reputation was the need to balance profits with communal expectations of economic honesty. There was a fundamental contradiction, a set of irreconcilable imperatives, in what Craig Muldrew has described as an "economy of obligation" which bound neighboring households together in networks of credit and debt. As Muldrew has rightly

---

44 Stevenson et al. (eds), *Records of … Nottingham*, vol. 5, p. 158; Caulton was fined 12d.

45 In addition, alehouse owners often had to find people who were willing to enter into bonds guaranteeing that the alehouse owner followed regulations and kept good order; see e.g. CUA, T.I.11, no. 101.

46 Hearnshaw and Hearnshaw (eds), *Court Leet Records [Southampton]*, vol. 2, p. 315.

47 Hearnshaw and Hearnshaw (eds), *Court Leet Records [Southampton]*, vol. 3, p. 470.

48 CUA, V.C.Ct.III.38, nos 27 and 29; for a similar case, see CUA, V.C.Ct.III.36, no. 130.

49 Hardy (ed.), *Sessions Rolls [Hertfordshire]*, vol. 1, p. 290. Unfortunately, it is not recorded whether or not her efforts to regain her license were successful.

stressed, the creditworthiness of a household was in large part determined along moral lines. For instance, in the course of fining unlicensed bakers and brewers, the Liverpool town government decided to grant a license to a widow, Katherin Dyall, not only because she had no other way to maintain her "poore familye," but also because of her "honest" reputation.[50] And yet neighbors could not afford to assess the creditworthiness of households along moral standards alone. Traders selling on credit expected to be repaid, and this often put pressure on female traders to make profits, sometimes by employing underhanded tactics. Indeed, a reputation for rapaciousness, in certain circumstances, could be an advantage.

These dual imperatives—the need for profit versus the need to maintain a reputation for economic honesty—colored the contradictory ways in which individual women's reputations were described by themselves and their adversaries. John Sherman, the plaintiff in a debt case heard by the Cambridge Vice-Chancellor's court in 1620, characterized one hostile witness, Suzanna Averill, a married woman who operated independently as a pawnbroker, as someone "who did gett mony of every man & woman into her hands & Cosoned them of the same." But it was precisely her sharpness in trading and pawnbrokering that made Averill's neighbors comfortable with lending her the money. In explaining how she raised money in order to engage in pawnbrokering, Averill admitted that many men and women gave her money "uppon hope of extraordinary gayne & increase which they should have" when she repaid them the principle with interest.[51] Agnes Shaw (previously Agnes Vepen before her second marriage), the wealthy Cambridge fishmonger, was resented by her neighbors and was often targeted by market authorities for her hard business practices. But John Atkin, who sued Agnes and her husband in 1597 for a large amount of fish he had sold to Agnes, chose to emphasize not her rapaciousness but her savvyness. In an attempt to establish that she and her husband had the ability to repay the debt, Atkin, in an interrogatory put to John Shaw, described Agnes as "A great dealer bargainer byer and seller of diver things and especially [of] fish … and one that is very provident and carefull in such her bargains for to make profitt and comodity."[52] As these conflicting perceptions of Agnes Shaw's career suggest, the line between competence and covetousness was not necessarily clear, for behavior that courted the anger of customers and competitors could be necessary to keep creditors happy.

Conflicting views also surrounded the career of Judith Delamotte, a wealthy clothier who had inherited the shop of her late husband, Phillipe Delamotte, minister of the Huguenot church in Southampton. Though widows were not allowed to hold office in the clothier's guild, Delamotte seems to have been influential in the company, organizing a scheme in 1615 by which the clothiers agreed amongst themselves to employ the poor children of the town rather than hiring apprentices

---

50 Twemlow (ed.), *Liverpool Town Books*, vol. 2, pp. 237–8.

51 *John Sherman c. Richard Ashby*, CUA, V.C.Ct.II.22, fos 14, 35, 36.

52 *John Atkin c. John and Agnes Shaw*, CUA, V.C.Ct.III.9, no. 56; see also Comm. Ct.II.8, fo. 30^{r-v}.

and workers who came from outside the town.[53] And yet, as some suspected, her motives were not entirely philanthropic. In a presentment made to the mayor against Delamotte in 1633, the jurors of the leet court complained that:

> although some may thinke her to be a good member of this towne in employeng the poore of this towne, yet we conceiue otherwise of her; for she taketh upon her diuerse trades as sellinge by retayle, sope, starch, pines, poynts, buttons, lockram, fustian, & many other things; giuing those & the like comodities to poor worke folke instead of readie mony.

By branching out into all of these different types of businesses, Delamotte was threatening the livelihoods of other shopkeepers. In addition, the court leet alleged that because her workers had to sell the goods they received in lieu of pay at whatever prices they could get in order to support themselves, they often did not receive their full earnings.[54] The ways in which members of her community assessed Delamotte—on the one hand, she put the poor to work, but on the other, she pursued business practices which had the potential to endanger the community—were similar to the ways in which contemporaries would have assessed any prominent, profit-oriented male trader.

How representative is the Cambridge and Oxford University court evidence, and do the legal peculiarities of these courts give us reason to doubt the ability to generalize from this evidence? It would have been somewhat harder for wives in other communities to resort to court in order to defend their economic good names, for such suits were confined to borough courts, and these women would have needed to gain the consent and support of their husbands to have their day in court. Because borough courts almost never used written evidence, it is impossible to assess the frequency with which husbands brought defamation suits to borough courts—either by themselves or jointly with their wives—in order to defend their wives' economic good names. But it is telling that, when given the opportunity, women defined their honesty and good name in multiple ways, and not just in terms of sexual morality or feminine obedience to male authority; this is reflected in the broad range of insults which prompted women in Cambridge and Oxford to bring suits to the university courts. Indeed, the evidence we have from the university courts may be more representative than the records of ecclesiastical courts of the types of insults which provoked litigation because both male and female litigants had the opportunity to bring suits regarding a wider range of insults than litigants resorting to ecclesiastical courts.[55] As Laura Gowing, Timothy Stretton, and others have argued, the ways in which litigants and witnesses crafted their testimony was powerfully influenced by the need to conform to the prejudices and gendered

53 Horrocks (ed.), *Assembly Books of Southampton*, vol. 4, p. 3.

54 SCA, SC 6/1/46, fo. 19.

55 Shepard, *Meanings of Manhood*, ch. 6.

expectations of court officials.[56] That middling and plebeian women insisted on defending their reputations as honest workers and traders in their testimony before university court officials is a powerful indication that magistrates recognized the economic necessity of female work and commercial activities in keeping the household afloat.

Demands that women restrict themselves to the household did not worry ordinary women or men much. Nevertheless, women involved in commerce faced conflicting imperatives. For market women, the need to buttress the household's resources and economic credit by making profits in the market and driving hard bargains had to be balanced with the need to abide by the values of Christian charity, good neighborliness, and economic honesty. As we shall see,[57] it was this dynamic which placed female traders at the center of the tensions and conflicts which urban communities and neighborhoods experienced as England underwent the processes of the price revolution and commercial expansion.

---

56 Gowing, *Domestic Dangers*; Stretton, *Women Waging Law*; see also Natalie Zemon Davis, *Fiction in the Archives: Pardon Tales and Their Tellers in Sixteenth-Century France* (Stanford: Stanford University Press, 1987).

57 Chapter 7 below.

Chapter 7
When to Give and When to Gouge: Bargaining, Neighborliness, and the Limits of the Moral Economy

In his 1577 book *A Description of England*, the clergyman William Harrison observed that "There are … few great townes in England, that haue not their weeklie markets … in which all manner of prouision for the household is to be bought and sold." Lamentably, however, these markets are "in many places too too much abused: for the reliefe and ease of the buier is not so much intended in them, as the benefit of the seller."[1] Harrison's belief that he was living in a particularly rapacious commercial climate was conventional wisdom, and some historians would be inclined to agree with his assessment.[2] But over the last several decades some social and cultural historians, including Keith Wrightson and John Walter, have come to question the assumption, held by contemporary observers such as Harrison and economic historians alike, that commercialization inexorably led to the rise of economic individualism and undermined the communal values of charity and good neighborliness.[3] These scholars have argued a case for symbiosis, and have shown that the values of good neighborliness and the extension of informal charity to poor neighbors not only helped to hold early

---

1 William Harrison, *The Description of England*, (ed.) Georges Edelen (Ithaca: Cornell University Press, 1968), p. 246.

2 See, for instance, clerics' responses to economic change: T. Adams, *The Barren Tree* (London, 1623); I. Dyke, *A Covnterpoison Against Covetovness* (London, 1619); I. Bourne, *The Godly Mans Guide: With Directions for all, especially Merchants and Tradesmen* (London, 1620). Joyce Appleby argued some time ago that commercial change was accompanied by a shift toward a more market-oriented economic thought: *Economic Thought and Ideology in Seventeenth-Century England* (Princeton: Princeton University Press, 1978). For an attempt to track this ideological change amongst members of parliament, see David Pennington, "Beyond the Moral Economy: Economic Change, Ideology and the 1621 House of Commons," *Parliamentary History Review* 25, no. 2 (2006): 214–31.

3 Wrightson, in his recent survey, has rightly stressed the relative importance of impersonal factors such as population growth, unemployment and inflation rather than rapacious economic practices of landowners and merchants in explaining rising levels of relative poverty; see *Earthly Necessities*, pp. 145–9. For a recent study of a somewhat later period which asserts the continued importance of moral notions of economic communities, see Brodie Waddell, *God, Duty and Community in English Economic Life, 1660–1720* (Woodbridge: Boydell Press, 2012).

modern communities together but also facilitated economic change. As Craig Muldrew has demonstrated, because many market transactions in this expanding, yet cash poor economy involved the use of credit, an increasingly vital market, "far from breaking up communities, actually created numerous bonds which held them together." Given the early modern household's dependence on ever-larger credit networks, the values of plain dealing, trust, and cooperation amongst neighbors were, Muldrew suggests, necessary preconditions for commercial growth.[4]

An exploration of the complex activities of provincial market women provides crucial insight into the meaning of what we have come to think of as the early modern moral economy. Because they were often in charge of managing the household's consumption and resources, women from plebeian and middling households were amongst the firmest supporters of the values of neighborly charity and Christian love. Largely excluded from the most profitable sectors of long-distance trade, and from high-status organized crafts and trades, ordinary women have been seen as the most stalwart defenders of the pre-capitalist order, the ones most likely to reject a commercial culture which placed individual profits above the needs of the community.[5] Women organized and participated in informal charity networks, in which reciprocation was expected. Equally important to communal harmony were attempts by trading women to act as informal mediators in economic disputes which arose amongst neighbors, family, and friends. There were, as we shall see, informal, yet powerful conventions against "cozening" neighbors and receiving goods stolen from within the community.

All the more revealing, then, is the fact that women's marketing practices often contradicted the strictures of an idealized and idealistic moral economy. Charitable giving and honest dealing were important neighborhood values; but they had little purchase beyond the confines of women's immediate neighborhoods. A different standard often obtained in women's dealings with the wealthy or those from outside the neighborly community. When negotiating with strangers, or those well able to bear the cost, trading women, like their male counterparts, were inclined to drive hard bargains, to take advantage of short-term price fluctuations, and to receive and sell stolen goods which came from outside the neighborhood without asking too many questions—anything, indeed, to keep the household solvent in a period of economic uncertainty and inflation. This meant that trading women were often willing to break marketplace and fair rules, the very strictures which were

---

[4] Craig Muldrew, "Interpreting the Market: The Ethics of Credit and Community Relations in Early Modern England," *Social History* 18 (May 1993): 169.

[5] This claim has been most often made when historians have investigated female consumers who participated in food riots. See for instance John Walter, "Grain Riots and Popular Attitudes to the Law: Maldon and the Crisis of 1629," in *An Ungovernable People*, (ed.) Brewer and Styles, pp. 47–84; Sharon Howard, "Riotous Community: Crowds, Politics and Society in Wales, c. 1700–1840," *The Welsh History Review* 20 (December, 2001): 680–84.

supposed to express the community's paternalistic commitment to ensuring that customers be given a fair deal.

Women were necessarily active in the informal charity networks which accompanied the webs of credit and obligation which bound households together. But the gender-related division of labor within the household and patriarchal authority structured the ways in which women participated in these networks. Because the husband had legal control over the household's resources, wives rarely had a free hand to give large amounts of money to, or arrange large loans for, neighbors and friends who were suffering hard times. In 1620, Marmaduke Toulson, a Cambridge baker, helped Richard Ward, an impoverished friend, set up as a cobbler by taking out a loan for £6-worth of leather, which he delivered to Ward. Toulson later shouldered the expense of the funerals of Ward and Ward's wife. Toulson's wife, on the other hand, played a supporting role, delivering food, bedding and other "necessaryes to the sayd Richard Ward his wyfe & Children to helpe to norish & Comfort them" during their time of sickness.[6] Though they may not have often been able to lend large sums in their own right, wives could exercise considerable influence over their husbands. Upon receiving repayment for a debt of 56s. 10d., Thomas Hodilowe gave as a gift half of the sum to one of his neighbors, the widow of John Caldcott, at the "earnest request" of his wife "to the relyef of [Caldcott's widow] & hir poore children."[7] Women, it seems, may have been likely to give or loan to needy neighbors household goods which could be pawned or small sums of money.[8]

Women's handouts may have been small, but they played an important role in the informal charity networks which strengthened the communal bonds of the neighborhood. In a cash poor economy in which under-employment was a constant threat, many households depended on small handouts from time to time. Indeed, though both established householders and authorities were always suspicious of able-bodied vagrants,[9] the willingness of neighbors to offer occasional support to poor residents of the community could be surprising; they occasionally extended charity to even the so-called undeserving poor. When in 1590 a widow Harrison lent a tapster, Thomas Thompson, a silver spoon to pawn, and when the wife of Robert Newmarshe gave 12 table napkins to the same man, they could not have been very hopeful of repayment, for Thompson was a "poore man" and a notoriously unsuccessful gambler. And when Thompson died a pauper's death, his neighbors took up a collection amongst themselves to have him buried.[10]

---

6 *Marmaduke Toulson c. Richard Ward*, CUA, V.C.Ct.II.22, fos 24ᵛ, 25, 23ᵛ.

7 *Richard Parker c. Roger Vaughan*, CUA, Comm.Ct.II.4, fo. 123.

8 See, for instance, CUA, Comm.Ct.I.1, fol 174ᵛ; Comm.Ct.I.3, fo. 34ᵛ; Comm.Ct.I.8, fo. 170.

9 A.L. Beier, *Masterless Men: The Vagrancy Problem in England 1560–1640* (London: Methuen, 1985); Peter Clark, "The Migrant in Kentish Towns 1580–1640," in *Crisis and Order in English Towns*, (ed.) Clark and Slack.

10 *Roger Hylls c. Richard Stevenson*, CUA, Comm.Ct.II.4, fos 10ᵛ, 11ᵛ.

Such small charitable donations, given outside of the framework of the poor law, helped ease communal tensions and created bonds of reciprocity which women could draw upon in their own times of need.

Just as important as informal charity in relieving the communal tensions which accompanied commercialization were attempts by neighbors to resolve disputes between households over unpaid debts or unfulfilled obligations. Informal mediation was not necessarily an alternative to the use of law in dispute settlement; bringing a suit and informal mediation complemented each other as household strategies.[11] Bringing or threatening to bring a suit was just as often a way of speeding up the negotiation process as it was a way of extending the dispute, and the great majority of cases were settled out of court.[12] Often, negotiators tried to influence one party to forgive part of the debt or to accept a new payment schedule in order to settle the matter. Women at times facilitated such agreements. Ralph Atkinson and his wife in 1584 successfully negotiated an agreement between William Abarrowe, merchant of Southampton, and his creditor, John Barwick, a chandler. According to the agreement, Abarrowe was to pay Barwick six pence a week until he had paid off the entire debt of 28 shillings. Atkinson's wife played a central role as intermediary between the disputants by holding Barwick's bill (presumably so that Barwick could not renege on the new deal and enter a suit of debt) on condition that she deliver the weekly payments to Barwick on Abarrowe's behalf.[13] Margaret Pemberton oversaw a negotiation in 1613 between William Wilton, a "very poore man," and his landlord, Agnes Hall. While Wilton agreed to pay 20 shillings in cash or goods, Hall, for her part, would consider "all other covents reckonings & advantages that [she] had agaynst … William Wilton … voyde and of noe effecte." It is significant, however, that before Wilton and Hall consented to the deal, Francis Shilborne, a tailor, was called into the room to serve as a witness to the agreement.[14] As Craig Muldrew has noted, few women served as formal, court-appointed mediators with the power to decide disputes because coverture prevented married women from going to court in their own right. Women were therefore "at an obvious disadvantage as mediators if a suit was threatened" by one of the parties against the other.[15]

That does not mean, however, that women were unimportant in communal dispute settlement; but rather that instead of serving as neutral arbiters *between* households, they more often drew on their economic and social positions from *within* the household or neighborhood in attempting to resolve disputes. In other words, they tended to serve more as representatives for their friends, households

11 See J.A. Sharpe, "'Such Disagreement Betwixt Neighbours': Litigation and Human Relations in Early Modern England," in *Disputes and Settlements*, (ed.) Bossy.

12 Shepard, "Litigation and Locality," p. 24.

13 SCA, SC 9/3/5, unfoliated, deposition of John Barwick, 8 April 1584.

14 *Agnes Hall c. William Wilton*, CUA, Comm.Ct.II.15, fos 23^{v}, 24^{v}.

15 Craig Muldrew, "The Culture of Reconciliation: Community and the Settlement of Economic Disputes in Early Modern England," *Historical Journal* 39, (Dec., 1996): 933.

and family members than as court-appointed neutral arbiters granted the power to resolve disputes. In 1625, when Samuel Cockeram, an Oxford mercer, could not convince his landlord to extend his lease because of the opposition of the landlord's wife, Ellen Cole, a regular customer of Cockeram's and niece of the landlord's wife, offered to intervene on his behalf, and "endevour to perswade Mr Martin [the landlord] and her Aunte Mrs Martin to lette him a lease ... for some terme."[16] Martin rebuffed Cole's entreaty, but in other instances disputants recruited female family members as negotiators. Alice Revet, a widow of Ipswich, met with one Walter Jervys in order to persuade him to repay the £3 5s. he owed to her son-in-law.[17] Given their vulnerable economic and social positions, spinsters and female servants had a particular need to enlist allies and negotiators to help in resolving economic disputes. In 1608, Thomasina Corbett, on behalf of her sister, a servant of the Cambridge printer Cantrell Legg, demanded 4s. worth of unpaid servant's wages. When Legg refused to pay the 4s. and rashly called Thomasina Corbett a whore, Corbett threatened to expose Legg as an adulterer and the father of a bastard, and bring him to "Courte for a knave."[18] As a result, Legg sued Corbett in the Commissary's court for defamation. This case reminds us that while negotiation could be a valuable means to end a dispute, it did not invariably lead to reconciliation, and negotiators themselves could become embroiled in legal disputes because of their participation.

Women were perhaps on firmer ground when trying to resolve disputes between their husbands and other men. Such intermediaries were of course not disinterested, but they were of use when their husbands were unable to keep their animosity toward their opponent from clouding their judgment. Thus, customers who could not persuade a creditor to come to a settlement sometimes approached their creditor's wife to open negotiations. For instance, when John Halliwell was sued in 1604 by Robert Browne, a draper, for a debt owed for silk and buttons, he tried to resolve the dispute by first visiting Helen Browne. Appealing to her to intervene on his behalf, he asked her "must your husband ... goe to lawe? There be other measure[s] to come by his mony then thus for I am in better recolection to now paye him then ever I was."[19] In other instances, women took the initiative in attempting to negotiate settlements. According to one witness, when Margery Ellwood's husband sued Henry Mase, a brewer, for 20 bushels of sea coals that Margery and Henry had sold to Mase, she said on several occasions "that if Maise would paye the one halfe of the monie due for the coales sewed for, that she woulde paye the other halfe for quietnes sake." Complicating the case was Margery Ellwood's attempt to resolve the dispute herself. Margery Ellwood, apparently without her husband's knowledge, came to a reckoning with Mary, the wife of Henry Mase, in which she accepted money and a quantity of beer for the

16 *William Martin c. Samuel Cockeram*, OUA, Hyp/B/5, fo. 194^{v}.

17 ESRO, C/2/3/8/1, p. 6.

18 *Cantrell Legg c. Thomasina Corbett*, CUA, Comm.Ct.II.13, fos 95^{v}, 96.

19 *John Halliwell c. Robert Browne*, CUA, V.C.Ct.II.10, fos 10^{v}, 11.

20 bushels of sea coals.[20] The line separating dispute resolution and charitable giving was often unclear.

The extension of charity to neighbors and extra-legal attempts to negotiate and resolve economic disputes reflect more than just efforts to live up to the ideals of good neighborliness: they also constituted crucial strategies in the economic preservation of the household. Wives engaged in informal negotiations, sometimes even as a court case was pending, in order to repair the valuable economic relationships which bound households to each other. Margery Elwood was clearly reluctant to give up her commercial contacts with Mary Mase, who seems to have been her main supplier of beer. In addition, reaching a quick settlement could limit the expenses a household incurred in fighting legal battles to recover debts. Charitable giving could also be spurred by considerations of self-interest. The household that could afford from time to time to dispense gifts to those suffering hard times was more likely to be seen by neighbors as prosperous, able to pay its debts, and thus creditworthy. Giving an occasional gift or loan to a neighbor, therefore, was one of the ways in which women could help to build the social and economic credit of their households amongst their neighbors. Several witnesses, for instance, found it hard to believe Richard Ward's claim that Marmaduke Toulson was indebted to Ward's late father, given the Toulsons' generosity to the Ward family over the years. As one neighbor, Mary Parker, pointed out, it was likely that in fact "Ward [Richard Ward's father] was much indebted to Toulson & his wyfe for … [the Toulsons] were like father & mother to … Richard ward & his wyfe & children."[21] Living in charity and "christian love" with neighbors was in the interest of the household.

And yet women always had to walk a fine line between the demand that they live up to charitable values on the one hand, which could improve the household's social and moral position within the local community, and on the other the need to make a profit. These were not always reconcilable goals. There had to be limits to charity, for according to one adage, "A nice wife, and a back door will soon make a rich man poor."[22] Many trading women (or at least their husbands) recognized the truth of this proverb. Middling and plebeian women felt pressure to engage in hard bargaining and even deceptive commercial practices in order to keep the household afloat. When dealing with neighbors who were not in dire need, women, like men, engaged in hard bargaining. "Cozening" neighbors—that is, for instance, cheating customers by selling poor quality goods or using false weights and measures—and receiving stolen goods were riskier strategies. As we have seen, earning a reputation for deception could prove disastrous to a trader's

[20] *Richard Elwood c. Henry Mase*, CUA, Comm.Ct.I.2, fos 54, 96, 97ᵛ–8, 100; the witnesses were unsure of how much she accepted for the coals.

[21] *Marmaduke Toulson c. Richard Ward*, CUA, V.C.Ct.II.22, fo. 25ᵛ; see also fos 29, 32.

[22] Smith (ed.), *Oxford Dictionary of English Proverbs*, p. 23; dated between 1450 and 1640.

credit within her own community. But neighborhood sanctions—including the loss of credit because of the spreading of unfriendly gossip and the threat of lawsuits—were less of a threat when traders dealt with strangers from outside the neighborhood. In addition, consumers and retailers alike ignored or skirted regulations which departed too far from the real play of supply and demand. The economic culture of the period was flexible; the context of a particular economic transaction was important in shaping the way people dealt with each other.

The ways in which women discussed prices of consumer goods illustrate the divergence between the standard set of market regulations found in most towns and a popular, flexible commercial culture. Buyers and sellers had to bargain aggressively because short-term price fluctuations and the long-term rise of food and commodity prices relative to wages were dangers that households had to face throughout the period.[23] Far from holding fast to a customary notion of a "just price," female consumers and traders in urban communities had a good working knowledge of price fluctuations, and recognized that local conditions and impersonal factors of supply and demand determined prices. A common recognition of the contingency of prices is indicated in the ways in which women in debt disputes recounted, without reference to regulations or assizes, the prices of various commodities. In a 1584 debt case in Cambridge involving coal, one witness, Agnes Barlye, a Cambridge laundress, was careful to recall that "a bushell of sea coales aboute Candlemas tyme last past ... was worthe in Cambridge iiiid [4d.], & not above."[24] In answering allegations in a 1587 debt case, the widow Agnes Stagg, who had already paid part of the alleged debt in 1584 in corn, asked that it be considered that during the course of the year the price of a peck of milled corn had risen from 4d. to 8d.[25] Similarly, in a debt case heard in 1587 by the Chancellor's court of Oxford University regarding 28 bushels worth of malt purchased by Cicilia Jackman from William Buttle, Joan Ladyman testified that "barley hath bene worth xxiiii s. a quarter this deare yeare, but nowe it is not worthe above xi s a quarter."[26] Unsurprisingly, then, leaving aside cases of charitable giving, female consumers and traders bargained for the best prices they could to maximize household resources and profits.

As a result, many of the purchases and sales made by men and women broke the rules of the regulated marketplace and fair. As we have seen, women who made their living by buying and re-selling provisions commonly evaded marketplace rules designed to protect the right of consumers to have the first opportunity to buy necessities. Southampton's court leet juries complained throughout the sixteenth and seventeenth centuries of hucksters who failed to buy their "provizion abroade & not ... bye so such [vicutals] as rep^{ar}eth to this m^{ar}ket except" after 11 a.m. when

---

23 For reactions to the price revolution, see Wrightson, *Earthly Necessities*, p. 118.

24 *Richard Elwood c. Henry Mase*, CUA, Comm.Ct.II.2, fo. 55.

25 *John Nixon c. Christopher and Agnes Stagge*, CUA, Comm.Ct.II.3, fo. 91^{v}; Stagge had remarried by the time of the trial.

26 *Cicilia Jackman c. William Buttle*, OUA, Hyp/B/3, fo. 92^{v}.

the market opened.[27] The bakers' wives of York also impinged on the rights of the marketplace customer. In 1567, the city's government found it necessary to bar all bakers' wives from buying "any maner of corne as wheat, rie or beans" in the public market, "onlesse hir husband be syke [sick] or forth of this Citie soo that at noo tyme there be above one of a hows of any of the said bakers in the markett to buye any corne."[28]

Selling staples such as bread or beer over the allowed price was another common offense. For instance, widow Bembridge in 1620 was fined by Cambridge University's Vice-Chancellor's court for selling strong beer in pots that did not contain a full quart.[29] Margaret Lorkin was fined for the same offense after her servant testified that her mistress sold beer by uninspected, small pots.[30] Bakers, including widows who took over their husbands' shops, were regularly fined for selling underweight bread.[31] The regularity of such prosecutions in market towns suggests that bakers and drink peddlers had few qualms about disregarding regulations when they thought they could get away with it.[32]

Vending light loaves and small pots of beer defrauded those customers who thought they were getting their full measure, but in other instances, consumers agreed to pay prices higher than allowed by regulatory price ceilings if that was the only way they could procure the goods they needed. Elizabeth Heskett of King's Lynn, for instance, was called to court in 1601 for selling a barrel of overpriced beer at her husband's stall in Stourbridge Fair.[33] In 1606, Hellen Curtise was prosecuted in the Vice-Chancellor's court for selling 1,200 oysters at the rate of 6d. per 100, 2d. over the maximum price.[34] Firewood was another commodity particularly prone to price fluctuations. In 1622, Hellen Vaughan was amerced for selling bundles of faggots which were "very little, & not accordinge to the sise [as legally specified]."[35] Despite a recent order made by Cambridge University

---

27 Hearnshaw and Hearnshaw (eds), *Court Leet Records [Southampton]*, vol. 1, pp. 65, 76–7 and passim. The concern of the Southampton leet jurors that traders sought to buy up supplies before the market opened were hardly unusual. For example, see Ferguson and Nanson (eds), *Records of ... Carlisle*, p. 87; Ferguson (ed.), *Recorde of Kirbie Kendall*, p. 170; Twemlow (ed.), *Liverpool Town Books*, vol. 1, p. 199; Michael Power (ed.), *Liverpool Town Books 1649–1671* (The Record Society of Lancashire and Cheshire, vol. 136, 1999), p. 78.

28 Angelo Raine (ed.), *York Civic Records* (9 vols, Yorkshire Archaeological Society, 1948), vol. 6, p. 131.

29 *Office v. Bembridge*, CUA, V.C.Ct.I.9, fo. 236v.

30 *Office v. Margaret Lorkin*, CUA, V.C.Ct.I.10, fo. 13; see also *Office v. Wright*, CUA, V.C.Ct.I.10, fos 260v–61.

31 For example, see *Office v. Jackson*, CUA, V.C.Ct.I.10, fo. 258v; Earwaker (ed.), *Court Leet Records ... of Manchester*, vol. 4, p. 46.

32 On this point, see also Boulton, *Neighbourhood and Society*, pp. 75–6.

33 *Office c. Elizabeth Heskett*, CUA, Comm.Ct.V.7, p. 280.

34 *Office c. Helen Curtise*, CUA, V.C.Ct.I.36, fo. 87v.

35 *Office c. Hellen Vaughan*, CUA, V.C.Ct.I.10, fo. 19v.

that set the price of candles at 3d. ob. per pound, one Richard Pinder informed the Vice-Chancellor's court that Walter Metcalfe's wife refused to sell him candles at the statutory price. Metcalf's wife was following common practice: two other witnesses noted that no traders in and around Market Hill would sell them candles at the prices set by the University.[36] Female retailers, then, were willing to risk occasional amercements in pricing their commodities. In times of shortage, many customers found it necessary to buy from traders who ignored artificially low statutory prices, though it seems likely that they later found recourse by informing authorities of those who ignored price ceilings.

It is of little surprise that wholesalers—corn badgers and other long-distance merchants—were able to obtain cut-rate prices unavailable to most consumers. But even petty retailers, including hucksters and regraters, were able to bargain for prices below those paid by consumers. The regularity of their purchases prompted producers to offer discounts. For instance, Southampton leet jurors reported in presentments from 1626, 1627, and 1628, hucksters procured bread at a cheaper price than consumers; they were typically able to buy 14 or 15 loaves for the price of a dozen. The same complaint was made by Manchester's court leet.[37] Stourbridge Fair officials confronted a similar situation. John Fidlin, a baker, complained in 1589, a year of relatively low corn prices, that "goodwife Miller of Barnewell," a victualer in Stourbridge Fair, refused to buy his bread unless he lowered his price. She informed him that she regularly received 14 loaves for the price of a dozen from Richard Scott and other bakers.[38] In the same year, Scott's wife seems to have urged her servant to inform the Stourbridge Fair officials of the activities of Elizabeth Helsden, a widow and a baker who was also undercutting the price of bread. Scott's servant, John Yaxley, along with the servant of another baker, testified that a woman who was operating a victualing booth in Stourbridge Fair had returned the bread Yaxley delivered because he "would not deliver to her seaven penyworthe of white breade to the halfe dozen"; he then witnessed Elizabeth Helsden's servant deliver seven loaves for the price of six to the booth.[39] For local buyers and sellers, then, haggling over prices was a normal part of business, as was threatening to inform market or fair authorities of transactions which violated regulations.

The effectiveness of market and fair officials in regulating prices for goods such as beer and bread is hard to measure, but the cases brought against Richard Scott and Elizabeth Helsden, recorded in unusual detail, are illustrative. Most of the records of office cases for marketplace and fair infractions do not provide detailed

---

36 *Office c. Walter Metcalfe*, CUA, V.C.Ct.I.3, fo. 224^{v}. The university's reason for setting an artificially low price for candles is obvious: studiousness at all hours must be encouraged.

37 SCA, SC 6/1/41, fo. 15^{v}; SC 6/1/42, fo. 18; SC 6/1/43, fo. 14^{v}; Earwaker (ed.), *Court Leet Records of ... Manchester*, vol. 3, p. 289.

38 *Office c. Richard Scott*, CUA, Comm.Ct.V.7, p. 69.

39 *Office c. Elizabeth Helsden*, CUA, Comm.Ct.V.7, p. 71.

allegations or depositional evidence. But as these two cases suggest, Stourbridge Fair officials may have had to rely on traders to inform on their competitors, for there would have been far too few officials to oversee all the business done in the fair. But if the pattern of regulation in this particular fair was patchy, it must have been even more so in the numerous smaller, local fairs, many of which were held outside of the jurisdictions of regulated town markets.[40] The regulation of town markets was in most cases undoubtedly tighter, but the enforcement efforts of market clerks could nevertheless be sporadic. Joan Cox, the wife of a baker in Oxford, testified in a 1596 case brought against a clerk of the market that "the clerks do not weigh her husbands bred everie day but sometymes two or thre daies together somtymes not in a weeke together."[41] In some towns, authorities lacked the will or desire to strictly enforce marketplace regulations. Jurors of Southampton's court leet in the late-sixteenth and early seventeenth centuries regularly accused the mayor and his "discreets"—four townsmen appointed by the mayor to oversee the buying and selling of victuals in the market—of shirking their duties.[42] Given the limited effectiveness of regulation, the informal pressure neighbors exerted on each other and the need to maintain a good reputation within the community by being charitable and by not cozening neighbors were probably more important in restraining market traders than the occasional risk of prosecution by market and fair officials.

But if the values of neighborliness constrained women from dishonest commercial activities when dealing with members of their community, dealings with strangers offered greater opportunities for women to turn a profit. As we have seen, women frequently acted as fences and receivers of stolen goods. While engaging in such activity was particularly dangerous if the goods were stolen from within the community, many women had little compunction about receiving goods they believed had come from outside the community. As keepers of inns and alehouses, women would have had plenty of opportunities to obtain such goods from travelers, sometimes in lieu of payment for food, drink, and lodging. Indeed, because early modern England was cash poor, innholders and alehouse keepers who catered to travelers probably had to accept second-hand goods rather than coin in order to do a brisk business. In 1623, Alice Symons of Reading accepted from three traveling lodgers a white hat, a pair of breeches and two napkins, all of which were found to have been stolen.[43] A sense of the boundaries of the moral community is given in the testimony of a quarter sessions trial for theft brought

---

40 Everitt, "Marketing of Agricultural Produce," p. 534.

41 *Day and Butler c. Thomas Collins*, OUA, Hyp/A/26, fo. 22^{v}; as in Cambridge, clerks of the market were appointed by the university. For more on the pattern of marketplace regulation, see Thwaites, "Corn Market and Economic Change;" Thwaites, "Women in the Market Place," pp. 30–31.

42 Hearnshaw and Hearnshaw (eds), *Court Leet Records [Southampton]*, vol. 1, pp. 65, 76–7, 104; vol. 2, pp. 300, 316, 341, 371; vol. 3, pp. 379, 400, 425, 432.

43 Guilding (ed.), *Reading Records*, vol. 2: pp. 145; see also pp. 157–8.

against a Staffordshire woman in 1695. After pawning a stolen kettle to a female neighbor, Stevens offered to steal some yarn from a woman who lived nearby for her pawnbroker to spin. Her pawnbroker answered that she could not accept the yarn, for that would be "devil's work," because "they should not steal from any of their own parish."[44]

But dealing with strangers offered opportunities for short-changing and passing on defective goods. For instance, in 1654 two pewterers, Roger Willoughby and Samson Bourne, complained to the Tolzey court of Bristol that they had been cheated by Edith Skinner, a long-distance trader from Exeter, who had sold them a quantity of tin which had turned out on closer inspection to be largely dross.[45] The use of false weights and measures in selling goods at events such as Stourbridge Fair, where most of the customers and traders were from other counties, was common.[46] Unscrupulous traders would also have had plenty of opportunities to bargain with strangers in town markets and fairs, which were frequently visited by traders and consumers from outside the community.

But did the behavior of female traders differ significantly from that of male traders? Records from the University's Stourbridge Fair court suggest that women were just as willing as men to break commercial regulations and defraud customers. Of the 2,001 prosecutions heard by the University's Stourbridge Fair court from 1575 to 1625, the type of offense could be determined for 1,865 cases. Table 7.1 categorizes these 1,865 cases by seven types of offenses and by gender.

At first glance, the most striking aspect of the data is the paucity of female defendants: women made up just 5.6 percent of all defendants. But, as we saw in Chapter 3, there is much evidence to suggest that wives and female servants commonly tended male householders' booths. In addition, women who wanted to trade independently in the fair got their husbands to hire a booth for them, or, if they were single, paid a male householder to be able to operate out of his house or booth. In such cases, the men would have been legally responsible for the activities of women trading under their names. Such arrangements are indicated by the occasions in which the court clerk recording fair court prosecutions crossed out the name of a married woman, and inserted the name of her husband as the defendant. For instance, John Vepen was charged in 1571 for his wife's sale of 200 "stynkynge" fish; similarly, Thomas Hawkins in 1629 was charged for his wife's sale of meat on a prohibited day.[47] Therefore, while the court records can give us

---

44 Patricia Crawford and Laura Gowing (eds), *Women's Worlds in Seventeenth-Century England* (London and New York: Routledge, 2000), p. 108.

45 Nott and Ralph (eds), *Deposition Books of Bristol*, vol. 2, p. 165.

46 For examples, see *Office c. Alice Pattyn,* CUA, V.C.Ct.I.29, fo 9; *Office c. [Agnes] Leonard*, CUA, V.C.Ct.I.29, fo. 40, and CUA, Comm.Ct.V, various, passim.

47 *Office c. John Vepen*, CUA, Comm.Ct.V.5, fo. 65, for his wife's sale of insalubrious fish; and *Office c. Thomas Hawkins*, CUA, Comm.Ct.V.9, fo. 111. Similar slips, in which the clerk was unsure whether or not to record the woman who violated the regulation, or her husband, could well have occurred in other towns. See, for instance, Richard Savage

Table 7.1 Prosecutions of male and female traders in Stourbridge Fair, 1575–1625[48]

Type of Offense	**Male**		**Female**		**Totals**	
Poor Quality Goods	390	22%	13	12%	403	22%
Uninspected Measures/Goods	377	21%	22	21%	399	21%
False Measures/ Underweight Goods	261	15%	7	7%	268	14%
Overpriced Goods	251	14%	19	18%	270	14%
Regrating/ Forestalling/ Engrossing	172	10%	5	5%	177	9%
Public Order/ Moral Offenses	164	9%	25	25%	189	10%
Unlicensed Trading	145	8%	14	14%	159	9%
Totals	1760		105		1865	

Source: CUA, Comm.Ct.V, 5–9.
Notes: Public Order/moral offenses include defying fair officials, selling meat on prohibited days, sexual impropriety, gambling, and illicit shows. Unlicensed trading offenses include trading in wares without having served the appropriate apprenticeship, selling butter or cheese without having a badger's license, or holding a booth without being an independent householder.

some indication of the types of offenses committed by men and women, they are not an accurate measure of female participation in the commerce of the fair.

The data suggest that while there were some gender-related patterns of prosecution, many men and women committed the same types of offenses. Prohibitions against prostitution and "dressing flesh"—the preparation and sale of meat on prohibited days—account for the over-representation of women prosecuted for moral offenses or infractions against public order. A higher percentage of cases involving women than of cases involving men concerned accusations of unlicensed trading; in particular, women were accused of infringing on the rights of vintners by selling wine without license. Nevertheless, both men and women were accused of a variety of offenses which harmed consumers. Not all of these infractions involved the deliberate cheating of customers. The same proportion (21 percent) of woman as men were prosecuted for failing to have their goods or weights and measures inspected. Some of these defendants were motivated

(ed.), *Minutes and Accounts of the Corporation of Stratford-Upon-Avon* (4 vols, Oxford: Dugdale Society, 1921–1929), vol. 1, p. 42, in which the clerk records: "Henry Syndall for brwynge aell [brewing ale] in *hyr* [*sic*: her] hous & syllynge [selling] out by the pot *he* standes amercyd." Emphasis is mine.

48 CUA, Comm.Ct.V.5–9.

by nothing more than an unwillingness to pay the proctors and gaugers' fees.[49] Stourbridge Fair was a major venue for the selling of perishables—including butter, cheese, fish, and hops—and so it was inevitable that many prosecutions stemmed from the attempted sale of spoiled goods. But some prosecutions reveal premeditated deceptions. Some hop sellers were found to have mixed dirt, leaves, and other debris in with good hops. In 1645, the court amerced Mary Stockes 13s. for "deceiptfully" packing together two types of hops—one of high quality and one of low quality.[50] Similarly, widow Greene, a local fishmonger, was found in 1624 to have mingled "bad" fish along with her good fish.[51] Both men and women engaged in price-gouging as well. Although men were more likely to be prosecuted for using false measures or selling underweight goods, women were more likely to sell their goods at prices higher than allowed by statute. Overall, 29 percent of cases involving male defendants, and 25 percent of cases involving female defendants related to charges of selling goods at inflated prices or using deceptive weights, measures, or containers.

Women in Stourbridge Fair were surprisingly less likely than men to be prosecuted for practices designed to corner the market on a particular type of good, and thus drive up the price. While 10 percent of cases involving male defendants involved accusations of forestalling, engrossing, or regrating, only 5 percent of cases involving women (just five cases in all) concerned these infractions. This finding is anomalous when compared to the relatively large number of women prosecuted for these offenses in local courts leet.[52] It seems likely that while women appear frequently in the records of local markets, fair officials focused their efforts on wealthy merchants who could muster the cash and credit to buy very large amounts of corn and other commodities, thus creating severe food shortages.

Some particularly well-positioned women nevertheless attracted the attentions of authorities for commercial practices which threatened the food supply of the community. Elizabeth Wallis, for instance, was prosecuted in 1583 for purchasing a large shipment of wheat before it reached the market in Cambridge, depriving marketplace consumers, and again two years later for forestalling another 15 quarters of wheat.[53] Agnes Fypennie, the wife of a corn merchant, was charged in Stourbridge Fair in 1583 as an engrosser. A prominent fishmonger in her own right, she had bought 500 cod from Thomas Elderye of Ipswich at Stourbridge Fair, which she then tried to sell in the same fair, presumably after the price of fish had risen.[54] The prominence of women in the sale of beer by retail has been

---

49 Presentments which accused traders of using uninspected measures or containers that were *also* deficient in size have been categorized in Table 4 as falling under "false weights/ underweight goods."

50 *Office c. Mary Stockes*, CUA, Comm.Ct.V.11, fo. 8^{v}.

51 *Office c. Greene*, CUA, Comm.Ct.V.9, fo. 54.

52 See above, Ch. 4.

53 CUA, Collect.Admin.6a, pp. 220, 304; Wallis's marital status is not given.

54 *Office c. Agnes Fypennie* [aka Vepen], CUA, Comm.Ct.V.5, fo. 111^{v}.

long observed, but some women also sold beer wholesale. The wife of John Goodman, for instance, was prosecuted in 1634 for buying six barrels of beer and re-selling them in the fair for a higher price.[55] Many fair visitors came for fun as well as business, and this created opportunities for beer middlemen. One trader, widow Barnes, turned a handsome profit by buying five barrels for 10s. a barrel just outside the fair and selling them at the fair to one Richard Lasenbey for 22s. a barrel.[56]

Most women operated on a smaller scale than widow Barnes, but they were no less hard-nosed in their pursuit of profit. The Midsummer Fair court amerced Widow Tompson in 1632 for buying a barrel of beer for 10s. and selling it in the same fair for 18s.[57] Marketplaces also offered opportunities for crafty middlemen. Marian Batterson, a Cambridge widow, turned a small profit in 1601 by buying 12 pigeons for 16d. and then selling them in the same market to another widow, Margaret Woodward for 18d. Woodward, however, could not have been too upset in paying the higher price, for she in turn sold the birds to a man for 2s. 4d.; both women were fined 22d. for forestalling and regrating.[58] Southampton's leet jurors believed that the town's hucksters reaped profits by buying bakers' light loaves at discount prices, and selling them for the full price of a penny, a practice which constituted "A greate wronge to the poore" who bought bread on the streets.[59] Marketplace regulations were not just ignored by wealthy, profit-seeking merchants, but also by humble hucksters.

These commonplace infractions cast doubt on the notion that market regulations reflected a common consensus that profit-seeking had to be controlled for the good of the local community. Certainly, in some of the cases described here, market women were creating artificially high prices by buying goods and re-packaging and re-selling them in the same market.[60] Yet regrators and forestallers provided what could be seen as a useful service in transporting goods over short distances, and vending them in the places most convenient for consumers. Hucksters, forestallers, and regrators earned their profits by transporting daily necessities and selling them where they were most needed in packages that even the poorest consumers could afford. Consumers—if not market officials—may have recognized that these humble traders deserved to profit for their labors.

The London apprentices' riot in Southwark in 1595 is particularly revealing of the gap between regulations and consumers' expectations. The conflict between the London apprentices and the Southwark market women was not one which

---

55 *Office c. John Goodman and his wife*, CUA, Comm.Ct.V.9, fo. 161.

56 *Office c. Barnes*, CUA, Comm.Ct.V.9, fo. 163.

57 *Office c. Tompson*, CUA, Comm.Ct.V.3, fo. 72^{v}.

58 *Office c. Marian Batterson* and *Office c. Margaret Woodward*, CUA, V.C.Ct.I.5, fos 101^{v}, 102.

59 SCA, SC 6/1/43, fo. 14^{v}.

60 See also, for instance, Stevenson et al. (eds), *Records of ... Nottingham*, vol. 4, p. 153.

pitted consumers against traders in the abstract, but one in which the interests of one community was at odds with an adjacent community. The London apprentices, sent by their masters to buy fish in Billingsgate market, arrived only to find that all of the fish had already been bought at the docks by Southwark fishwives "against orders" (Southwark was the suburb to the immediate south of London). The apprentices, numbering between 60 and 80, then rushed across the Thames and pressured the fishwives to sell the fish to them at a low price. Although the apprentices certainly intimidated the sellers, there was little or no fighting. The only reported violence involved a fishwife who struck an apprentice with her basket.[61] Whereas the fishwives attempted to deprive the consumers of Billingsgate, they were bringing fish to their own customers of Southwark.

It remains possible that our argument for the limits of the moral economy rests on atypical evidence. Legal records, as Susan Amussen notes, by their very nature highlight deviance and conflict.[62] We know much more about deals made in the markets and fairs which violated regulations than those bargains which conformed to the rules. It should be noted, however, that many—and perhaps toward the end of the seventeenth century even most—deals were made not in public markets or fairs, but in private places, such as shops and alehouses, out of view of public market officials.[63] Such private dealing carried with it greater freedom to ignore the rules. In addition, the cost of an occasional fine may have been more than made up by profits which had been reaped in the meantime. This is indicated by the career of widow Stevenson, who was prosecuted three times—in 1611, 1612 and 1622—for unlicensed wine trading in Stourbridge Fair. It seems likely that she escaped prosecution for unlicensed wine trading in the intervening years between 1612 and 1622.[64] While dishonest dealing with neighbors provoked dangerous conflicts, moral constraints in dealings with traders from outside the community were weaker.

But instances of hard dealing with outsiders may too be anomalous, for it has been argued that the same moral imperatives which influenced the way one dealt with neighbors—the need for trust, plain dealing, and charitable understanding—were just as crucial in shaping the deals made by members of regional and national trade networks.[65] But if reputation was a fragile commodity within any local community, it was an even more fragile commodity (and thus less valuable) in long-distance trade networks whose members were not well

61 LMA, COL/RMD/PA/01/002: *Remembrancia*, vol. 2, fo. 50r.

62 Amussen, *An Ordered Society*, p. 6.

63 Everitt, "Marketing Agrarian Produce," p. 552–3.

64 CUA, Comm.Ct.V.6, p. 530; Comm.Ct.V.8, p. 24; Comm.Ct.V.9, fo. 23. Many other women were prosecuted for unlicensed wine trading, and it seems unlikely that they would have come to the fair if they did not feel confident of making a profit, whether or not they suffered a fine.

65 Everitt, "Marketing Agricultural Produce," 553–7; Muldrew, "Interpreting the Market," p. 180.

acquainted. We can glimpse the tenuousness of reputation in long-distance trade networks in one trader's complaint in Stourbridge Fair to his creditor that he would have paid his debt on time "but for your talke, for you have used suche speaches of me here amongst the Londoners, that they wyll not trust me."[66] On the other hand, dealing with strangers one might meet once or twice a year at a fair also offered unique possibilities for hard dealing and cozening with little chance of repercussions to be suffered from outraged neighbors. Strangers at a fair with ready cash must have been seen as targets.

The early modern household faced contradictory imperatives: the need to turn a profit always had to be balanced with calls to deal charitably with neighbors. We should thus question the standard description of the economy as part of a national, pre-modern and anti-capitalist plebeian culture. Given the typical early modern household's dependence on good credit and neighborly charity, it was in the interest of market women to treat neighbors well, if only to build a good social and economic reputation within their local communities and to establish a network of neighbors whose charity could be drawn on in times of need. Nevertheless, rapacious economic practices were not just typical of wealthy, well-positioned middlemen and landowners. In this period of commercialization, inflation and rising poverty, the most humble of chapwomen had to engage in unsavory business practices to survive. But just as intriguing is the possibility that consumers recognized that female hucksters, regardless of their infractions against market regulations, provided a valuable service in helping to link consumers and producers within the marketplace. If the values of neighborliness, trust and charity helped ease England's transition toward a commercial economy for middling and poor households, so too did a healthy regard for self-interest, a keen eye for profit, and a discerning willingness to turn a blind eye to the tenets of the economic morality.

---

66 *George Brooks c. John Hurste*, CUA, Comm.Ct.II.2, fo. 41.

Chapter 8
The Potency of Women's Words: Gossip, Slander, and the Enforcement of Plain Dealing

"Yo[u]^{r} Husband ... is not so honest as my Husband, for he carried false weights in his pocketts, and bought butter w[i]th them."[1] So declared Margerie Reade to the wife of Reuben Fitches in Jesus Lane, Cambridge before a number of spectators. Reade's words seem at first glance to underscore the purchase of the gendered order, and particularly the deference women were supposed to show to married men; the most effective way in which Reade felt she could challenge Reuben Fitches's honesty before the crowd on Jesus Lane was by comparing him to her own, more honest, husband. And yet the case also reveals the influence women could wield in the micro-politics of the neighborhood and marketplace. In addition to confronting Fitches's wife on the street, Reade, the Fitches alleged, had engaged in a whispering campaign, spreading the word from March to June of 1620 that Reuben Fitches and his wife used false weights. Reuben Fitches was worried enough by Reade's assertions to sue her for defamation before Cambridge University's Commissary's court. He was hardly alone in sensing the power of women's words. Townswomen's varied commercial roles placed them in a position to wield powerful influence in the early modern marketplace and neighborhood. Female gossip networks were important distributors of information and rumors about neighbors who were bad credit risks, unscrupulous lenders, or dishonest traders. Chapter 6 showed that contemporaries judged women's reputations by their economic as well as sexual behaviors. This chapter shows how townswomen, as distributors of gossip and news, participated in the construction of their neighbors' "common fame." These gossip networks—informal associations of female kin, friends, and neighbors—played a crucial role in the enforcement of economic good neighborliness.

A reputation for industriousness, creditworthiness, and plain dealing was a valuable but fragile commodity that could be easily undermined by gossip or public insult. "Common fame," according to Pamella Algate, a deponent in a 1591 debt case heard before Cambridge University's Commissary's court, "ys that which ys reported by halfe a dozen persones or more."[2] Algate's definition, given in the course of testimony which cast aspersions on the plaintiff's economic

1 *Reuben Fitches c. Margerie Reade*, CUA, Comm.Ct.III.13, no. 28.

2 *John Harvye c. Thomas and Joan Wraye*, CUA, Comm.Ct.II.4, fo. 169.

honesty, suggests that ill-fame amongst even a small segment of one's neighbors could easily spread, and undermine a trader's reputation. A bad reputation could not only turn the course of a debt case, but also damage a trader's standing in his or her local community, for rumors traveled fast in England's crowded urban neighborhoods. Most traders relied on their immediate neighbors to buy their goods and extend them credit; and it was thus imperative that they maintained a reputation for industriousness and plain dealing amongst their neighbors if they hoped to thrive. A study of how townswomen undermined those neighbors they deemed to be dishonest or rapacious helps explain how honesty and plain dealing remained such important and widely held values in a period which saw the rise of a consumer society, wild price fluctuations, and increased commercial opportunities for unscrupulous traders. A commercial environment in which trust and credit regularly had to be extended to neighbors could not survive without enforcers looking out for themselves and their neighbors' interests.

While scholars of women's participation in neighborhood disputes have recognized the potency of women's words, their preoccupation with explaining how women "negotiated" and found "accommodation" with patriarchy has led them to focus too narrowly on disputes which concerned domestic propriety and sexual morality. As Bernard Capp has persuasively argued, gossip networks "offered [women] … a means of coping with patriarchal pressures and alleviating them, and a powerful weapon for both defense and attack."[3] Women could turn patriarchal maxims of female sexual purity to their advantage to undermine the sexual reputations of female enemies.[4] Women had to be more careful in confronting men with accusations of sexual immorality. Men were hardly immune to imputations against their sexual honesty, but, as Laura Gowing and others have pointed out, accusations of sexual impropriety stung women with more force than they did men. Women reputed to be sexually dishonest could lose their marriage prospects, or, if married or widowed, lose their customers and be shamed and shunned by their neighbors. But a very different dynamic obtained in disputes which revolved primarily around suspicions of shortchanging and "cozening." Gossip and public insult could undermine the position of even the most comfortable male householder. Market traders had to take account of the opinions of their female neighbors if they hoped to earn and retain trust.

We have yet to look hard enough for evidence that women regularly participated in commercial disputes; historians' focus on the records of ecclesiastical courts has only served to confirm the impression that women were primarily concerned with issues of sexual and domestic morality. These courts after the early sixteenth century were barred from hearing defamation cases involving accusations of temporal offenses. As a result, the power of women to shape the commercial reputations of traders, male and female, has received little attention. However,

---

[3] Capp, *When Gossips Meet*, pp. 25, 381. Capp, however, does not focus on commercial disputes.

[4] Gowing, *Domestic Dangers*.

an examination of the evidence from the university court records, which were entitled to hear defamation cases regarding accusations of temporal infractions, demonstrates that women were just as able to retaliate against dishonest traders and unreliable borrowers as they were to expose violators of domestic and sexual mores. The records of these courts provide a wealth of incidental evidence of the ways in which women helped to make, and break, the economic reputations of their neighbors. After discussing women's social networks and the role insult and gossip played in perceptions of common fame, this chapter examines the intersection between women's gossip and the operation of urban credit networks. It concludes with a consideration of the ways in which women identified and undermined dishonest craftsmen and traders, both male and female.

Gossips and Their Social Environment

A glance at the origin of the noun "gossip" would hardly suggest that women's social networks placed them at the center of the economic tensions which afflicted England's growing urban communities. In its original meaning, gossip, or "godsib," referred to a kinsman or kinswoman who co-sponsored a child's baptism.[5] By the early modern period, however, the noun had come to mean any loose association of female friends and neighbors; and the verb "to gossip" had entered common parlance. The expanding meanings of "gossip" are arguably reflective of the ways in which women's commercial activities brought them into the town's public spaces. Just as women did not confine their work to the home, so they played a highly visible role in the social life of their neighborhoods. The illustration accompanying the satirical 1603 broadside "Tittle-Tattle; Or, the several Branches of Gossiping" shows townswomen talking, carousing, and fighting in a myriad of places in which business was conducted: the street and marketplace, outside the alehouse and parish church, and around the communal well.[6] Slander cases heard by the university courts confirm the impression that women regularly exchanged news, rumors, and assessments of their neighbors' honesty in places of commerce. For instance, Joan Ringe, the wife of a Cambridge saddler, deposed in 1602 that she had heard from many of her neighbors in the town's market that Dorcas Swettson, who sued a neighbor who accused her of stealing a book, was "a filcher of other mans goods."[7] As Ringe's deposition suggests, women gossiped about their female as well as male neighbors. We should therefore resist the temptation to ascribe a nascent feminist solidarity to the "subculture" of early modern women's gossip

---

5 *OED*, s.v. "gossip."

6 Mendelson and Crawford, *Women in Early Modern England*, pp. 206–7.

7 She was a witness for the plaintiff, and the quote comes in response to an interrogatory: *Margaret Cotton c. Dorcas Swettson*, CUA, Comm.Ct.II.10, fo. 71; see also Comm.Ct.II.11, fo. 3. Alehouses were also sites of damaging gossip: e.g. *Thomas Wylkinson c. Jane Johnson*, CUA, Comm.Ct.II.3, fos 21^{v}–4.

networks.[8] Women's loyalties to their households often trumped their sympathies toward fellow tradeswomen; and, as we shall see, meetings of gossips could be sites of conflicts as well as conviviality.

Despite prejudices against loquacious and verbally combative women, tradeswomen had room to maneuver in their conflicts with their neighbors. Although commentators often worried that women's rumormongering had the potential to undercut the patriarchal authority of husbands,[9] male householders nevertheless had reasons to tolerate their wives' loose tongues. Gossips connected households in a common social network, and provided much needed information regarding the honesty of local borrowers and traders. Public insult was for women a riskier strategy, for scolding was conceived as a gender-specific crime, with gender-specific punishments.[10] But, as Martin Ingram has demonstrated, scold prosecutions were relatively rare: usually only those women who had offended a large number of their neighbors, or a particularly prominent town citizen, were punished with the scold's bridle or cucking stool.[11]

Those who wished to combat a female neighbor's insults more commonly sought satisfaction from the ecclesiastical and temporal courts which heard defamation cases. Women made up a sizable minority of defendants in defamation cases. From 1615 to 1629, women constituted 40 percent of defendants brought before Salisbury's bishop's court.[12] The percentages of female defendants were also large in courts entitled to hear defamation cases regarding accusations of temporal infractions. In cases for which depositions survive for the period 1580–1640, women appear as defendants in 19.5 percent of Cambridge University's Vice-Chancellor's defamation cases and 32.9 percent of the Commissary's defamation cases.[13] That women constituted such a large number of defendants suggests the power of women's words to determine their neighbors' common fame. The defendants in these cases risked paying monetary damages and the humiliation of donning a white cloak in the parish church and apologizing to the offended party; but the fact that most cases did not result in a final judgment, but were

---

8 Compare with Mendelson and Crawford, *Women in Early Modern England*, ch. 4.

9 Foyster, *Manhood in Early Modern England*, pp. 58–61.

10 Underdown, "Scolding Woman Cucked and Washed;" but for one exception, see a 1561 regulation in Carlisle: the mayor was to fine both women (4s.) *and* men (6s.) who "scold rayll or misreport any man or women." See Ferguson and Nanson (eds), *Records of ... Carlisle*, p. 62.

11 Martin Ingram, "'Scolding Women Cucked and Washed': A Crisis in Gender Relations in Early Modern England?," in *Women, Crime and the Courts*, (ed.) Kermode and Walker, pp. 48–80. Ingram's conclusions that convicted scolds' behavior can be equated to present day notions of "harassment," and that many scolds were mentally unbalanced, are hard to substantiate—and perhaps overdrawn—because records of scolds defending their conduct are rare.

12 Martin Ingram, *Church Courts, Sex and Marriage in England, 1570–1640* (Cambridge: Cambridge University Press, 1987), p. 304.

13 Shepard, "Litigation and Locality," p. 18, table 3.

instead abandoned or settled out of court, indicates that courts served as much to ameliorate conflicts as to punish offenders.[14] The records of the defamation cases heard by the university courts give us little reason to suspect that they were effective in controlling women's speech; they do, however, offer plenty evidence of the role women played in assessing the commercial reputations and practices of their neighbors.

Gossip, Insult, and the Economy of Credit

As J.R. Wordie has rightfully observed, "no merchant or individual could operate on credit indefinitely." Borrowers at some point had to be able to come to periodic reckonings with their lenders and suppliers if their credit was not to be deemed "worthless."[15] But even relatively prosperous craftsmen and traders lacked the cash on hand to repay all of their debts at once. Consumers and traders whose willingness or ability to repay their debts on time came into doubt faced the threat of being confronted by multiple creditors at once, all of whom were eager to obtain repayment. Common fame, as much as the actual wealth of a trader or consumer, determined one's creditworthiness, and thus the extent of one's economic agency; according to one mid-seventeenth-century aphorism, "credit lost is like a Venice-glass broken."[16] In a society that had to place importance on economic common fame, gossips and rumormongers were in a powerful position to participate in the local politics of informal credit networks.

Women regularly gauged the wealth and creditworthiness of their neighbors, and their neighbors valued—or feared—their judgments. One way they could express their opinion of the creditworthiness of neighbors was by providing testimony and depositions in debt cases.[17] Occasionally, litigants asked female deponents to give their assessments of the creditworthiness of persons involved in debt cases. Elizabeth Hylls, the innkeeper's wife, deposed in a debt case brought by her husband against Richard Stevenson that Thomas Thompson, the man Stevenson urged the Hylls to hire as a tapster, was reported by her neighbors to be "a poore man, and soe poore yt he is commonly accompted reported and taken in Cambridge

---

[14] Sharpe, "Such Disagreement Amongst Neighbors," pp. 172–3; Ingram, *Church Courts, Sex and Marriage*, pp. 317–18.

[15] Wordie, "Deflationary Factors in the Tudor Price Rise," p. 34; however, the author's supposition that debts had to always be repaid in "hard cash," rather than in, say, other consumer items, is more applicable to long-distance merchants than traders operating on a local level.

[16] Smith (ed.), *Oxford Dictionary of English Proverbs*, p. 81.

[17] For example, see *Thomas Barker c. Robert Heylocke*, CUA, Comm.Ct.II.6, fos 68^{v}–9, 72^{v}–3; *William Carowe c. Richard Blunte*, CUA, Comm.Ct.II.2, fos 12^{v}–13; *William Gough v. Roger Robinson*, OUA, Hyp/B/5, fo. 111.

not to be able to paye his debtes."[18] Male householders were particularly sensitive to attacks against their ability to provide for their families.[19] In 1584, John Hopton, a Southampton woolen draper who had recently gained burgess status, appealed to Southampton's assembly to punish as scolds Mary Janverin, the wife of the sheriff and proprietor of the Star Inn, and Sara Abarrow, Janeverin's daughter. According to several witnesses, Mary, for reasons unknown, "revylled" John Hopton in the "open streat," and amongst other insults called him "banckroutt knave." Janeverin's daughter added rather cryptically that she had seen Hopton's "fryes [*sic*: friezes] flee once out of his shoppe and hopid to see yt flye agayne"; presumably she was predicting that Hopton's creditors would soon come to seize his wares.[20] Anne Robathman of Oxford, while visiting an alehouse with several male and female friends, was angered by the proprietor's demand that she keep quiet so as not to attract the proctor's watch, and responded by challenging any pretensions he had to being economically self-sufficient; she called him a "puppie, two pennie shab, & halfe pennie boye, [and] aletap lickspicket." According to witnesses who gave depositions on behalf of Robathman, her words drove the proprietor into a violent rage, during which he punched Anne Robathman in the nose and threw her out of the house.[21] As such cases suggest, townswomen were more willing to challenge the pretensions of their male neighbors than might be suspected.

Borrowers who gained a reputation for escaping from their debts could find themselves in an even more precarious position amongst their neighbors than those who were merely impecunious. Many creditors, after all, would have felt more sympathy for those "honest poor" who had fallen on hard times than borrowers who out of greed sought to dodge their obligations. Women who believed they had been cheated out of repayment for goods and services were quick to take the offensive. When Mary Dickenson, a widow of Cambridge, failed to obtain payment for £11 12s. 10d. worth of meat and other commodities, she confronted her customer, one Edmund Wenham, on the street, and accused him of being a "forsworne fellowe;" perhaps anticipating his denial of the debt for which she was about to sue him, she added that he would "forsweare they selfe as thou hast done before."[22] According to Nicholas Gouldsborough, one of "divers other persons" who witnessed the exchange of words and provided a friendly deposition on behalf of Wenham, Dickenson's accusation damaged Wenham's "good name and fame;"

---

18 *Roger Hylls c. Richard Stevenson*, CUA, Comm.Ct.II.4, fo. 10^{v}.

19 *Frances Thompson c. William Parrye*, CUA, Comm.Ct.II.4, fo. 197.

20 A.L. Merson (ed.), *Third Book of Remembrance 1514–1602*, vol. 3, *1573–1589*, Southampton Record Series, 2, 3, 8 (3 vols Southampton: Southampton University Press, 1965), 3: 32, 109.

21 *Lawrence Bradill c. Ann Robathman*, OUA, Hyp/B/6, fos 113^{v}, 114^{v}–15.

22 *Edmund Wenham c. Mary Dickinson*, CUA, Comm.Ct.III.18, no. 77; for the debt case brought by Dickinson shortly after this incident, see *Mary Dickinson c. Edmund Wenham*, CUA, Comm.Ct.III.18, no. 78; V.C.Ct.II.32, fo. 106.

he was "much hurte & … very disgraced" amongst his neighbors.[23] Dickinson's attack on Wenham's good name may well have given his neighbors pause before they sold him goods on credit.

Public confrontations provided a dramatic way for women to call a neighbor's honesty into question, but they carried risks: women who accosted their opponents on crowded streets and markets hazarded violent retaliation, and would have hardly been able to deny their words if called to court. Many women therefore chose the more discreet option of quietly spreading their side of the story and seeking allies amongst their neighbors in the more private spaces of homes and shops. For instance, Christopher Clinkard, a wine vendor who operated in Stourbridge Fair alleged that Alice Leadham secretly warned his servant that Clinkard was a "cheatinge fellow" who could not be trusted to pay his servants' wages.[24] After Henry Trouton denied under oath that he owed Mary Pinder, a widow shopkeeper of Cambridge, £3 15s. 11d. for lace and clothe, Pinder visited the house of a neighboring widow, Margaret Wright, and allegedly told Wright that Trouton was "the most forsworne knave in the towne." Trouton was concerned enough by Pinder's characterization that he brought a defamation case against her in which he sought £40 in damages.[25]

As Trouton's case suggests, townswomen commonly attacked unreliable borrowers by reference to the debtor's "base" social status. Courts were usually reluctant to hear defamation cases which involved the slights "knave" and "rogue" alone, for such terms did not denote a specific temporal offense. Nevertheless, these terms had powerful connotations for contemporaries, for they signified the mirror opposite of the solid, honest, and respectable male householder.[26] Such terms constituted, therefore, a weapon which women could use to erode a male householder's social status and economic fortunes. When one female defendant in a defamation case was required to define what the words "Roague, knave &

---

23 *Edmund Wenham c. Mary Dickinson*, CUA, V.C.Ct.II.32, fos 101ᵛ–2. The deponent claimed not to remember what issue drove Dickinson to anger.

24 *Christopher Clinkard c. Alice Leadham*, CUA, Comm.Ct.V.9, fo. 169ᵛ. The court absolved Leadham, probably because Clinkard in a previous defamation case had been found to have damaged Leadham's reputation by calling her a "base woman base Jade & base queene divers tymes over"; *Alice Leadham c. Christopher Clinkard*, CUA, Comm. Ct.V.9, fo. 165ᵛ. Clinkard was sentenced to pay 40s. in damages and £2 7s. 4d. in court costs.

25 *Mary Pinder c. Henry and Elizabeth Trouton*, CUA, Comm.Ct.III.15, no. 20; *Henry Trouton c. Mary Pinder*, CUA, Comm.Ct.III.15, no. 21.

26 Women often threw in accusations of roguishness, vagrancy, knavery, or churlishness when accusing men of temporal offences; see for example *Roger Dawson c. Joan Hammell*, CUA, Comm.Ct.I.7, fo. 51, Comm.Ct.II.fo. 28 V.C.Ct.I.34, fo. 33; *Barnabe Clayden c. Elizabeth Parris*, CUA, Comm.Ct.III.9, no. 61; *Thomas Clarke c. William Bull*, CUA, Comm.Ct.II.1, fo. 53; *Joan Masey c. Margaret Smith*, CUA, Comm.Ct.III.19, no. 69; *William Banckes c. Lydia Tillet*, CUA, V.C.Ct.II.38, fo. 9; *William Crane c. Christine Crow*, Helmholz (ed.), *Select Cases on Defamation*, p. 15.

base knave" meant, she responded that they applied to "a man of dishonest lyfe & conversacion & one that is a vagabonde."[27] Those men who failed to pay their debts, whatever their occupational or social status, risked being described in such terms. As Nicholas West was pursuing a cause of debt against Sir Thomas Wright, a BA of St. John's College,[28] West's wife, Grace, sought to undermine Wright's good name. According to Wright's allegation, Grace West said in the shop of John Dorrington, a tailor, and in other places that Wright was "a vile rascally vyllaine & that ... [Wright] did ... deserve to have his eares cutt of[f] & nayled vppon the pyllorie."[29] If the designation of "knave," "rogue," or "vagabond" stuck, it could have immediate impact on economic fortunes of the targeted person. Ann Glascock had thought "very well" of James Huitson, who owed her husband seven or eight pounds for horses. But after hearing that Huitson was reputed to be a "crafty, cosonynge knave," she convinced her husband to call in Huitson's debt as soon as possible.[30]

Women too, as shown in Chapter 5, were vulnerable to attacks against their creditworthiness and commercial honesty. The attentiveness with which tradeswomen assessed each others' economic standing is evident in a confrontation in Cambridge's fish market between the crafty, wealthy, and combative fishmonger Agnes Shaw and Joan Atkin, a younger, less established rival. After Shaw dismissed Atkin as an "Imppe of the world," Atkin retorted that if she was an imp, then Shaw was "the scumme of the world." Attempting to turn the tables on the wealthier trader, Atkin continued: "thowe arte a hard harted woman, thowe arte loathe ... [that] enye bodye should lyve by thee, I am a poore woman, and I would fayne lyve by thee to keepe my selfe & my children[.] the poore Imppe would lyve as well as ye scu[m] of the world."[31] We might expect such verbal contests between marketplace rivals, but private gatherings of gossips could also serve as occasions for disputes over socio-economic status. After attending a churching, Jane Gates of Cambridge found that her purse had been picked; she immediately suspected one of her fellow gossips, Elizabeth Kerby, for not only had Kerby "served her 2 or 3 tricks"[32] in the past, but also she was "the poorest woman in the company," and thus presumably would have had the greatest motive to steal. Certain that Kerby had picked her pocket but uncertain of being able to prove it in court, Gates retaliated against Kerby by recounting her version of the incident "in secrett" to her fellow gossip Helen Rabe and Rabe's servants and suggested that

27 *Robert Grime c. Ann Semar*, CUA, V.C.Ct.II.25, fo. 84^v.

28 *Nicholas West c. Thomas Wright*, CUA, Comm.Ct.I.1.

29 *Thomas Wright, BA c. Grace West*, CUA, Comm.Ct.III.3, no. 36.

30 *James Huitson c. William Cotton*, CUA, Comm.Ct.II.3, fo. 162.

31 *Agnes Shaw c. Joan Atkin*, CUA, Comm.Ct.II.6, fo. 8^v; see also Comm.Ct.I.4, fos 45, 47^v, Comm.Ct.III.6, no. 112; Atkin settled the dispute by apologizing to Shaw. Unfortunately, the evidence does not suggest a specific reason for why the two had a falling out, but it does seem likely that competition for customers led to flared tempers.

32 Unfortunately, what these "tricks" were was left unspecified in the depositions.

Kerby should be known as a "black sheep" amongst the gossips.[33] When Gates's words reached her ears, Kerby felt she had to bring a defamation suit against Gates to restore her good name.

Records of civil litigation, by their very nature, highlight conflicts between self-interested parties. But incidental evidence from the university courts suggests that townswomen harbored resentments against unscrupulous characters who would defraud and cheat their friends and neighbors. Katherine Hawkins, the wife of a Cambridge chandler, was keeping her "gossip" Helen Browne, the wife of a draper, company in the Brownes' shop when John Halliwell asked Helen to sell him wares on credit. Hawkins, who had little regard for Halliwell's honesty, advised Browne—in Halliwell's presence—that "if you will lett [Halliwell] … have that pile of Cloath without mony … you will never have your mony without Trouble." Halliwell then "wrangled" with Hawkins, and managed to convince Helen to sell him the goods on credit. Helen should have followed her friend's advice; her husband was eventually forced to bring a debt suit against Halliwell to obtain payment for the draperies.[34] Conflicts over loans could divide women just as easily as bring them together in common cause. Hellen Evans, the wife of the head cook of Queen's College in Oxford, provoked the disapproval of her neighbors when she failed to return a large kettle she borrowed on behalf of her husband from her neighbor Mrs. Johnson. In 1591, she was finally confronted on the crowded street between the two houses by one Mary Fillis. In front of Johnson, "goodwife" Robinson, and many others, Fillis called Evans's husband an "arrant theife" for failing to return the kettle, and said that even if Hellen or her husband returned the kettle now, they should still suffer "shame enoughe" for having kept it so long.[35] It is unclear from the testimony whether Fillis had gathered her female neighbors to witness the confrontation, or if she simply waited until Johnson and others were present to shame Evans. But in either case, Hellen and Hugh Evans had little doubt that the incident had damaged the reputation and credit of their household.

Townswomen's sympathies did not always rest with the lender. Pawnbroking and money-lending were common and accepted commercial activities throughout the period, but women had little sympathy for lenders who engaged in usury—charging rates somewhere above the legal minimum punishable by law[36]—or who were unreasonably inflexible in their demands that the terms of the agreement be observed. The ideals of honesty and plain dealing offered women a compelling way of framing their complaints against predatory lenders. When Elizabeth Matrin was confronted on a crowded street by her husband's creditor, Adam Underwood,

33 *Elizabeth Kerby c. Jane Gates*, CUA, V.C.Ct.II.22, fos 69^{v}–71, 76.

34 *Robert Browne c. John Halliwell*, CUA, V.C.Ct.II.10, fo. 10^{v}.

35 *Hugh Evans c. Mary Fillis*, OUA, Hyp/B/3, fos 268^{v}, 275, 276.

36 For the history of usury statutes, and the ineffectiveness of enforcement efforts, see Norman Jones, *God and the Moneylenders: Usury and Law in Early Modern England* (Oxford: Oxford University Press, 1989).

Martin called Underwood a thief, and—in reference to a standard-sized corn container Underwood had received in exchange for the loan—told him to carry home the brass bushel which he had already "stollen."[37] Predatory lenders did not just impoverish the borrower; they inspired enmity and strife amongst their neighbors. A 1597 suit brought against George White, a wealthy moneylender of Oxford, gave several women a chance to undermine White's reputation. One of the deponents, Jane Cavin, a widow, deposed that she sent one Elyzabeth Monday to deliver two pawns—a gown and petticoat—to White. When Cavin later visited White to redeem the petticoat, White, perhaps hoping to retain the pawned goods by causing a disagreement between Monday and Cavin, claimed that Monday had not pawned the gown, but rather had sold it outright. It was only after she obtained an order from the University Chancellor that Cavin was able to redeem the coat, but White still pocketed a profit of six pence.[38] Ruses such as these made White an unpopular figure amongst his neighbors. In another deposition, Joan Brown charged that White was a "comon usurer" who took "extreme use for his money." She went on to argue that White was a "dissentious fellow" who looked for ways to profit from the "badd striff & co[n]tention" he sowed "amongst his neighbores."[39]

The Perils of False Dealing

Hard bargaining by itself brought no disrepute, but traders were expected to deal with their customers honestly and plainly. Women's efforts to identify and expose to communal opprobrium those who cheated and defrauded their neighbors were therefore of crucial importance to the maintenance of an often fragile communal harmony. Women's gossip networks provided one venue for the airing of complaints. Just as crucial, however, to the enforcement of economic morality was the success female consumers had in building alliances with market authorities or traders against dishonest vendors.

Townswomen regularly alerted their neighbors to the deceptive ways of local "cheaters," "cozeners," and "Judases." Those men accused of false dealing were anxious to protect their good names.[40] When Joseph Dodson of Cambridge sent his servant to the house of Alice Woods to fetch Tuck, a butcher, Woods allegedly

---

[37] *Elizabeth Martin c. Adam Underwood*, CUA, Comm.Ct.II.2, fos 47, 51; see also *Adam Underwood c. Elizabeth Martin*, Comm.Ct.I.1, fo. 205.

[38] *John Hill c. George White*, OUA, Hyp/A/26, fos 87^{v}. White responded to Brown's testimony by questioning her honesty, calling one Helen Kingswell, who deposed that Brown was a receiver and seller of stolen goods, and that she illicitly bought goods from students against University rules: fo. 113^{v}.

[39] OUA, Hyp/A/26, fos 86^{v}–7.

[40] For example, see *Robert Lyne v. John and Mary Stanyforth*, in *Records of Doncaster*, vol. 3, p. 114; *John Blomfield LLB c. Elizabeth Twelves*, CUA, Comm.Ct.III.10, no. 89; V.C.Ct.II.14, fo. 34.

warned the servant, in the presence of several other women, that Dodson was a "cheatinge Roague & one that lived by cheatinge & she would take her oath uppon a book of it." According to the servant, by such words, Woods meant that Dodson got the "goods and mony" of his neighbors by "fraudulent & cosoninge meanse," and that Dodson would have "been better [to] have lost a good some of mony" than to have "such a scandalous & slanderous reporte made of him."[41] Dodson and his witness had no doubt that Woods's assertions would soon spread throughout the neighborhood. Similarly, in 1585, Thomas Johnson, a Stourbridge Fair trader, was worried enough by Margery Sawnders's claim that he was a "Cosoner and I will proue yt," that he sued her for defamation.[42] Women too could be characterized in such terms. From March to May of 1617, the wife of one Dickinson of Cambridge spread the word through her neighborhood that widow Hayes was an "Ould roage," and an "ould co[s]ener," and on at least one occasion threw stones at Hayes's windows, causing 12d. worth of damage.[43]

The ideals of honesty and plain dealing offered townswomen a compelling way of framing their complaints against the enemies of their households. Disputes over even small sums could spark violent conflicts. In 1628, Ann Pitman accused a servant, Margaret Sampson, of cheating her out of 2d. by giving her less change than she was due in the course of a transaction. According to Sampson's allegations, Pitman falsely accused Sampson of "cozening" her, struck her face, and later beat Sampson with piece of wood.[44] It is likely that Pitman, a married woman, felt it was her right to physically discipline the wayward, younger servant. Women may have been more circumspect in confronting men, but they challenged those men whom they believed to be dishonest nonetheless. In order to support her accusation that Ralph Dunthorne, a trader of draperies, had stolen goods from her inn, Joan Johnson told her customers that Dunthorne was a "rooging knave & a cussoning knave [and] all the Towne knowes yt."[45] Because they were in regular contact with a large group of their neighbors, alewives and innkeepers would have been in an especially powerful position to impugn their opponents' common fame.

The accuracy of weights and measures was a particularly common cause of contention amongst neighbors. Use of proper weights and measures was a central component of a trader's reputation for honesty and plain dealing. Many of those traders accused of using faulty weights and measures felt the need to defend their good names in court in order to avoid losing the esteem, and business, of their neighbors. In 1587, Maria Lyne of Doncaster prompted a defamation suit by complaining that the corn merchant John Snell had "deceived" her by selling her

41 *Joseph Dodson c. Alice Woods*, CUA, V.C.Ct.II.28, fos 8^{v}–9; Comm.Ct.III.16, no. 8.

42 *Thomas Johnson c. Margery Sawnders*, CUA, Comm.Ct.V.7, p. 2.

43 *Hayes c. Dickinson*, CUA, Comm.Ct.III.12, no. 53.

44 *Margaret Sampson c. Ann Pitman*, CUA, Comm.Ct.III.15, no. 110.

45 *Ralph Dunthorne c. Joan Johnson*, CUA, Comm.Ct.I.2, fo. 34; Comm.Ct.II.2, fos 91–93^{v}.

corn with "false measures."[46] Cases such as this suggest that canny consumers double-checked the weight of their purchases. For instance, after buying a quantity of soap in Stourbridge Fair, Mary Benice deposed before the fair court that she had the soap weighed again by "legall waights," and found that it was underweight.[47] Accusations of using false weights carried dangers beyond a loss of good name and fame: consumers could retaliate against those who used false measures by alerting authorities. In one instance, fair officials relied on the information provided by Elizabeth Adams in their prosecution against Thomas Dowtdill, a soap maker, for using false weights. Adams testified that after purchasing soap from Dowtdill using Dowtdill's weights, she had her soap weighed and found that the six pounds of soap he sold to her was light by 12 ounces.[48] Although the clerks of Cambridge's fair courts rarely recorded oral evidence given by witnesses, it seems likely that female consumers provided much needed information to overstretched market and fair authorities who could scarcely monitor every vendor at once.

Traders also had to be careful not to pass on poor quality wares and goods to their local customers if they were to avoid damaging attacks on their competence and honesty. Female consumers were hardly shy about complaining about poor quality goods. When Francis Sawnders, a Cambridge brewer, sued William Sacker, who held a victualing booth in the 1595 Midsummer Fair, for beer he sold to Sacker, he had to contest the claim of Sacker's wife that his beer was of lesser quality and strength than he had promised.[49] Sacker's wife's complaint that the drink was "small bere, & not soe good as they could have had in another place," served notice to Sawnders that he was about to lose a customer who bought his product in large quantities. Dissatisfied customers could cripple the reputations of craftsmen who produced shoddy wares. In 1631, Christabell Williamson, looking to surprise her husband with a new suit, agreed with the tailor Robert Herbert to buy a quantity of Spanish cloth from the draper Thomas Buckle; Herbert would use his portion to make a cloak for himself, and he would use the rest for Williamson's suit. But when she came to retrieve the suit from the tailor, she found it to be short of cloth and of poor quality; and her anger grew greater when she spied the fullness of the tailor's cloak. According to two female witnesses, Williamson accused Herbert in his workshop of using her portion of the cloth meant for the suit to enhance his cloak. Herbert, worried that his dissatisfied customer's accusations would spread amongst his neighbors and other customers, brought a defamation suit against Christabell Williamson. But his plan backfired: three tailors called to inspect the wares found that Herbert had indeed used Williamson's material in the making

---

46 *Records of the Borough of Doncaster*, 3: 103.

47 *John Baxter c. Kiteley*, CUA, Comm.Ct.V.11, fo. 13^{v}.

48 *Office c. Thomas Dowtdill*, CUA, Comm.Ct.V.7, p. 464.

49 *Francis Sawnders v. William Sacker*, CUA, V.C.Ct.II.1, fos 196^{v}–7. One of Sawnders's witnesses, a servant who delivered Sawnders's beer to the booth, countered the Sackers' mitigating evidence by claiming that if any of the beer was tasted and disliked, it was taken back and exchanged for better beer.

of his cloak.[50] It is possible of course that Herbert's fellow craftsmen saw in Williamson's complaint a way of undermining a competitor. Female traders were certainly not above attacking their competitors. So heated was the competition and conflict amongst the butchers' wives trading in Northampton's market that in the hard year of 1558 the town made an order that no butcher's wife keeping a market stall was allowed to "fall out with anie other bocher's wyfe nor speake anie evill or slaunderous wordes of deffamation or otherwyse revaile or revile one another."[51]

Thus far, we have focused exclusively on the ways in which townswomen retaliated against "cozeners." But what of those householders who were able to maintain a reputation for honesty and good credit? Records from legal cases, focused as they are on alleged wrongdoing, rarely shed light on the benefits traders gained from dealing fairly with their customers, borrowers, and creditors. But there are glimpses in the depositional evidence from the university courts that women's words could bolster as well as erode reputations. Joan Filoe, the wife of a Cambridge draper, was prompted to come to the defense of her husband's trustworthy tenants, the apothecary Henry Cotton and his wife, during an encounter with John Swetson, who accused Cotton and his wife of failing to return borrowed goods. She declared to Swetson in the presence of several neighbors that "you talke much against them … to theire discredit, but yt would sett your roofe on fyer to meinteine the charge which they doe, and in suche sorte as they doe." Industrious, respectable, and prosperous, the Cottons, according to Filoe, would have no reason to withhold Swetson's property.[52] When in 1618 Richard Pekitt, a Cambridge hatter, came under suspicion of using false weights and measures, five of his neighbors, including two women, crafted a written statement in support of Pekitt. They argued that Pekitt was blameless, for it was his former apprentice who had used false weights and measures to "Cosen the Cuntry" without his knowledge. They claimed that the apprentice only informed Pekitt of his "cozening" after he left Pekitt's service.[53] Presumably, the apprentice was pocketing the ill-gotten gains, but why the apprentice would inform his former master remains unknown. Traders such as Pekitt were wise to gain the trust and favor of their female neighbors and customers.

Regular excoriations of gossips and scolds notwithstanding, traders and consumers—both men and women—listened when women passed judgment on the honesty and creditworthiness of well-known neighbors. Women's varied economic roles and their social networks placed them in a powerful position to participate in the micro-politics of neighborhood commercial disputes. As the records of defamation litigation in the university courts suggest, even economically comfortable householders found it difficult to dismiss attacks on their credit as

---

50 *Robert Herbert c. Christabell Williamson*, CUA, V.C.Ct.II.30, fos 19–22^v, V.C.Ct. III.32, nos. 36, 40.

51 Markham and Cox (eds), *Records of … Northampton*, vol. 2, p. 273.

52 *Margaret Cotton c. John Swetson*, Comm.Ct.II.11, fos 31–5.

53 CUA, V.C.Ct.III.23, no. 141.

mere women's words. Gossip networks provided women with an important source of information about their neighbors, and venue to pursue grievances against "cozeners." And it is hardly surprising that women often chose to argue with and insult their opponents in public places—in the streets, markets, alehouses—for such confrontations were sure to be observed and discussed by neighbors. Townswomen were at the center of the inevitable social tensions which arose as townspeople confronted the opportunities and pressures of commercial and economic change. Furthermore, the power they wielded extended beyond the immediate confines of their neighborhoods. As we shall see in the next chapter, women played critical roles in defending the economic interests of their communities. Town governments and the magistracy could hardly ignore women's interests in confronting the key problems of dearth and underemployment.

Chapter 9

Women, Protest, and Marketplace Politics

Until recently, historians maintained that food protests—the riots and petitioning campaigns that often accompanied dearth—were indicative of a widely held conception of a "moral economy," characterized by a popular distrust for the free play of supply and demand.[1] Middlemen whose activities threatened poor households could expect to encounter angry, occasionally violent resistance; these protests obliged local officials—and sometimes even national authorities—to consider the interests of consumers. An examination of women's participation in crowd actions is an ideal way to understand popular assumptions about marketing. Women, after all, did much of the shopping for the household, and were among the most sensitive to price fluctuations and marketplace shortages. Ordinary women had a direct stake in ensuring that the regulation of the public marketplace protected the household during dearth. But humble women traders recognized that a balance was needed between protections for consumers and a degree of freedom to operate in the market, for overly stringent oversight of the market during times of plenty hampered the ability of many poor and middling women to earn profits. What protests against middlemen and exclusionary regulations had in common was not a reflexive suspicion of the commercial economy, but rather an insistence that officials had an obligation to keep market venues open and viable.

The prominent role poor women played in crowd actions against middlemen and corn badgers who enhanced food prices has long been recognized, but their participation in economic protests have seldom been understood in terms of the varied commercial roles they played in their communities. Most historians have followed E.P. Thompson's explanation of the unusual assertiveness of female consumers during times of dearth: traditionally associated with unruliness, enjoying greater leniency under the law because of their status as *femes coverts*, propelled to violence by their inability to feed their families, poor women felt that they had the right to engage in riot and to collect *taxation populaire*. And fittingly—so the argument

[1] In an early critique, John Stevenson argued that eighteenth-century food riots had less to do with a national, plebeian "moral economy," and more to do with local attempts to maintain wage-earners' standards of living: "The 'Moral Economy' of the English Crowd: Myth and Reality," in *Order and Disorder in Early Modern England*, (ed.) Anthony Fletcher and John Stevenson, pp. 218–38. In a recent major study, John Bohstedt re-emphasizes the role of hunger, rather than moral outrage, as the root cause of riots: *Politics of Provisions*, pp. 10, 34.

goes—they often had the tacit support of sympathetic authorities.[2] Paradoxically, then, authorities' dim view of women gave women more license to engage in disorderly protests than men. However, the evidence of leniency toward female rioters *vis-à-vis* men is less compelling than is often assumed; women rioters too risked harsh punishments. It is unlikely that female participation in moral economy riots can be explained by supposed legal ambiguities regarding female criminality.

But that does not mean that female participation in urban economic protests arose out of distinctive female economic interests or exclusively female social networks.[3] The common picture of female dominance of the food riot obscures the fact that both men and women were involved in most sixteenth- and seventeenth-century food protests.[4] As we shall see, local economic crises most often brought poor men and women together in common cause. Female economic interests and social solidarities were not separate from, but rather inter-connected with the popular politics of poor men. Food protests took forms other than riot. Poor female consumers during periods of shortage supported and helped draw up formal, written petitions which were presented to local authorities, harried officials as they went about their business in the market, and spread gossip and uttered threats against middlemen and lax officials. The involvement of women in all of these types of protest—both legal and extra-legal—underscores the prominent role of female consumers in the market economy.

An exclusive focus on the politics of poor consumers, however, limits our understanding of the multivalent nature of the popular politics of the market economy. Poor men and women, when dearth threatened them and their families, were more than willing to refer to market regulations, statute, royal orders, and the laxity of officials to justify their seizures of corn from middlemen. But however much they were resented, middlemen were necessary, especially in growing communities that were distant from regulated markets. And the middlemen might be women. Women as well as men thus petitioned county justices for badger and maltster licenses on behalf of those neighbors they trusted, and women were sometimes candidates themselves for licenses. Market and town regulations were necessary to protect poor consumers from price gouging during dearth, but they could also create resentments when they unnecessarily prevented traders from earning a living in the marketplace. Women often joined with men to resist heavy-handed town officials, and they contested the policies of town governments that endangered their businesses or excluded them

---

2 Thompson, "Moral Economy of the English Crowd," pp. 115–17; Clark, "Popular Protest and Disturbance in Kent," pp. 376–7; Mendelson and Crawford, *Women in Early Modern England*, pp. 44, 385–6; Capp, *When Gossips Meet*, pp. 316–17.

3 Such a case has been made in Houlbrooke, "Women's Social Life and Common Action," pp. 171–89, and Mendelson and Crawford, *Women in Early Modern England*, pp. 380, 383–6.

4 This was also the case in eighteenth- and early nineteenth-century food riots; see J. Bohstedt, "Gender, Household and Community Politics: Women in English Riots 1790–1810," *P&P* 120 (1988): 88–122.

from markets. Female involvement in the micro-politics of the marketplace was not limited to times of dearth. An exploration of their quotidian concerns obliges us to reconsider the standard picture of the popular "moral economy."

***

Periodic food shortages exposed latent tensions in communities if they brought the activities of middlemen and profiteers, and lax enforcement by justices and market officials, to popular attention. As John Walter and Keith Wrightson have shown, petitioning and rioting over food shortages was most likely to occur in counties where regional trade networks were most sophisticated, and in which the impersonal economic imperatives of the corn trade tended to work against the immediate interests of local consumers.[5] Food protests were rare or nonexistent in the three largest cities (London, Norwich, and Bristol) because city authorities were usually successful in raising emergency funds to purchase imported corn and ensuring that corn badgers had licenses to buy corn in the surrounding counties to be transported to the major cities.[6] But the supplying of the big cities during dearth years left provincial markets underserved, and thus created resentments in counties, towns, and villages which exported corn or through which passed corn bound for the cities. As a result, food riots during the dearths of the late sixteenth and early seventeenth centuries were largely confined to southern counties and provincial ports that shipped food to the major cities or the continent. Though poor harvests were the most important cause of dearth,[7] hungry crowds and sympathetic

---

[5] John Walter and Keith Wrightson, "Dearth and the Social Order in Early Modern England," *P&P* 71 (1976): 22–42; Walter, "Grain Riots and Popular Attitudes to the Law;" Clark, "Popular Protest and Disturbance in Kent," pp. 373–4. Privation alone was not enough to spur crowds to riot; rioters were almost always provoked by the activities of corn merchants shipping food through communities. In addition, as John Bohstedt argues, riots tended to occur in regions which had developed a political culture of economic protest (see *The Politics of Provision*, p. 12). Thus, we have no records of food riots in the northwestern counties of Westmorland and Cumberland, for while privation in this region during dearth years was particularly severe, there were no major corn trade routes in these counties: see John Walter's presentation of the pattern of early modern riots in Andrew Charlesworth (ed.), *An Atlas of Rural Protest in Britain 1548–1900* (London: Croom Helm, 1983), p. 77. On the other hand, Cambridge, which enjoyed a particularly fertile hinterland, and thus suffered less than many towns during dearth years, nevertheless saw disorders and riots c. 1597–1598 which arose from resentments against middlemen: CUA, V.C.Ct.III.7, no. 189; CUR 37.2, no. 52.

[6] WRO, Q/S Great Roll, Trinity 1647, no. 188; *APC, 1630–1631*, p. 120; Walter and Wrightson, "Dearth and the Social Order," p. 27.

[7] Rising unemployment as a result of slumps in the cloth trade in the 1620s and 1630s also contributed to the climate of distress which provoked food riots. See Sharp, *In Contempt of All Authority*, ch. 2. Women too were thrown out of work as a result of trade depression; PRO, SP 14/130/73.

authorities agreed that tight regulation of the corn trade could solve, or at least mitigate, the problem of dearth. It was in those communities in which enforcement of market regulations was seen as too lax, or in which justices were all too willing to grant badger licenses, that crowds resorted to political action and riot.[8]

Who participated in food riots, and to what extent is the common picture of the food riot as dominated by poor women accurate? The patchy survival of legal records and the laconic nature of many descriptions of crowds in central government and local sources make it difficult to recover a detailed picture of who was involved in food riots. The evidence we have of the occupational backgrounds of those who engaged in crowd actions protesting food shortages is unsurprising: most petitioners and rioters came from the households of poor artisans, unemployed textile workers, and laborers.[9] The question of female participation in food riots is more complex. John Bohstedt has pointed out that in the late sixteenth and seventeenth centuries, food rioting was "not a peculiarly female province"; women were reported as participants in 22 of the 89 riots in Bohstedt's food riot census.[10] But this figure almost certainly underestimates levels of female participation because much of the documentary evidence fails to specify the gender of those of the crowd. In 29 riots from the period 1595 to 1642 documented in State Papers, quarter session records from a sample of counties prone to food riots (Somerset, Wiltshire, Hampshire, Kent, and Essex), and the corporation records of Southampton, Dorchester, and Reading, some indication is given of the gender of the rioters. Of the 29 cases, men alone were mentioned as participants in 8 riots (27.6 percent); women alone were mentioned concerning another 8 (27.6 percent); and in 13 cases, both men and women were reported as involved (44.8 percent). Thus, women were reported to have been involved in 21 of the 29 cases of riot (72.4 percent).[11] These numbers

---

[8] For example, see CUA, CUR 37.2, no. 52; WRO, Q/S Great Roll, Hilary 1648, no. 229.

[9] Clark, "Popular Protest and Disturbance in Kent;" Walter, "Grain Riots and Popular Attitudes to the Law;" Sharp, *In Contempt of All Authority*.

[10] Bohstedt, *Politics of Provision*, pp. 37, 44; for his census, see http://web.utk.edu/~bohstedt/, which is based on secondary sources.

[11] I have examined the primary documents for riots within a shorter chronological frame than Bohstedt's census for 1580–1650. Because of the nature of the documents, methodological issues remain, and I have had to make some assumptions. In documents in which only specific men were identified along with "others unknown," I have counted those as riots involving only men; I have done the same for riots which specify that women were involved along with "others unknown." For riots in which men alone were involved: BL, Harleian MS 2143, fo. 57v (for the same riot, see also LMA, COL/RMD/PA/01/002, *Remembrancia*, vol. 2, fo. 50); CKS, QM/SB 82 (for the same riot, see also *Records of Maidstone: Being Selections from Documents in Possession of the Corporation* [Maidstone, 1926], pp. 263–6); ERO, Q/SR 316/24; HampRO, Jervoise MSS 44 M69/63/115/1–2; Guilding (ed.), *Reading Records*, vol. 3, p. 379; WRO, Q/S Great Roll, Trinity 1614, nos. 168–171; WRO, Q/S Great Roll, Hilary 1631, nos. 12, 127; SRO, Q/SR 61.1/192. For riots in which women alone were involved: CKS, QM/SI/1595/2/1; CKS, QM/SIq/26–27

must remain provisional: given the paucity of evidence and the inexactness of surviving descriptions of crowds of food rioters, we shall never know with certainty the percentage of early modern food riots in which women participated. But because many of the crowds described in the records of the 29 riots contained "others unknown," the count given here probably underestimates the percentage of riots in which both men and women were participants.

However provisional, this count supports the impression of scholars of popular protest that women were particularly active in food riots. Women were involved in just 11 percent of the enclosure riots prosecuted in Star Chamber.[12] They were certainly more visible in food rioting than other major crimes such as murder and assault. By way of comparison, women comprised only 19.2 percent of those indicted for assault or assault and battery in early modern Cheshire.[13]

It was not the authorities' lenient attitudes toward female rioters but rather the engagement of women as consumers that spurred them to engage in food riots. Some historians have contended that, in both legal theory and popular opinion, women were allowed greater license to engage in assemblies and riots because they could not, as *femes coverts*, be considered fully responsible under common law for their actions. But as Peter Lawson has found in his case study of female criminality in late Tudor and early Stuart Hertfordshire, although *feme covert* status could provide female suspects a possible legal defense if they could show that they had been forced or incited to commit a crime by their husbands or male masters, it did not usually absolve women of responsibility for the crimes they committed.[14] An ostensible exception—in legal theory at least—to female

(2 riots); CKS, U951 C2611/22 (see also *APC, 1630–1631*, p. 268); DRO, B2/8/1, fos 100^{v}–1; ERO, D/B 3/3/208; PRO, SP 16/176/35 (see also PRO, SP 16/177/4 which relates to the same riot); PRO, SP 16/190/39. For riots in which both men and women were involved: Bod. Lib., MS Firth c.4, pp. 501–4; CKS, QM/SI/1605/13/29–32 (three riots); DRO, B2/8/1, fo. 59; Horrocks (ed.), *Assembly Books of Southampton*, vol. 1, pp. 61–3; PRO, SP 16/133/19I (two riots); PRO, SP 16/191/3; PRO, SP 16/191/4; SRO, Q/SR 63.2/146; SRO, Q/SR 64.2/210–14; WRO, QS Great Roll, Trinity 1614, 160–62. Perhaps more evidence could be found if more counties were included. Generic descriptions of disorder could conceal what were, in reality, several riots (For instance, PRO, S.P., 16/190/39, regarding assaults on boatmen at Sittingbourne, Kent, in 1631), but where a lack of detail leaves the matter in doubt, I have counted each of these cases as a single riot.

12 Roger B. Manning, *Village Revolts: Social Protest and Popular Disturbances in England, 1608–1640* (Oxford: Clarendon Press, 1988), p. 96.

13 Garthine Walker, *Crime, Gender and Social Order in Early Modern England* (Cambridge: Cambridge University Press, 2003), p. 25. For a study which finds similarly low percentages of women's involvement in violent crime, see Carol Z. Wiener, "Sex-Roles and Crime in Late Elizabethan Hertfordshire," *Journal of Social History* 8 (1974–5): 38–60.

14 Peter Lawson, "Patriarchy, Crime, and the Courts: The Criminality of Women in Late Tudor and Early Stuart England," in *Criminal Justice in the Old World and the New*, (ed.) Greg Smith, Allyson May, and Simon Devereaux (Toronto: Centre of Criminology, University of Toronto, 1998), pp. 34–6; see also Walker, *Crime, Gender and Social Order*, pp. 201–6.

culpability for felony crimes committed absent male coercion was the freedom of women to assemble legally on their own in protest. Thomas Marlowe, in his reading of Westminster 1 Cap. 1 in *De Pace Terre & Ecclesie & Conseruacione Eiusdem* (1503), asserted that if women and children assemble of their "own cause," it could not be considered a riot under the terms of the law. William Lambarde, in *Eirenarcha* (1581), drew the same conclusion. However, this allowance was tightly circumscribed in both legal theory and practice. As R.A. Houlbrooke has perceptively observed, Marlowe failed to specify if women could be prosecuted if they not only assembled, but also committed another crime, such as seizing goods or breaking an enclosure; Lambarde believed that in such cases, female rioters could be punished.[15] We should not be surprised if female rioters were punished in much the same way as male rioters, for, as Cynthia Herrup and Garthine Walker have shown, magistrates did not invariably show more mercy to women than men in sentencing for capital crimes.[16]

Magistrates and the central government had enough discretion under the law to mete out those punishments they thought fit to restore order, whether the rioters were men or women. When under pressure from the royal government, local authorities were particularly keen to demonstrate that they were taking all necessary measures to scotch unrest by punishing offenders, including female food rioters. In 1630, the Privy Council upbraided the justices of Berkshire for not taking strong action against disorders in and around the town of Newbury. The subsequent report of the justices to the council is revealing. Though the carriers of corn through the town could only charge two or three of the "Twelve or Thirteen poore Ragged woemen" who had assembled with the offence of stopping their wagons and ripping open their sacks of corn (the rest of the women had merely gathered the corn which had fallen into the street), the JPs nevertheless sentenced five of the women to a "severe whippinge … in the open streete for a further terror and example unto others;" the other women were subjected to the public shame of being carted through the town and then sent to the house of correction.[17] The commission of oyer and terminer sent to quell disorder at Maldon in 1629 singled out Anne Carter for execution in order to "terrify" the seditious poor after she was found to have mobilized and led two crowds which seized corn from ships moored at Burrow Hill.[18] The fact that Carter and her followers, in addition to seizing corn, assaulted the boatmen and threatened to murder the captain if he

15 Houlbrooke, "Women's Social Life and Common Action," p. 182.

16 Walker, *Crime, Gender and Social Order*, pp. 135–8; Herrup, *The Common Peace*, p. 176, table 7.3; Lawson, "Patriarchy, Crime, and the Courts," pp. 41–2, tables 2.6, 2.7, 2.8 .

17 *APC, 1630–1631,* p. 122; PRO, SP, 16/175/81; for a similar reaction by local authorities to female rioters, see William Hudson and John Cottingham (eds), *The Records of the City of Norwich* (2 vols, Norwich: Jarrold, 1906–1910), vol. 2, p. 165.

18 Bodl. Lib., MS Firth, c. 4, p. 503; Walter has given us an excellent case study of early modern food riots in "Grain Riots and Popular Attitudes to the Law."

did not pay a ransom surely influenced the commission's sentence. Whether or not authorities thought severe punishments, or mercy, were needed in order to re-establish order depended on the level of violence the crowd engaged in and the particular judgments of magistrates on the ground. Thus, authorities sometimes advocated leniency toward male rioters if they thought that "provoking men by … hard dealings" could spur yet more resistance.[19] For magistrates, the need to restore order trumped all other considerations.

But did popular expectations of the risk of punishment match up with patterns of enforcement? Did poor women, or their husbands, expect lighter treatment for women by virtue of their sex? It is perilous to argue from an absence of evidence, but it is nevertheless revealing that when justices interrogated women involved in seizures of foodstuffs, none of the women claimed that they held a special immunity under the law because they were women. Instead, they, like some men, cited dire want and the interests of their communities to secure an adequate food supply as mitigating circumstances. For instance, when the JPs of Essex asked Dorothy Berrye, the wife of a shepherd of Maldon, who "procured" her to participate in the 1629 Burrow Hill riot near Maldon, she gave no specific answer, but she explained that she was motivated by the "Crie of the Countey & hir owne want."[20] Perhaps not coincidentally, when criminal defendants answered in court, they put themselves "upon God and their country."[21] Certainly Berrye was claiming that her participation in the food seizure was in accordance with a legitimate communal consensus. But women who made such claims in front of nervous authorities engaged in a risky strategy, for husbands of women who engaged in food riots did not always assume that their wives would receive easy treatment from authorities. After a crowd of women in Norwich in 1532 intercepted a shipment of wheat and sold it off to other women at prices below the rate decreed by the city government, the husband of one of the rioters advised the women that they should not add to their crimes, but should "delyver the … money to Mr Mayer, and furder said to them, Ye are to blame and dede nat well in selling the … whete."[22] The most compelling evidence against the notion that lenient attitudes among magistrates encouraged female assertiveness in marketplace disturbances is that in most riots both men and women were involved, and in those cases the immunity for women engaged in unlawful assembly was null.[23]

19 BL, Lansdowne MS 71, fo. 28, a 1592 letter from the Lord Mayor of London to Lord Burghley regarding an uprising of apprentices. See also SRO, Q/SR 63.2/146.

20 ERO, D/B 3/3/208; see also the examination of a woman after a Gloucestershire riot in 1674: BrRO, JX/1/6, fo. 16. For examples of men pleading dire want for themselves and their families, see WRO, Q/S Great Roll, Trinity 1614, nos. 160, 161.

21 It should be remembered that "county" and "country" were synonyms in early modern England.

22 Hudson and Cottingham (ed.), *Records of Norwich*, vol. 2, p. 164

23 With the hypothetical exception of wives who could show that they had been coerced by their husbands to participate in riots. But their husbands would have, of course, been liable for punishment.

Early modern food rioters were not threatening to invert, even temporarily, the social or gender order.[24] Natalie Zemon Davis has argued that because women were popularly associated with disorderliness, early modern crowds, whether they were made up of men, women, or both, drew upon popular rituals of misrule and sexual inversion, and thus played upon patriarchal stereotypes in legitimizing their actions.[25] However, with the exception of the rather extraordinary Anne Carter, who assumed the title of "captain" in leading a crowd of unemployed weavers in the second Maldon riot, we have no cases of gender inversion in which women assumed male roles in leading food protests. Nor was it the case that male food rioters, whether or not they were accompanied by women, donned female dress as a way of escaping detection or punishment. There is thus very little evidential basis for using the handful of rural enclosure riots in which either women claimed that they were immune from prosecution because of their sex, or men disguised themselves as women to presumably escape punishment, to explain the prominence of women in food riots.[26] The pattern of participation in food riots hardly supports the conclusion that women rioters sought to exploit ambiguities in the criminal law in order to escape punishment. But that does not mean that crowds of men and women did not attempt to legitimate their actions to authorities in other ways.

As consumers, women necessarily had a good knowledge of marketplace rules, and were attentive to public proclamations that advertised statutes and royal policies against middlemen who exacerbated dearth.[27] They were thus central to food riots because, as Walter and Wrightson have shown, crowds sought to justify their actions by claiming the right to enforce the laws and customs of the marketplace when those regulations were ignored or unenforced. Indeed, on some occasions, rioters delivered the corn they had seized to local officials.[28] In several cases, women took their cue from official pronouncements in seizing corn from middlemen. On 11 April, 1608, the mayor and assembly of Southampton, worried about sharply rising grain prices, ordered that a ship owned by one of the aldermen laden with corn bound for London be stayed and the corn brought ashore. Just after the town government decided to detain the ship, several women, with the help of the town crier, boarded the hoy on which the corn was stored and

[24] On the discipline and restraint showed by most crowds, see Wrightson, *English Society*, pp. 173–9.

[25] Davis, *Society and Culture*, ch. 5.

[26] For the enclosure riot cases, see Sharp, *In Contempt of All Authority*, p. 90; Manning, *Village Revolts*, pp. 97–9. For the argument that men disguised themselves as women to elude punishment, see Davis, *Society and Culture*, p. 146; Clark, "Popular Protest and Disturbance in Kent," p. 377 and n. 1.

[27] John Walter, "Public Transcripts, Popular Agency and the Politics of Subsistence in Early Modern England," in *Negotiating Power in Early Modern Society: Order, Hierarchy and Subordination in Britain and Ireland*, (ed.) Michael Braddick and John Walter (Cambridge: Cambridge University Press, 2001), p. 126.

[28] Walter and Wrightson, "Dearth and the Social Order," p. 33.

carried it off before it could be cellared.[29] The women of Norwich who seized corn from badgers in 1532 seem to have been prompted by the recent efforts of the mayor and aldermen of the city to search out hoarded grain and bring it to the market.[30] When justifying their assaults against middlemen, crowds of women and men referred to the law against forestallers or otherwise claimed to have the backing of authorities. For instance, in a failed attempt in 1674 to stop a barge in Gloucestershire transporting corn to Bristol via the river Wye, local men and women cried out to the sailors that the crowd "had Orders to stopp [the barge] till [the bargemen] Came before" county authorities. Later, when a justice of the county demanded their orders, members of the crowd on the other side of the river called back that "they had Orders, butt would not come over the River to show them."[31] The vigilantism of early modern female food rioters represented not a direct challenge to the social order, but rather an insistence by poor women that the interests of their communities be considered during times of dearth.

This parochially oriented notion of a moral economy had surprisingly little to do with the notion of a customary, static "just price." There were thus important differences between crowd actions in the sixteenth and seventeenth centuries and the food riots of the eighteenth century. In his seminal study of eighteenth-century food protests, E.P. Thompson identified *taxation populaire*—the intimidating or forcing of middlemen, bakers, and millers to accept a low, customary price—as a common tactic. As Thompson observed, when angry female consumers intercepted corn and bread traders, the confrontation very soon became a "bargaining-situation," in which the crowd threatened violence if the traders did not reduce their prices.[32] However, sixteenth- and seventeenth-century crowds rarely offered traders even nominal payment when they seized corn supplies. The only clear example of *taxation populaire* that we know of from our period is an apprentices' riot in the market of Southwark during the hard year of 1595; these unpaid laborers would have been sensitive to even minor price fluctuations.[33] The legal peculiarities and economic exigencies of the sixteenth and seventeenth centuries played a decisive role in shaping the ways in which poor women and men defended their communities from dearth.

---

29 Horrocks (ed.), *Assembly Books of Southampton*, vol. 1, p. 62–3.

30 Hudson and Cottingham (eds), *Records of ... Norwich*, vol. 2, p. 163.

31 BrRO, JX/1/6, fos 15ᵛ–16; see also SRO, Q/SR 64.2, no. 210, CKS, QM/SB 82.

32 Thompson, "Moral Economy of the English Crowd," 108–14, 117. Specifically, Thompson argued that eighteenth-century crowds harkened back to the grain prices mandated by government regulations of the early seventeenth century. For a critique of this argument, see Stevenson, "The 'Moral Economy' of the English Crowd: Myth and Reality," pp. 218–38.

33 BL, Lansdowne MS 71, fo. 28. This finding is confirmed by Bohstedt's riot census, which is based on secondary sources for this period: http://web.utk.edu/~bohstedt/. The 1532 Norwich riot cited above does not fit the pattern of *taxation populaire* riots because the women who seized and sold the corn in the market did not offer the proceeds to the middlemen.

The legal context changed between the late sixteenth century and the end of the eighteenth century. Many corn badgers in the sixteenth and seventeenth centuries offered no corn for sale as they passed through towns and villages; these traders either expected that larger profits could be made if they sold all of their corn in larger markets, or they were under contract by city governments to supply city markets.[34] Because crowds often believed that these traders had violated the forestalling statute or royal orders, they claimed that the corn should be forfeited to the poor, as was often mandated by royal proclamations. Statutes and orders controlling the activities of middlemen were inconsistently enforced in the sixteenth and seventeenth centuries, but food shortages and protests usually prompted local officials and the Crown to take action. By the mid-eighteenth century, however, commercial practices such as engrossing and selling by sample were more widespread than in the sixteenth and seventeenth centuries, and enforcement of market regulations, even before the Edwardian forestalling statute was repealed in 1772, was sporadic at best even during times of crisis.[35] Eighteenth-century consumers were probably less certain than sixteenth- and seventeenth-century crowds that they could appeal to the law to legitimate their actions, and so their demand that middlemen lower their prices was less assertive than the demands of most sixteenth- and seventeenth-century crowds.

Rioters believed they had the law on their side; but what arguably incensed them most was not the middlemen's disregard for marketplace rules, but the unwillingness of middlemen during hard years to sell them corn on credit, which normally was common practice. But middlemen passing through towns and villages were often unwilling to extend credit to hungry strangers whose creditworthiness they could hardly gauge with any accuracy. Even middlemen prudent enough to offer corn at discounted prices to hungry crowds could be victims of riot. Those same middlemen would have had an easier time in dealing with crowds of the eighteenth century, by which time even poor consumers sometimes had cash to offer as nominal payment for corn. In most instances of riot in the sixteenth and seventeenth centuries, the "just price" of the corn in question was not the matter of dispute. A badger's demand for "ready money" alone could provoke crowds of angry consumers to seize corn supplies.[36] Women food rioters were not attempting to reinstate a "moral economy," but rather were attempting to restore working markets.

The role humble women played in the local politics of dearth extended well beyond their participation in riots. They did much of the work necessary to mobilize

---

[34] For example, see CKS, U951 C261, regarding rioters who were provoked by a trader who would not sell his corn, even for ready money.

[35] Thompson, "Moral Economy of the English Crowd," p. 88; R.B. Outhwaite, "Dearth and Government Intervention in English Grain Markets, 1590–1700," *EcHR,* new series, 34 (August, 1981): 389–406.

[36] HampRO, Jervoise MSS, 44 M 69/G3/188; WRO, Q/S Great Roll, Trinity 1614, nos. 160–62; PRO, SP 16/187/13.

their communities to protest food shortages. With their knowledge of prices, traders, and commercial practices, women passed on news of commercial dealings and built local support for protests against middlemen. As we have seen, these gossip networks were not gendered closed circles: women gathered information from men, and passed information along to men. When JPs of Somerset examined Florence Peryn and Susan Dole of Bishop Sutton regarding a conspiracy in 1630, the two women recalled that when they met one Edward Kirton, a mason, on their way to church, they "talked of the dearth of corn." Peryn told Kirton that "shee heard [corn] was sold att Exeter for 5*s*. a bushell," prompting Kirton to complain that corn "would be cheaper heere if it were not for the heard hearts of miserlie men and that if a hundred were of his minde they would kill some of those rich men that the rest might sell corne cheaper."[37] Female proprietors of alehouses and their servants were also in a position to pass along news of prices and popular discontent, for alehouses were important centers of local gossip.[38]

In addition to spreading information regarding prices and corn shipments, female consumers attempted to focus popular resentments by naming specific middlemen for censure. When poor widow Dente was told by a "collector for the poor" that he could not give her any wheat because a middleman named Caley had bought up wheat supplies in Hitchin, Hertfordshire, she informed her female neighbors. These women conspired "to beat him [Caley]" if he returned to the market.[39] Middlemen took such threats seriously. In 1587, Richard Breackes brought a defamation suit to the borough court of Doncaster against William Murgadred and Elizabeth his wife. Breackes accused Elizabeth of declaring falsely in public that Breackes had sold engrossed peas at a high profit after having bought them from a local gentlemen under the pretense that he would sell the peas at a discount to the poor who "weare lyke to be famished."[40] The fears of middlemen were often justified. In Dorchester in 1631, Margaret Porter helped to rally a crowd of women to stay carts of John Blachford. Blachford, Porter exclaimed in the market, "did send away the best fruits" of the county, including cheese and wheat, "ouer the seaes."[41] The information provided by female gossip networks focused general complaints against high food prices by providing specific information on middlemen and commercial practices that endangered the local community.

The part women played in petition campaigns also testifies to the importance of their involvement in what John Bohstedt terms the "politics of provision." During dearth years, petitioners lamented the number of licenses given to maltsters, who converted corn to malt for brewing, and corn badgers, who engrossed local food supplies, driving up prices. At first glance, women did not seem to play a prominent

---

[37] SRO, Q/SR 64.2, 253.

[38] For example, see ERO, Q/SR 131/35.

[39] Lawson, "Patriarchy, Crime, and the Courts," p. 32; Lawson notes that the plan did not come to fruition, for there are no subsequent reports of a riot.

[40] Records of Doncaster, vol. 2, p. 103.

[41] DRO, B2/8/1, fo. 101.

role in drawing up or supporting petitions. In a Somerset petition presented to JPs during the winter of 1648, the poor complained of a superfluity of alehouses and rich men who "doe Joyne & conplott together to starve us, thiere poore distressed bretheren" by engrossing corn; only five of the 350 people who signed the petition were women, and all of these women were widows.[42] Other petitions presenting similar complaints had no female signatures.[43] Only heads of households seem to have signed most petitions, which is unsurprising, since under common law married women were legally represented by their husbands. That does not mean, however, that women did not play important roles behind the scenes in spurring their men to action, and in helping them to articulate their complaints. According to the weavers and laborers who presented a petition to Essex JPs during the dearth of 1642, "when the Market day comes, we send our wives to the Market Crosse to buy a pecke of corne and we can [only] have it according to a great rate … although there is corne enough." At the least, these male petitioners relied on the reports of marketplace conditions they received from their wives. Furthermore, there were shortages in bread, butter, cheese, and eggs, because forestallers and "Higlers"—by "what license of authority … we know not"—were buying goods in the market before the allowed time (noon) and exporting them to London. The artisans' and laborers' wives who had difficulty in finding food to purchase in the market must have kept close watch over the traders in the market, for the petition went on to list middlemen whose activities endangered the community.[44]

While the Chelmsford petition indicates that women wielded influence behind the scenes in petitioning campaigns, it also shows that female traders themselves could be targets of food protests.[45] Four of the 14 badgers singled out for censure in the petition were women, including goodwife Fisher and goodwife Canan, both of whom "buy a horse load [of victuals] every market day" to ship to London markets. Though these two women had been commanded by market officials a month previously not to come to the market, "they haue come every friday since."[46] The complaint of the petitioners was not spurred by any generalized suspicion of female hucksters or badgers; rather it was the large scales of these export operations that angered the petitioners. The poor resented widows and wives who unnecessarily engaged in part-time work that exacerbated food shortages. In 1648, the poor of Warminster claimed that many inhabitants of the town, despite having "sufficcient meanes & trades (w[hi]ch they vse)" to maintain themselves, exacerbated corn shortages by making malt. Among the accused was Elinor

42 SRO, Q/S PET/1/AA.

43 WRO, Q/S Great Roll, Hilary 1615, no. 192; WRO, Q/S Great Roll, Hilary 1648, no. 220.

44 ERO, Q/SR 332/106.

45 I should note, however, that I have found no instance of food rioters attacking female traders.

46 ERO, Q/SR 332/106.

Rawlins, a baker who earned extra money by making and selling malt.[47] We should thus avoid making simplistic generalizations regarding the economic mentality of trading women, for while the market restrictions called for by petitioners could protect the access of households to food supplies, they could also close down commercial activities for wives and widows trading on the side.

In many cases, poor female consumers approached middlemen and officials directly to warn or threaten them before a serious riot broke out. Grumbles, threats, and curses uttered against middlemen put middlemen and officials on notice that crowd actions were imminent if the complaints of poor consumers were not addressed.[48] In a 1622 deposition given by John Oliver, a husbandman, before the mayor of Weymouth regarding the accidental injuring of a child, Oliver claimed that he had been warned by several women of the town that had his cart carried wheat instead of peas, he would have been in danger of having his sacks cut and his corn taken by the women of the town.[49] Similarly, in 1631, the women of Sittingbourne, Kent, spread "Terror" throughout the area by intimidating and threatening boatmen shipping food to London. According to one worried magistrate, "if they meete with Barley meale in a boate, they throw it away, saying they must haue better stuffe. Gascoyne the boatman is much threatened by them, & they tell his wife, they will fetch the butter & cheese out of her house."[50] When a corn badger named Vere encountered a group of angry women in Bishop Stortford, Hertfordshire, the women began by "insulting" him, and when he apparently refused to give in to their demands, they wounded him and took his corn.[51] Women also voiced their complaints directly to market officials and justices. Descriptions by authorities of the crowds which presented written petitions were usually laconic and generic, but there is little reason to suppose that women were not present at many of these showings of communal solidarity, just as they were present at many food riots. In 1591, Henry Cocke, a justice of Hertfordshire, was harried several times by the "poorer sorte" of people of the county, including "vagar^{a}unte women w[hi]ch in truthe … I never knewe to be soe many," who complained that millers, bakers and others "greedylie doe buye vppe the Corne in Marketts & els wher as the poorer sorte are skarce able to gett eny for ther moneye." These crowds of poor men and women declared that if market regulations continued to go unenforced,

47 WRO, Q/S Great Roll, Hilary 1648, no. 254; see also Stocks (ed.), *Records of … Leicester*, p. 196.

48 For example, the complaints of the poor to the University against John Vepen, a gentleman of Cambridge and an engrosser of peas: CUA, V.C.Ct.III.7, no. 189.

49 H.J. Moule (ed.), *Descriptive Catalogue of the Charters, Minute Books and Other Documents of the Borough of Weymouth and Melcombe Regis A.D. 1252 to 1800*, (Weymouth: Sherren and Son, 1883), p. 67.

50 PRO, S.P. 16/190/39.

51 Lawson, "Patriarchy, Crime, and the Courts," p. 32.

the offending millers would "be pulled out of the m[a]rketts by the eares."[52] Because, of course, the early modern state lacked a regular police force, magistrates had to take such threats seriously.

The only factor that can explain the deep engagement of poor women in the popular politics of dearth is their role as consumers in the marketplace. They not only joined with men when riots broke out, but worked to mobilize their communities against lax officials and greedy traders. But we should be wary of extrapolating from food protests during times of crisis a general popular economic mentality, and reading into these disturbances an unbending, "traditional" backlash against profit-making in the marketplace. After all, many of these same women would have also depended on the profits they made in the marketplace to keep their households afloat. Market women pursued a wider agenda than has heretofore been recognized.

***

It was not only during dearth years that women felt compelled to make their voices heard. Rather, women, as consumers *and* retailers were intimately involved in the everyday politics of the marketplace, and their demands shifted according to the economic context; they were thus active in local efforts to loosen restrictions on commerce. While proper enforcement of regulations could mitigate dearth, overly stringent commercial restrictions could prevent communities from being supplied with malt and corn and humble households from making profits in the market. Ordinary women did not always assume that giving a degree of freedom to middlemen to participate in the market economy and protecting poor consumers were mutually exclusive prospects. Furthermore, plebeian and middling women were aggressive in protecting their commercial activities from official interference. Food protests have received the most attention from historians, but these protests were part of a broader politics of the marketplace in which plebeian and middling households sought to influence the way in which markets were governed for the good of their households.

Local maltsters and middlemen were sometimes able to enlist their female neighbors and customers in petitioning authorities for licenses. Badger and maltster petitions were probably most common in the growing communities of the woodland/pasture regions of the western counties, because these villages were often some distance from regulated town markets and depended on corn imports from the midland counties. Castle Combe and its surrounding villages was one such area. In 1648, the inhabitants of the community successfully petitioned the Wiltshire JPs to grant John Morrice a license to convert "a reasonable quantity of

52 BL, Lansdowne MS 66, fo. 64^{v}. In many cases, petitioners hinted that social disorder would be likely if magistrates did not act quickly to alleviate dearth. For instance, see WRO, Q/S Great Roll, Hilary 1615, no. 192; SRO, Q/S PET/1AA; Bodl. Lib., Firth MS c4, 495, pp. 504–5.

barley into Malt for the only use of us the neighbours theire & of the poor people of the villages adjacent neither wee nor they having any Market neere us to Supply our wants."[53] A large number of the signatures, 20 out of a total of 69 (29 percent), were made by widows. It is likely that many of these widows were brewsters or alehouse-keepers, and thus saw the advantage of having a local maltster who could supply their community with malt. Women too were candidates for corn badger and maltster licenses. In 1648, residents of Westbury—including 64 men and seven women—requested a license for Margery Iles, a widow who owned a mill and "hath for many yeares nowe … vsed to provide and serve the poor w[i]th all manner of Corne and grayne."[54] Provided that their appetites were satisfied, poor consumers did not always regard middlemen with suspicion.

Communal support for badgers' and maltsters' licenses was therefore conditional. Traders who transported malt and provisions through communities without offering any for sale were targets of popular resentment, as were middlemen who offered to sell corn for ready money only. On the other hand, badgers, millers, and maltsters who satisfied local demand, were willing to extend credit to neighbors, and refrained from price gouging during times of dearth gained the appreciation of their communities. John Edwards, constable for the parish of Stockelane, Wiltshire, recommended that Edward Morris be granted a maltster's license, for Morris was "an honest concionable man" who furnished "the pore both with barly & maulte at an indifferante rate."[55] Margery Iles's neighbors lauded her as one who dealt "very Conscionably in all respects" with the poor of her community, and thus "lyveth in good creditt and reputac[i]on."[56] Neighbors clearly appreciated such necessary and conscientious traders. We can see in these petitions a qualified acceptance by the poor of commercial society. The private economic initiatives of small middlemen were essential to the survival of communities not well served by markets. Adherence to the tenets of charity and good-neighborliness did not just constrain profit-making, but also opened economic opportunities for male and female traders serving local communities.

We should not assume from such petitions a universally deferential attitude of women toward town officials. Despite the risks, women who felt unfairly targeted by officials grumbled, cursed, and threatened authorities who prevented them from earning a living. Quite often, town and court clerks failed to record the specifics of insolent speeches, but occasionally we can glimpse the nature of the complaints women had against town officials. For instance, Margery Ellwell, called before

---

53 WRO, Q/S Great Roll, Hilary 1648, no. 227; Morrice was allowed to convert twelve bushels of barley into malt every week "to sell it to his neighbours that shall want it." For a petition by a community for a license for a local corn badger, see HampRO, Jervoise MS 44 M 69/G3/194.

54 WRO, Q/S Great Roll, Hilary 1648, no. 249. Women were candidates for licenses in other counties: HertRO, HAT/SR 13/106–7.

55 WRO, Q/S Great Roll, Hilary 1648, no. 238.

56 WRO, Q/S Great Roll, Hilary 1648, no. 249.

the mayor and aldermen of Devizes in 1586 for buying bread in the countryside and selling it in the town, chided the mayor for his hypocrisy. In a "lewed" speech delivered in the Guildhall, she observed that the mayor "sold bread hymself w[hi]ch came from Fitsall," and that he bought candles in the countryside which he sold in town. She concluded her speech by asking the mayor if he would "lett her have a loffe to lay under her heade to sleepe on;" the clerk noted that for this speech, "Margery was committed to pryson."[57] Women sometimes greeted town officials sent to distrain goods in lieu of market fines or to investigate disorderly alehouses with threats and insults.[58] The wife of John Browne of Southampton warned the beadle of St Michael's ward that "she would thrust her knife in him" at her door if he came again in the middle of the night to search her tippling house for drunkards.[59] Such resentments, though common, rarely erupted into major protests, because prosecutions against individual households for various types of infractions or unauthorized trading most often failed to unite significant numbers of neighbors in common cause.

In a couple of cases, female retailers succeeded in building communal support to protest corporate efforts to enclose the common land of the town. At first glance, enclosure riots in towns may seem to have little to do with the popular politics of the marketplace. However, as we have seen, urban women engaged in part-time dairy farming both to supplement household food supplies and produce a commodity that could be sold in the town market. Enclosures of town commons threatened this largely female by-employment. In 1517, the mayor of Southampton alienated a large number of women by enclosing half of the saltmarsh in order to protect a strategic highway from the sea. In addition to angering dairy women, the mayor's decision also threatened the interests of butchers and the town porters who also pastured their animals on the salt marsh. Thus, three hundred women and men cast down the enclosures and confronted the mayor at his law court and residence, asking "yff Master Meyer have any more wurke for us."[60] In Cambridge, women enlisted their customers to protest the erection of a fence around a patch of common ground called Parker's Piece. A scholar of Pembroke Hall testified in Cambridge University's Commissary court that he heard several women say to a group of students that the women "did hope that the schollers would take there parts" in breaking down a new enclosure erected by the University around the

57 Cunnington (ed.), *Annals of ... Devizes*, part 2, p. 21. "Fitsall" is of course not a place name, but is an abbreviation of the phase "one fits all." The clerk failed to communicate the joke/barb in a coherent manner. Obviously, this trader was asserting her right to trade, just as the mayor had a right to trade.

58 For example, see *Office c. Richard Hull* (1617), CUA, V.C.Ct.I.8, fo. 308^{v}; *Office c. the wife of John Goodman* (1632), CUA, Comm.Ct.V.9, fo. 126^{v}; *Office c. John Edwards* (1641), CUA, Comm.Ct.V.10, fo. 26.

59 Hearnshaw and Hearnshaw (eds), *Court Leet Records [Southampton]*, vol. 3, p. 485 (1615).

60 Merson (ed.), *Third Book of Remembrance*, vol. 1, pp. 21–5.

land; and indeed, later in the day, several students and women broke the gates and fences around the plot.[61] We cannot be certain of the scholars' motives from the existing testimony, but given the frequency with which women were prosecuted for trading with scholars or serving them in alehouses,[62] it is likely that the scholars could expect rewards more tangible than the fun of breaking down fences.

While women were resourceful in finding male allies to help them contest the authorities, they also at times succeeded in finding common ground with local magistrates. One of the ways in which women could gain the support of town and county authorities was to point out that the exclusion of poor women from commerce could only exacerbate the problem of poverty. In 1616, the brewers of Bury St Edmund's complained that innholders and alehouse-keepers were undermining the brewers' company by brewing their own beer. The attempt of the brewers to prevent alehouse-keepers from brewing on the side provoked a petition from "a great number of poor people" to the justices of assize. The petitioners, including widows of the town, claimed that by prohibiting "so many charitable [poor] persons" from brewing small beer for retail, the brewers would "undo a great number of poor men … [and] widows."[63] Authorities could not afford to ignore the vital role market women played in supplying the market with provisions. In 1615, the jurors of the Southampton court leet took up the cause of the traders of the women's section of the market, where women from both the town and the surrounding countryside came to sell provisions such as butter, cheese, poultry, and eggs. According to a presentment by the jurors delivered to the town government, the bakers of the town had taken to setting up stalls in the women's sector of the market, "whereby to expullse" female traders. The jurors were concerned that this was a "disincouragment of manye [of] the Countrye people" to bring their provisions to the market, which could only lead to shortages. The jurors thus recommended that a separate section be designated for the bakers of the town to trade in.[64] As this case suggests, town authorities at least did not dismiss out of hand the complaints of trading women.

Women also took action against overzealous or greedy market officials whose enforcement of regulations cut too deeply into profits. The "poore people of the contrey" who came to sell provisions in Southampton complained in 1581 against the wife of Robard Kennig, a market toll-collector. According to the petitioners, Kennig's wife took an "exessyve toule" for corn, poultry, oatmeal, and

61 CUA, Comm.Ct.I.18, fos 88–9a.

62 For example, *Office c. Margaret Pinder*, CUA, Comm.Ct.I.18, fo. 39, *Office c. Emma Moody*, CUA, Comm.Ct.I.18, fo. 42^{v}, *Office c. Margaret Lichfield*, CUA, Comm. Ct.I.18, fos 42^{v}–3. University students were forbidden to sell goods to townspeople or visit alehouses.

63 *HMC*, Lincoln, Bury St. Edmund's, Hertford, and Great Grimsby (1895), pp. 141–2.

64 Though the town assembly agreed to this request, nothing was done, and the same complaint was heard the next year: Hearnshaw and Hearnshaw (eds), *Court Leet Records [Southampton]*, vol. 1, pp. 489, 509.

other victuals brought to the woman's section of the market, "w[hi]^{ch} was nev^{er} accostomed heertofore." The traders gained the support of the court leet, which claimed (perhaps with some hyperbole) to be concerned that if such complaints should reach the queen, she might reconsider the town's liberty to regulate its own markets.[65] In a petition delivered to the mayor, aldermen, and Common Council of London in 1699, women who sold provisions in the Leadenhall and Newgate markets complained of the high stall tolls charged by the fee-farmers. Joan Laxton, a widow who had kept a stall for 18 years in Leadenhall Market, noted that until recently she had only had to pay 2d. for each day that she set up her stall in the market, but now fee-farmers were demanding that she pay the fee even for days she did not trade in the market.[66] But resentments and protests against market officials were not confined to the issue of excessive toll collecting.

While strict enforcement of price ceilings and standard weights and measures could mitigate dearth, it could also prevent humble retailers from making profits in the market. Price controls and consumer protections occasionally provoked collective protests. In 1577, the town government of Beverly levied a fine of 20d. against Richard Blanchard, warden of the fraternity of oatmeal makers, because his wife had "made a ryot" in the town. While the specific circumstances of the disorder are not given, Blanchard's wife may have been provoked by recent orders by the mayor and his governors that put a ceiling on the price of oatmeal and required that oatmeal makers' houses be searched to prevent hoarding.[67] Protests against price ceilings were, however, relatively rare, because most households had a greater interest in keeping food prices at reasonable levels than ensuring profits for individual traders and regulated companies.

This communal conflict of interest between the need to protect consumers and ensure profits could be overcome, as was the case in Cambridge during the Civil Wars. The traders of Stourbridge Fair, including the many local women who vended food and drink to fair visitors, had a common interest in curbing the regulatory powers of University officials. The outbreak of civil war gave the traders and Cambridge's town government, which had long resented the University's privileges, an opportunity to attack the University's power to prosecute economic infractions committed in the fair. With the Crown's authority now in question, retailers began to question the legal basis of the University's economic privileges.

---

[65] Hearnshaw and Hernshaw (eds), *Court Leet Records [Southampton]*, vol. 2, p. 216. For similar complaints in York in 1564, see Raine (ed.), *York Civic Records,* vol. 6, pp. 76–9.

[66] "The petition of the oppressed market people, humbly offer'd to the consideration of the Lord Mayor, Aldermen, and Common Council of the City of London" (London, 1699), reprinted in Crawford and Gowing (eds), *Women's Worlds*, pp. 81–3.

[67] J. Dennett (ed.), *Beverly Borough Records, 1575–1821* (York: Yorkshire Archaeological Society, 84, 1933), pp. 13, 5; see, also, for instance, the complaints of the bakers and butchers of York in Raine (ed.), *York Civic Records*, vol. 5, pp. 98, 127–8; vol. 6, p. 1.

As one man prosecuted in 1642 for vending meat in his house during the Sabbath claimed, "there was but one Courte & yt was the p[ar]liament." In the same year, a woman whose husband failed to appear before the Commissary court for selling beer in unsealed pots argued that the University had no right to prosecute her husband.[68] Resistance to the University's privileges in the fair came to a head in 1644, when a bailiff of the town, apparently at the behest of the town government, refused to let the University proctors inspect the weights and measures used for measuring hops. The bailiff also encouraged traders not to report to the proctors' booth, and several traders assaulted court officials who warned them to appear before the court.[69] Significantly, the leaders of the Stourbridge Fair protest appealed to female as well as male vendors in building support. For instance, Philip Wickham pressured Jane Britton not to have her beer pots inspected, and another man tried to convince Ann Laurence and the wife of one Harrold, from King's Lynn, not to report to the proctors' booth. Of the 30 traders who refused to attend the proctors' booth or answer charges before the Commissary court, at least eight were women.[70] Women do not seem to have led the protests at that year's Stourbridge Fair, but the fact that they were recruited by male traders to resist University officials suggests of men's desire to maintain a united front, for women played a crucial role in the fair by supplying food and drink.

***

Did the protests of female consumers and retailers affect the way markets were governed? The extent to which protests against market and corporate officials were successful is difficult to measure, but, as we saw in Chapter 4, at least it is clear that authorities in charge of markets were not always hostile to female traders on the grounds that it was somehow unseemly or illegitimate for women to earn a living trading in the public market. And it is possible that protests such as the traders' resistance to University officers in Stourbridge Fair in 1644 made officials more wary of interfering with retailers' businesses and discouraged them from holding too strictly to the letter of the law, though this reaction would not have left much of an imprint on the historical record.[71] But the unusually well documented records of the Southampton court leet and town government do suggest that authorities did not always reject the demands of female retailers out of hand. Though the court leet did attempt to keep tight control over the price-gouging activities of hucksters

68 *Office c. John and Mary Duisborough*, CUA, Comm.Ct.V.10, fo. 34; *Office c. Roger Harrison*, CUA, Comm.Ct.V.10, fo. 34^{v}.

69 CUA, Comm.Ct.10, fos 45^{v}, 46^{v}.

70 CUA, Comm.Ct.10, fo. 45^{v}.

71 There did appear to be a decline of business in the Stourbridge Fair court after 1644, but whether this was a result of the protest, poorer record keeping, the disorders surrounding the civil wars, or some combination of the three, is uncertain; CUA, Comm. Ct.V.10.

(many of whom were women), they also accepted the fact that female retailers played a crucial role in supplying the town with provisions and had to have access to the market to earn a living.

The impact of food rioters in shaping the policies of local and national authorities during times of dearth should not be underestimated. By the early seventeenth century, consensus around the inherited body of Tudor economic regulation was breaking down; it was the fear of social disorder during dearth that prevented the nation's rulers from abandoning traditional protections for consumers. The Crown and the Privy Council, of course, remained committed to a "carrot-and-stick" approach designed to preserve the social order by both maintaining local corn supplies during dearth and cracking down on hungry rioters.[72] But two decades of relatively low food prices after the disastrous harvests of 1594–1597 led to rising opposition among landowners to the regulation of the corn and cattle trades. Members of the House of Commons in 1621, in particular those MPs representing midland constituencies, pushed for measures to limit the importation of corn and cattle from overseas and even proposed repealing the Edwardian forestalling statute. Fear of the mob—that "many-headed monster"—was the primary reason why most of these measures failed to pass; more MPs than not believed that "we must not make a law for the farmer that we may make the poor to curse us."[73] Local authorities felt the fear of social disorder with great immediacy. Though they blamed the shortage of 1592 on the "visitac[i]on of god," JPs from Kent, in a letter to their colleagues in Sussex regarding a series of riots along the Kent-Sussex border, nevertheless requested that royal directions for the control of the markets be strictly observed "so that it might appeare [that] hir Ma[jes]tie hath A princely care to p[ro]vide as much as may bee for the Relief of hir loving Subiects."[74] When confronted by crowds of unruly poor men and women in Hertfordshire in 1591, Henry Cocke took energetic action: he suppressed several millers accused of hoarding corn, posted the Privy Council's orders issued during the last dearth, and requested a letter from Lord Burghley reaffirming those orders.[75] Protests by poor consumers were crucial in spurring authorities to consider the interests of the poor well before the rise of a coherent *laissez-faire* ideology in the eighteenth century.

At first glance, it seems contradictory to argue that market women at times supported constraints on profit-making activities, and at other times opposed officials when they went about enforcing regulations. Popular notions of

---

72 Steve Hindle, *The State and Social Change in Early Modern England, c. 1550–1640* (London: Macmillan, 2000), ch. 2.

73 Wallace Notestein, Frances Relf, and Hartley Simpson (eds), *Commons Debates 1621* (7 vols, New Haven: Yale University Press, 1935), vol. 2, p. 178; this statement, made during debate to prohibit the importation of corn from overseas except during dearth, is a reference to Prov. 11.26. MPs did raise the price ceiling for grain in 1624; Outhwaite, "Dearth and Government Intervention," p. 391.

74 BL, Harleian MS 703, fo. 101v.

75 BL, Lansdowne MS 66, fo. 64v.

economic morality, however, should not be equated with a "traditional" suspicion of commercial society or an uncritical acceptance of market regulations codified by Tudor statutes and royal proclamations. The women who protested against stringent regulations, market fees, busy officials, and oppressive town governments were, for the most part, not the type of traders who endangered the survival of the local community. Though hucksters and small retailers often ignored the rules against forestalling and regrating, or sold food over-price or under-weight, they nevertheless earned their livings by serving their neighbors in times of plenty and dearth. Sharp market practices created resentments and led to innumerable disputes between neighbors, but it was only when a middleman threatened to starve the market of food by engrossing supplies either for re-sale at a later time or for export that local men and women resorted to the threat of collective violence; many food riots were in fact attempts by the crowd to enforce the laws themselves. But it was not only during periods of crisis that women felt compelled to engage in public protests. In many towns, there was a low-level, quotidian resentment among traders against meddling market officials. Women fought to ensure not just that they had supplies of food during shortages, but also to prevent town governments and market officials from threatening or closing down their commercial activities.

Women played crucial roles in these protests because, as consumers and traders, they were integral members of their local economies and neighborhoods. It is significant that their participation in economic protests was not confined to efforts to alleviate food shortages; their demands shifted according to the economic context and the nature of the threat to their household economies and communities. The early modern moral economy was thus not defined by any particular "class" interest or a "traditional" suspicion of commercialization; it was instead based on local contingencies. Middlemen who enhanced prices and officials who closed down commercial opportunities to female traders who served markets constituted threats to local communities. That women were often successful in working with male neighbors and authorities to protect their interests from a diverse range of economic threats obliges us to reconsider both the concept of a "traditional" economic mentality and the strength of patriarchal prejudice in early modern provincial towns.

Chapter 10
Conclusion:
To "Runneth & Raveth" after Markets

As Adam Smith famously intoned in 1776:

> It is not from the benevolence of the butcher, the brewer, or the baker that we expect our dinner, but from their regard to their own self-interest. We address ourselves not to their humanity but to their self-love, and never talk to them of our own necessities, but of their advantages.[1]

It has been tempting to see Smith's call for *laissez-faire*, rooted as it was in his vision of a profit-oriented English people and a rejection of paternalistic market regulations, as reflecting a new commercially rapacious, or at least competitive, age.[2] Yet Smith was less a prophet than he was a keen observer of his own day; and the commercial culture he knew had very old historical roots indeed. Almost two centuries before Smith, John Wheeler, writing on behalf of the Merchant Adventurers Company, observed that "there is nothing in the world so ordinarie, and natural" as for people to "truck, merchandise, and traffike." He captures something of the joy and anticipation his contemporaries felt when they sensed that a good deal was at hand: "Children, assoone as euer their tongues are at libertie, do season their sports with some merchandise, or other … the Husband with his wife, Women with and among themselues, and in a word, all the world choppeth and changeth, runneth & raueth after Marts, Markets, and Merchandising."[3] Women were not marginal, but were rather, as Wheeler suggests, central players in early modern England's commercial life.

Historians have tended to explain the involvement of women in commerce in one of two ways. The first generation of studies, influenced by Alice Clark, saw women's commercial activities as an outgrowth of their domestic chores. Women supplemented the household economy by selling the produce of their gardens and dairies after household appetites had been satisfied; and they marketed

[1] Adam Smith, *An Inquiry into the Nature and Causes of the Wealth of Nations*, (ed.) R.H. Campbell and A.S. Skinner (2 vols, Oxford: Oxford University Press, 1976), vol. 1, p. 17.

[2] Thompson, "Moral Economy of the English Crowd;" A.W. Coats, "Contrary Moralities: Plebs, Paternalists, and Political Economists," *P&P* 54 (1972): 130–33.

[3] John Wheeler, *A Treatise of Commerce* (New York: Columbia University Press, 1931), p. 6; originally published in 1601.

their expertise as managers of household consumption by shopping for others and hawking goods.[4] Other scholars have argued that a gendered "dual labor market" existed, one which shunted women into the lower rungs of commercial activities.[5] This study suggests that neither model sufficiently explains the scope and variety of women's trading activities. Many women did market surplus foods and goods they produced for their families, but many others also engaged in commercial practices which had little or no direct relationship to their domestic duties. Female creditors, hucksters, pawnbrokers, and second-hand goods traders certainly drew upon their knowledge and experience as household managers to make wise business decisions, but they were driven foremost by profits rather than the sense that they were engaged in uniquely "women's work"—as suggested by the fact that plenty of men engaged in these kinds of trades as well. Both male and female traders were adept at exploiting new commercial opportunities and niches in England's burgeoning provincial towns. Doing so required household economies to be flexible and willing to engage an array of productive and commercial activities at once. Far from hemming women workers in, the household as an institution lent legitimacy to women's multi-faceted commercial endeavors; and the fact that many wives participated in vital aspects of their husbands' business—keeping debt books, arranging deals with creditors, handling customers, and assisting in production—suggests that they cannot be dismissed as mere "adjuncts" or, to use Dekker's term, "kitchen-stuff." Their reproductive and affective purposes aside, early modern urban households operated in much the same way as a small firm.

Indeed, as surprising as it seems, residents of early modern urban communities were probably more profit-oriented and commercially adept than today's everyday consumer or employee. Almost every transaction created a potential bargaining situation. While Craig Muldrew and others have reminded us that credit was often judged in moral as well as financial terms, and that charity and honesty remained key values, it is nevertheless the case that the primary purpose of trucking and trading was to make a profit; and the purpose of "cheapening" was to get a good deal. Today, prices are mostly set and adjusted by professional forecasters: there is no bargaining at Safeway, and asking the boss for a raise is an often perilous gambit. England's commercial growth in the sixteenth and seventeenth centuries may have been less noticeable than the industrial take-off

---

4 See Clark, *Working Life of Women*, and, for example, Tilly and Scott, *Women, Work, and Family*, ch. 3; Hill, *Women, Work and Sexual Politics*, ch. 3.

5 Honeyman and Goodman, "Women's Work, Gender Conflict and Labour Markets;" the essays in Duffin and Charles (eds), *Women and Work in Pre-Industrial England*; McIntosh, *Working Women in English Society*; Judith Bennett, "Medieval Women, Modern Women: Across the Great Divide," in *Feminists Revision History*, (ed.) Ann-Louise Shapiro (New Brunswick: Rutgers University Press, 1994).

of the late eighteenth and early nineteenth centuries, but it was important and had deep grassroots.[6]

The tradeswomen of the provincial English towns studied here were hardly unique. There were striking parallels between the experiences of English townswomen and their continental counterparts. Certainly local circumstances influenced the occupational roles open to women, most clearly in the production sectors of the economy. So strong was the association of craftwork with masculinity in early modern Germany that women were rarely able to break into the ranks of skilled artisans. The guilds of German cities steadily restricted women's work opportunities in the sixteenth and seventeenth centuries by limiting the amount of time widows could carry on their husbands' shops and barring women from the craft workshop; these restrictions were rarely promulgated or enforced in English towns.[7] On the other hand, Paris and other French cities, unlike England, had guilds exclusively for women; these companies were recognized by the crown, and allowed at least some women to pursue a regulated craft independently of a male householder.[8] Despite these regional variations, if we look toward the many trades which fell outside guild structures, we see strong parallels between the work done by English female traders and the trades dominated by continental women. As Merry Wiesner has shown, women selling all manner of victuals and wares populated the markets of German cities. Many of these women also operated as pawnbrokers and creditors.[9] Similarly, female residents in French towns sold a wide variety of victuals and foods, either as producers or middlemen.[10] P.J.P. Goldberg has argued that because they married relatively early, women in Mediterranean societies had fewer options to earn money than in northern Europe. But recent work suggests that ordinary women's commercial opportunities in Italy and Iberia have been underestimated; in fact, the model of the flexible household economy seen in English towns—in which women commonly pursued commercial work in partnership with, and independently from, their husbands—best describes the household economies of Italian and Iberian cities. As Monica Chojnacka has found in her study of working women in early modern Venice, while cultural prejudices

---

6 Furthermore, historians have come to see the gains and changes wrought by the "first" Industrial Revolution as having been previously overstated. For a convincing attempt to link the economic developments of the early modern period with the nineteenth century, see Richard Price, *British Society, 1680–1880* (Cambridge: Cambridge University Press, 1999).

7 Wiesner, *Working Women in Renaissance Germany*; see also Ogilvie, *A Bitter Living*.

8 Carol Loats, "Gender, Guilds, and Work Identity: Perspectives from Sixteenth-Century Paris," *French Historical Studies* 20 (Winter 1997): 15–30; Daryl M. Hafter, "Female Masters in the Ribbonmaking Guild of Eighteenth-Century Rouen," *French Historical Studies* 20 (Winter, 1997): 1–14.

9 Wiesner, *Working Women in Renaissance Germany*, pp. 134–42.

10 Loats, "Gender, Guilds, and Work Identity," pp. 21–3, 27; James B. Collins, "The Economic Role of Women in Seventeenth-Century France," *French Historical Studies* 16 (Fall, 1989): 442, 456.

and legal disabilities helped to restrict women of elite households to the "private sphere" of the household, women of the *popolani* classes regularly ventured out of doors to ply their wares and trade in the marketplace.[11] The traditional notion of English uniqueness did not obtain when it came to women's working roles.

Women's varied commercial roles had important implications for the ways in which they participated in the micro-politics of the neighborhood and marketplace. Female consumers in England and on the continent were prominent participants in food riots, but as the English case suggests, the economic mentality of market women was more complex and nuanced than has been supposed. When dearth was not threatening the community, women traders had a healthy eye for profit. A consideration of women's bargaining tactics and their demands that they be guaranteed access to markets suggest that Adam Smith's vision of a self-regulating market driven by profit motive did not spring Prometheus-like out of his head, but instead had deep roots in popular culture. That women saw no contradiction between defending their trades in terms of the defense of the household economy and communal interest suggests that the popular "moral economy" left plenty of room for the pursuit of profit. Women were not only affected by the commercial revolution, but were crucial participants in shaping its course.

[11] Monica Chojnacka, *Working Women of Early Modern Venice* (Baltimore and London: Johns Hopkins University Press, 2001), pp. 45–9. Samuel K. Cohn has made similar findings in his work on women and work in Florence and Tuscany: "Women and Work in Renaissance Italy," in *Renaissance Italy*, (ed.) Judith C. Brown and Robert C. Davis (New York: Longman, 1998). For Portugal, see Abreu-Ferreira, "Fishmongers and Shipowners," and her article "From Mere Survival to Near Success;" for women workers in Spain, see Mary Elizabeth Perry, *Gender and Disorder in Early Modern Seville* (Princeton: Princeton University Press, 1990), ch. 1.

Bibliography

Archival Sources

Bristol Record Office

JX/1/3:	Deposition Book, 1654–1657
JX/1/6:	Deposition Book, 1673–1687

British Library

Harleian MS 703:	Warrants and Orders Relating to the County of Sussex
Lansdowne MS 66:	Lord Burghley Papers
Lansdowne MS 71:	Lord Burghley Papers
Lansdowne MS 161:	Caesar Papers, Court of Requests

British Museum

SAT 61:	*Tittle-Tattle; Or, the Several Branches of Gossiping*

Bodleian Library, Oxford University

Bodl., MS Firth, c. 4

Cambridge University Archive

Commissary's Court

Comm.Ct.I.1–31:	Act Books, 1559–1642
Comm.Ct.II.1–22:	Deposition Books, 1580–1639
V.C.Ct.II.30:	Deposition Book, 1632–1634
V.C.Ct.II.32:	Deposition Book, 1633–1640
V.C.Ct.II.37:	Deposition Book, 1641–1642
Comm.Ct.III.1–20:	Exhibita, 1579–1649

Vice-Chancellor's Court

Collect.Admin.13:	Act Book, 1549–1578
Collect.Admin.6a.:	Act Book, 1577–1589
V.C.Ct.I.1–36:	Act Books, 1551–1645
V.C.Ct.II.1–19:	Deposition Books, 1593–1619

V.C.Ct.II.22–30:	Deposition Books, 1620–1630
V.C.Ct.II.33–36:	Deposition Books, 1634–1645
V.C.Ct.II.38–40:	Deposition Books, 1646–1682
Comm.Ct.II.8–9:	Deposition Books, 1596–1597, 1600
V.C.Ct.III.:1–40:	Exhibita, 1540–1660

Stourbridge Fair Court

Comm.Ct.V.1:	"Jurisdiction at Sturbridge Fair" manual
Comm.Ct.V.5–11:	Court Books, 1562–1656

Midsummer Fair Court

Comm.Ct.V.2–4:	Court Books, 1583–1656

University Proctor's Leet

CUR 17:	Court Leet Rolls, 1382–1616

Town Documents

CUR 37.2:	1564–1662

Registry of Alehouses and Victualling Houses

T.I.1:	Registry of Alehouses, 1616
T.I.10:	Registry of Victuallers, 1552
T.I.11:	Registry of Victuallers, 1606–1641
T.I.12:	Registry of Victuallers, 1644–1700
T.IX.1:	Registry of Victuallers, 1608–1856

Centre for Kentish Studies, Maidstone

Quarter Sessions Records

QM/SB 82
QM/SI/1595/2
QM/SI/1605/13
QM/SIq/26–27
U951 C2611/22

London Metropolitan Archives

COL/RMD/PA/01/002

Remembrancia

MCD 1/1–133:	Mayor's Court Depositions, 1641–1646

Dorset Record Office, Dorchester

B2/8/1: Dorchester Court Book, 1629–1637

East Suffolk Record Office, Ipswich

C/2/3/8/1–2: Petty Court Deposition Books, 1573–1651

Essex Record Office, Chelmsford

Quarter Sessions Records
D/B/3/3/208
Q/SR 131
Q/SR 316
Q/SR 332

Hampshire Record Office, Winchester

Jervoise MSS 44: Sheriff and Justices of the Peace Papers

Hertfordshire Record Office, Hertford

HAT/SR 13: Quarter Sessions Papers

Oxford University Archive

Chancellor's Court
Hyp/B/1–6: Deposition Books, 1566–1592, 1604–1638
Hyp/A/26: Deposition Book, 1596–1605

Public Record Office, Kew

SP 14: State Papers, James I
SP 16: State Papers, Charles I
STAC 8: Star Chamber Papers, James I and Charles I

Somerset Record Office, Taunton

Quarter Sessions Papers
Q/SR 61.1
Q/SR 63.2
Q/SR 64.2

Petitions to the Justices of the Peace
Q/S PET/1/AA

Southampton City Archives

SC 6/1/2–61:	Court Leet Presentments, 1550–1665
SC 9/3/2:	Quarter Sessions Depositions, 1575–1576
SC 9/3/5–7:	Quarter Sessions Depositions, 1583–1587
SC 9/4/6:	Quarter Sessions Papers, 1587

Wiltshire Record Office, Trowbridge

Quarter Sessions Rolls
Q/S Great Roll, Trinity 1614
Q/S Great Roll, Hilary 1615
Q/S Great Roll, Hilary 1631
Q/S Great Roll, Trinity 1647
Q/S Great Roll, Hilary 1648

Primary Sources, Published

A Calendar to the Records of the Borough of Doncaster. 4 vols, Doncaster, 1900–1902.

Acts of the Privy Council

Adams, T. *The Barren Tree*. London, 1623.

Alley, Hugh. *Hugh Alley's Caveat: Markets of London in 1598*, (ed.) Ian Archer, Caroline Baron, and Vanessa Harding. London: London Topographical Society, 1988.

Anderson, R.C. (ed.), *The Assize of Bread Book, 1477–1517*, Southampton Record Society, 23. Southampton: Cox and Sharland, 1923.

Anderson, R.C. (ed.), *The Book of Examinations and Depositions, 1622–1644*, Southampton Record Society Publications. 4 vols, Southampton: Cox and Sharland, 1929–1936.

Anon. *The Bloody Butcher, And the two wicked and cruel Bawds*. London, 1667.

Anon., *The Gossips meeting, or, The Merry market-women of Taunton.* London?, 1674.

Anon. *The Life of Long Meg of Westminster* 2nd edn. London, 1635.

Bateson, Mary (ed.), *Records of the Borough of Leicester*. 7 vols, London: C.J. Clay, and Cambridge: Cambridge University Press, 1905.

Bourne, I. *The Godly Mans Guide: With Directions for all, especially Merchants and Tradesmen*. London, 1620.

Chapman, George, Ben Jonson, and John Marston, *Eastward Ho*. In *The Roaring Girl and Other City Comedies*, (ed.) James Knowles and Eugene Giddens. Oxford: Oxford University Press, 2001.

Chappell, W.M. and J. Woodfall Ebsworth (eds), *The Roxburghe Ballads*. 8 vols, London and Hertford: The Ballad Society, 1871–1897.

Connor, W.J. (ed.), *The Southampton Mayor's Book of 1606–1608*, Southampton Record Series, 21. Southampton: Southampton University Press, 1978.

Crawford, Patricia and Laura Gowing (eds), *Women's Worlds in Seventeenth-Century England*. London and New York: Routledge, 2000.

Cunnington, B. Howard (ed.), *Some Annals of the Borough of Devizes*. Devizes: George Simpson and Company, 1925.

Dekker, Thomas. *The Dramatic Works of Thomas Dekker*, (ed.) Fredson Bowers. 4 vols, Cambridge: Cambridge University Press, 1953–1958.

———. *The Roaring Girl* (1611). In *The Dramatic Works of Thomas Dekker*, (ed.) Fredson Bowers. Cambridge: Cambridge University Press, 1953–1958, vol. 3.

———. *The Shoemaker's Holiday*. In *The Dramatic Works of Thomas Dekker*, (ed.) Fredson Bowers. Cambridge: Cambridge University Press, 1953–1958, vol. 1.

Dekker, Thomas and Thomas Middleton. *The Honest Whore, part I.* In *The Dramatic Works of Thomas Dekker*, (ed.) Fredson Bowers. Cambridge: Cambridge University Press, 1953–1958, vol. 2.

Deloney, Thomas. *The Works of Thomas Deloney*, (ed.) Francis Oscar Mann. Oxford: Clarendon Press, 1912.

Dennett, J. (ed.), *Beverly Borough Records, 1575–1821*. York: Yorkshire Archaeological Society, 84, 1933.

Dod, John and Robert Cleaver. *A Godly Forme of Houshold Gouernment for the Ordering of Priuate Families, According to the Direction of Gods Word*. London, 1630.

Dyke, I. *A Cvnterpoison Against Covetovness*. London, 1619.

Earwaker, J.P. (ed.), *The Court Leet Records of the Manor of Manchester*. 12 vols, Manchester: H. Blacklock and Co., 1884–1890.

Ebsworth, Joseph Woodfall (ed.), *The Bagford Ballads: Illustrating the Last Years of the Stuarts*. 2 vols, Hertford: Stephen Austin and Sons, 1878.

Etherege, George. *The Man of Mode*. In *Restoration Plays*, (ed.) Robert Lawrence. London: Everyman, 1994.

Ferguson, R.S. (ed.), *A Boke off Recorde of Kirbie Kendall*. Cumb. And Westm. Ant. And Arch. Soc., e.s. VII, 1892.

Ferguson, R.S. and W. Nanson (eds), *Some Municipal Records of the City of Carlisle*. Carlisle: Cumb. And West. Ant. and Arch. Soc., e.s. IV, 1887.

Gataker, Thomas. *Marriage Duties Briefely Couched Togither*. 2nd edn, London, 1620.

Gidden, H.W. (ed.), *The Book of Remembrance of Southampton*, Southampton Record Society, 27, 28, 30. 3 vols, Southampton: Cox and Sharland, 1928.

Gouge, William. *Of Domesticall Duties* 3rd edn. London, 1634.

Griffith, Mathew. *Bethel: Or, A Forme For Families*. London, 1633.

Guilding, J.M. (ed.), *Reading Records. Diary of the Corporation*. 4 vols, London: James Parker and Co., 1892–1896.

Hannay, Patrack. *A Happy Husband or, Directions for a Maide to Choose Her Mate*. London, 1619.

Hardy, W.J. (ed.), *Notes and Extracts from the Sessions Rolls 1581 to 1698 [Hertfordshire]*. 3 vols, Hertford: C.E. Longmore, 1905–1910.

Harrison, William. *The Description of England*, (ed.) Georges Edelen. Ithaca: Cornell University Press, 1968.

Hearnshaw, F.J.C. and D.M. Hearnshaw (eds), *Court Leet Records [of Southampton]*, Southampton Record Society Publications 1, 2, 4, 6. 4 vols, Southampton: H.M. Gilbert & Son, 1905–1908.

Helmholz, R.H. (ed.), *Select Cases on Defamation to 1600*. London: Selden Society, 1985.

Heywood, Thomas. *The Fair Maid of the West*, (ed.) Katharine Lee Bates. Boston, New York, and Chicago: D.C. Heath, 1917.

Historical Manuscript Commission, Reports: Lincoln, Bury St. Edmund's, Hertford, and Great Grimsby. 1895.

Historical Manuscript Commission, Reports: Rye and Hereford Corporations. 1892.

Horrocks, J.W. (ed.), *The Assembly Books of Southampton [1602–1616]*, Southampton Record Society 19, 21, 24, 25. 4 vols, Southampton: Cox & Sharland, 1917–1925.

Hudson, William and John Cottingham (eds), *The Records of the City of Norwich*. 2 vols, Norwich: Jarrold, 1906–1910.

Jonson, Ben. *Epicoene,* (ed.) L.A. Beaurline. Lincoln: University of Nebraska Press, 1966.

———. *Bartholomew Fair*, (ed.) Simon Trussler. London and New York: Methuen, 1986.

Knowles, James and Eugene Giddens (eds), *The Roaring Girl and Other City Comedies*. Oxford: Oxford University Press, 2001.

Lawrence, Robert (ed.), *Restoration Plays*. London: Everyman, 1994.

Markham, Christopher A. and J. Charles Cox (eds), *The Records of the Borough of Northampton*. 2 vols, Northampton and London: Northampton, 1898.

Marston, John. *The Dutch Courtesan*, (ed.) M.L. Wine. Lincoln: University of Nebraska Press, 1965.

Merson, A.L. (ed.), *Third Book of Remembrance 1514–1602*, Southampton Record Series, 2, 3, 8. 3 vols, Southampton: Southampton University Press, 1952–1965.

Moule, H.J. (ed.), *Descriptive Catalogue of the Charters, Minute Books and Other Documents of the Borough of Weymouth and Melcombe Regis A.D. 1252 to 1800*. Weymouth: Sherren and Son, 1883.

Notestein, Wallace, Frances Relf, and Hartley Simpson (eds), *Commons Debates 1621*. 7 vols, New Haven: Yale University Press, 1935.

Nott, H.E. and Elizabeth Ralph (eds), *The Deposition Books of Bristol*. 2 vols, Bristol: Bristol Record Society, 1935–1948.

Power, Michael (ed.), *Liverpool Town Books 1649–1671*. The Record Society of Lancashire and Cheshire, vol. 136, 1999.

Raine, Angelo (ed.), *York Civic Records*. Wakefield: Yorkshire Archaeological Society, 98, 103, 106, 108, 110, 112, 115, 119, 138, 1946.

R.B. *The Description of a good Wife: Or, A rare one amongst Women*. London, 1619.

Records of Maidstone: Being Selections from Documents in Possession of the Corporation. Maidstone, 1926.

Rollins, Hyder Edward (ed.), *A Pepysian Garland: Black-Letter Broadside Ballads of the Years 1594–1639*. Cambridge: Cambridge University Press, 1922.

———. (ed.), *The Pepys Ballads*. 8 vols, Cambridge, Mass.: Harvard University Press, 1929–1932.

Rowlands, Samuel. *Tis Merrie When Gosips meete*. London, 1602.

———. *The Complete Works of Samuel Rowlands*. 3 vols, Glasgow: Hunterien Club, 1880.

Sachese, William (ed.), *Minutes of the Norwich Court of Mayoralty 1630–1631*. Norfolk Record Society, 25, 1942.

———. (ed.), *Minutes of the Norwich Court of Mayoralty 1632–1635*. Norfolk Record Society, 36, 1967.

Savage, Richard (ed.), *Minutes and Accounts of the Corporation of Stratford-Upon-Avon*. 4 vols, Oxford: Dugdale Society, 1921–1929.

Shadwell, Thomas. *Bury Fair: A Critical Edition*, (ed.) John C. Ross. New York and London: Garland Publishing, 1995.

Smith, Adam. *An Inquiry into the Nature and Causes of the Wealth of Nations*, 2 vols, (ed.) R.H. Campbell and A.S. Skinner. Oxford: Oxford University Press, 1976.

Smith, Sir Thomas. *De Republica Anglorum*, (ed.) Mary Dewar. Cambridge: Cambridge University Press, 1982.

Smith, William George (ed.), *The Oxford Dictionary of English Proverbs*. Oxford: Clarendon Press, 1935.

Stevenson, W.H., W.T. Baker, E.L. Guilford, Duncan Gray, and V.W. Walker (eds), *Records of the Borough of Nottingham*. 9 vols, Nottingham and London: Thomas Forman & Sons and Bernard Quaritch, 1889.

Stocks, Helen (ed.), *Records of the Borough of Leicester*. Cambridge: Cambridge University Press, 1923.

Tawney, R.H. and Eileen Power (eds), *Tudor Economic Documents*. 3 vols, London: Longmans, 1924.

Thomson, Sheila D. (ed.), *The Book of Examinations and Depositions Before the Mayor and Justices of Southampton 1648–1663*, Southampton Record Series 37. Southampton: Southampton University Press, 1994.

Tilley, Morris Palmer (ed.), *A Dictionary of the Proverbs in England in the Sixteenth and Seventeenth Centuries: A Collection of the Proverbs Found in English Literature and the Dictionaries of the Period*. Ann Arbor: University of Michigan Press, 1950.

Tilney, Edmund. *A Brief and Pleasant Discourse of the Duties of Mariage.* London, 1571.

Twemlow, J.A. (ed.), *Liverpool Town Books 1550–1862.* 2 vols, London: University of Liverpool, 1918.

Whatley, William. *A Bride-Bush or, a Direction for Married Persons.* London, 1619.

Wheeler, John. *A Treatise of Commerce.* Facsimile; New York: Columbia University Press, 1931.

Secondary Sources, Published

Abreu-Ferreira, Darlene. "Fishmongers and Shipowners: Women in Maritime Communities of Early Modern Portugal." *The Sixteenth Century Journal* 31 (Spring 2000): 7–23;

———. "From Mere Survival to Near Success: Women's Economic Strategies in Early Modern Portugal," *Journal of Women's History* 12 (Summer, 2001): 58–79.

Amussen, Susan Dwyer. *An Ordered Society: Gender and Class in Early Modern England.* Oxford: Basil Blackwell, 1988.

Appleby, Joyce. *Economic Thought and Ideology in Seventeenth-Century England.* Princeton: Princeton University Press, 1978.

Barry, Jonathan. "Introduction." In *The Tudor and Stuart Town: A Reader in English Urban History 1530–1688,* (ed.) Jonathan Barry. London and New York: Longman, 1990.

———. (ed.), *The Tudor and Stuart Town: A Reader in English Urban History 1530–1688.* London and New York: Longman, 1990.

———. "Bourgeois Collectivism? Urban Association and the Middling Sort," in *The Middling Sort of People: Culture, Society and Politics in England, 1550–1800,* (ed.) Jonathan Barry and C.W. Brooks. New York: St. Martin's Press, 1994.

Barry, Jonathan and Christopher Brooks (eds), *The Middling Sort of People: Culture, Society and Politics in England, 1550–1800.* New York and London: Palgrave Macmillan, 1984.

Beier, A.L. *Masterless Men: The Vagrancy Problem in England 1560–1640.* London: Methuen, 1985.

Ben-Amos, Ilana Krausman. "Women Apprentices in the Trades and Crafts of Early Modern Bristol." *Continuity and Change* 6 (Aug., 1991): 227–52.

———. *Adolescence and Youth in Early Modern England.* New Haven and London: Yale University Press, 1994.

Bennett, Judith M. "Medieval Women, Modern Women: Across the Great Divide." In *Feminists Revision History,* (ed.) Ann-Louise Shapiro. New Brunswick: Rutgers University Press, 1994.

———. *Ale, Beer, and Brewsters in England: Women's Work in a Changing World, 1300–1600.* New York: Oxford University Press, 1996.

———. *History Matters: Patriarchy and the Challenge of Feminism*. Philadelphia: University of Pennsylvania Press, 2006.
Bohstedt, J. “Gender, Household and Community Politics: Women in English Riots 1790–1810.” *Past and Present* 120 (1988): 88–122.
———. *The Politics of Provisions: Food Riots, Moral Economy, and Market Transition in England, c. 1550–1850*. Farnham and Burlington: Ashgate, 2010.
Bossy, John (ed.), *Disputes and Settlements: Law and Human Relations in the West*. Cambridge: Cambridge University Press, 1983.
Boulton, Jeremy. *Neighbourhood and Society: A London Suburb in the Seventeenth Century*. Cambridge: Cambridge University Press, 1987.
Braddick, Michael and John Walter (eds), *Negotiating Power in Early Modern Society: Order, Hierarchy and Subordination in Britain and Ireland*. Cambridge: Cambridge University Press, 2001
Brewer, John and John Styles (eds), *An Ungovernable People. The English and their Law in the Seventeenth and Eighteenth Centuries*. New Brunswick: Rutgers University Press, 1980.
Brewer, John and Roy Porter (eds), *Consumption and the World of Goods*. London: Routledge, 1993.
Brown, Judith C. and Robert C. Davis (eds), *Gender and Society in Renaissance Italy*. New York: Longman, 1998.
Bruster, Douglas. *Drama and the Market in the Age of Shakespeare*. Cambridge: Cambridge University Press, 1992.
Cahn, Susan. *Industry of Devotion: The Transformation of Women's Work in England, 1500–1660*. New York: Columbia University Press, 1987.
Capp, Bernard. “Popular Literature.” In *Popular Culture in Seventeenth-Century England*, (ed.) Barry Reay. New York: St. Martin's Press, 1985.
———. “Separate Domains? Women and Authority in Early Modern England.” In *The Experience of Authority in Early Modern England*, (ed.) Paul Griffiths, Adam Fox, and Steve Hindle. London and New York: Macmillan, 1996.
———. “The Double Standard Revisited: Plebeian Women and Male Sexual Reputation in Early Modern England.” *Past and Present* 162 (1999): 70–100.
———. *When Gossips Meet: Women, Family, and Neighbourhood in Early Modern England*. Oxford: Oxford University Press, 2003.
Carlin, Martha. *Medieval Southwark*. London and Rio Grande: Hambledon Press, 1996.
Carus-Wilson, E.M. (ed.), *Essays in Economic History*. 2 vols, London: Edward Arnold, 1962.
Charles, Lindsey and Lorna Duffin (eds), *Women and Work in Pre-Industrial England*. London: Croom Helm, 1985.
Charlesworth, Andrew (ed.), *An Atlas of Rural Protest in Britain 1548–1900*. London: Croom Helm, 1983.
Chojnacka, Monica. *Working Women of Early Modern Venice*. Baltimore and London: Johns Hopkins University Press, 2001.

Clark, Alice. *Working Life of Women in the Seventeenth Century*. 1919; repr., London: Routledge & Kegan Paul, 1982.

Clark, Peter (ed.), *The Cambridge Urban History of Britain* vol. 2, *1540–1840*. Cambridge: Cambridge University Press, 2000.

Clark, Peter. "The Migrant in Kentish Towns 1580–1640." *Crisis and Order in English Towns 1500–1700: Essays in Urban History*, (ed.) Peter Clark and Paul Slack. Toronto: University of Toronto Press, 1972.

———. "Popular Protest and Disturbance in Kent, 1558–1640." *The Economic History Review*, new series, 29 (August: 1976): 365–82.

———. *The English Alehouse. A Social History 1200–1830*. New York: Longman, 1983.

Clark, Peter and Paul Slack (eds), *Crisis and Order in English Towns 1500–1700: Essays in Urban History*. Toronto: University of Toronto Press, 1972.

———. "Introduction." In *Crisis and Order in English Towns 1500–1700: Essays in Urban History*, (ed.) Peter Clark and Paul Slack. Toronto: University of Toronto Press, 1972.

Clark, Stuart. *Thinking With Demons: The Idea of Witchcraft in Early Modern Europe*. Oxford: Oxford University Press, 1999.

Clay, C.G.A. *Economic Expansion and Social Change: England 1500–1700*. 2 vols, Cambridge: Cambridge University Press, 1985.

Coats, A.W. "Contrary Moralities: Plebs, Paternalists, and Political Economists." *Past and Present* 54 (1972): 130–33.

Cohn, Samuel K. "Women and Work in Renaisssance Italy." In *Gender and Society in Renaissance Italy*, (ed.) Judith C. Brown and Robert C. Davis. New York: Longman, 1998.

Collins, James B. "The Economic Role of Women in Seventeenth-Century France." *French Historical Studies* 16 (Fall, 1989): 436–70.

Corfield, Penelope. "Urban Development in England and Wales in the Sixteenth and Seventeenth Centuries." In *The Tudor and Stuart Town: A Reader in English Urban History 1530–1688*, (ed.) Jonathan Barry. London and New York: Longman, 1990.

Cox, Nancy. *The Complete Tradesman: A Study in Retailing, 1550–1820*. Burlington and Farnham: Ashgate, 2000.

Cressy, David. *Literacy and the Social Order: Reading and Writing in Tudor and Stuart England*. Cambridge: Cambridge University Press, 1980.

Davies, Kathleen. "Continuity and Change in Literary Advice on Marriage." In *Marriage and Society: Studies in the Social History of Marriage*, (ed.) R.B. Outhwaite. New York: St. Martin's Press, 1981.

Davis, Natalie Zemon. *Society and Culture in Early Modern France*. Stanford: Stanford University Press, 1975.

———. *Fiction in the Archives: Pardon Tales and Their Tellers in Sixteenth-Century France*. Stanford: Stanford University Press, 1987.

De Vries, Jan. "Between Purchasing Power and the World of Goods: Understanding the Household Economy in Early Modern Europe." In *Consumption and the World of Goods*, (ed.) John Brewer and Roy Porter. London: Routledge, 1993.

Donnison, Jean. *Midwives and Medical Men: A History for the Control of Childbirth.* 2nd edn. Stroud: Phillimore, 1999.

Duffin, Lindsey and Lorna Charles. "Introduction." In *Women and Work in Pre-Industrial England,* (ed.) Lindsey Duffin and Lorna Charles. London: Croom Helm, 1985.

Duffin, Lindsey and Lorna Charles (eds), *Women and Work in Pre-Industrial England.* London: Croom Helm, 1985

Dyer, Alan. "Small Market Towns 1540–1700." In *The Cambridge Urban History of Britain* vol. 2, *1540–1840*, (ed.) Peter Clark. Cambridge: Cambridge University Press, 2000.

Dyer, Christopher. "The Consumer and the Market in the Later Middle Ages." *The Economic History Review*, new series, 42 (Aug., 1989): 305–27.

Eales, Jacqueline. "Gender Construction in Early Modern England and the Conduct Books of William Whately (1583–1639)." In *Studies of Church History*, (ed.) R.N. Swanson, 34 (1998): 163–74.

Earle, Peter. "The Female Labour Market in London in the Late Seventeenth and Early Eighteenth Centuries." *The Economic History Review,* new series, 42 (Aug., 1989): 328–53.

———. *A City Full of People: Men and Women of London 1650–1750.* London: Methuen, 1994.

Epstein, S.R. "Regional Fairs, Institutional Innovation, and Economic Growth in Late Medieval Europe." *The Economic History Review*, new series, 47 (Aug. 1994): 459–82.

Erickson, Amy Louise. *Women and Property in Early Modern England.* London and New York: Routledge, 1993.

Everitt, Alan. "The Marketing of Agricultural Produce." In *The Agrarian History of England and Wales*, vol. 6, *1500–1640*, (ed.) Joan Thirsk. Cambridge: Cambridge University Press, 1967.

Finkelstein, Andrea. *Harmony and Balance: An Intellectual History of Seventeenth-Century English Economic Thought.* Ann Arbor: University of Michigan Press, 2000.

Flather, Amanda. *Gender and Space in Early Modern England.* Woodbridge: Boydell, 2007.

Fletcher, Anthony. *Gender, Sex and Subordination in England 1500–1800.* New Haven: Yale University Press, 1995.

Fletcher, Anthony and John Stevenson (eds), *Order and Disorder in Early Modern England.* Cambridge: Cambridge University Press, 1985.

Foyster, Elizabeth. "Male Honour, Social Control and Wife Beating." *Transactions of the Royal Historical Society*, 6th Series, vol. 6 (1996).

———. *Manhood in Early Modern England: Honour, Sex and Marriage*. London and New York: Longman, 1999.

Froide, Amy M. *Never Married. Singlewomen in Early Modern England.* Oxford: Oxford University Press, 2005.

Goldberg, P.J.P. *Women, Work, and Life Cycle in a Medieval Economy: Women in York and Yorkshire c. 1300–1520.* Oxford: Oxford University Press, 1992.

Goose, Nigel. "English Pre-Industrial Urban Economies," in *The Tudor and Stuart Town: A Reader in English Urban History 1530–1688*, (ed.) Jonathan Barry. London and New York: Longman, 1990.

Gowing, Laura, *Domestic Dangers: Women, Words, and Sex in Early Modern London.* Oxford: Clarendon Press, 1996.

———. "'The Freedom of the Streets': Women and Social Space, 1560–1640," in *Londinopolis. Essays in the Cultural and Social History of Early Modern London*, (ed.) Paul Griffiths and Mark S.R. Jenner. Manchester and New York: Manchester University Press, 2000.

Griffiths, Paul. *Youth and Authority: Formative Experiences in England, 1560–1640.* Oxford: Clarendon Press, 1996.

Griffiths, Paul, Adam Fox, and Steve Hindle (eds), *The Experience of Authority in Early Modern England.* New York: St. Martin's Press, 1996.

Gurr, Andrew. *Playgoing in Shakespeare's London*, 2nd edn. Cambridge: Cambridge University Press, 1996.

Guy, John (ed.), *The Reign of Elizabeth I: Court and Culture in the Last Decade.* Cambridge: Cambridge University Press, 1995.

Hafter, Daryl M. "Female Masters in the Ribbonmaking Guild of Eighteenth-Century Rouen." *French Historical Studies* 20 (Winter, 1997): 1–14.

Hanawalt, Barbara (ed.), *Women and Work in Preindustrial Europe.* Bloomington: Indiana University Press, 1986.

Haynes, Jonathan. *The Social Relations of Jonson's Theater.* Cambridge: Cambridge University Press, 1992.

Herrup, Cynthia. *The Common Peace: Participation and Criminal Law in Seventeenth-Century England.* Cambridge: Cambridge University Press, 1987.

Hill, Bridget. *Women, Work and Sexual Politics in Eighteenth-Century England.* Oxford: Basil Blackwell, 1989.

Hilton, R.H. "Lords, Burgesses and Hucksters." *Past and Present* 97 (1982): 3–15.

———. "Small Town Society in England before the Black Death." *Past and Present* 105 (1984): 53–78.

Hindle, Steve. *The State and Social Change in Early Modern England, c. 1550–1640.* London: Macmillan, 2000.

Hirst, Derek. "The Failure of Godly Rule in the English Republic." *Past and Present* 132 (1991): 33–66.

Holderness, B.A. "Credit in English Rural Society Before the Nineteenth Century, with Special Reference to the Period 1650–1720." *Agricultural History Review* 24, no. 2 (1976): 97–109.

———. "Widows in Pre-Industrial Society: An Essay Upon their Economic Functions." In *Land, Kinship and Life-Cycle*, (ed.) Richard M. Smith. New York: Cambridge University Press, 1984.

Honeyman, Katrina and Jordan Goodman. "Women's Work, Gender Conflict, and Labour Markets in Europe, 1500–1900." *The Economic History Review*, new series, 44 (Nov., 1991): 608–28.

Houlbrooke, R.A. "Women's Social Life and Common Action from the Fifteenth Century to the Eve of the Civil War." *Continuity and Change* vol. 1, no. 2 (1986): 171–89.

Howard, Sharon. "Riotous Community: Crowds, Politics and Society in Wales, c. 1700–1840." *The Welsh History Review* 20 (December, 2001): 656–86.

Hubbard, Eleanor. *City Women: Money, Sex, and the Social Order in Early Modern London*. Oxford: Oxford University Press, 2012.

Hufton, Olwen. *The Poor of Eighteenth-Century France, 1750–89*. Oxford: Oxford University Press, 1978.

Hughes, Diane Owen. "Sumptuary Laws and Social Relations in Renaissance Italy." In *Disputes and Settlements: Law and Human Relations in the West*, (ed.) John Bossy. Cambridge: Cambridge University Press, 1983.

Humphries, Jane. "Enclosures, Common Rights, and Women: The Proletarianization of Families in the Late Eighteenth and Early Nineteenth Centuries." *Journal of Economic History* 50, no. 1 (1990): 17–42.

Hunt, Margaret. *The Middling Sort: Commerce, Gender, and the Family in England, 1680–1780*. Berkeley: University of California Press, 1996.

Ingram, Martin. *Church Courts, Sex and Marriage in England, 1570–1640*. Cambridge: Cambridge University Press, 1987.

———. "'Scolding Women Cucked and Washed': A Crisis in Gender Relations in Early Modern England?" In *Women, Crime and the Courts in Early Modern England*, (ed.) Jenny Kermode and Garthine Walker. London: University of London Press, 1994.

Jardine, Lisa. *Worldly Goods: A New History of the Renaissance*. London: Macmillan, 1996.

Jenner, Mark and Paul Griffiths (eds), *Londinoplis: Essays in the Cultural and the Social History of Early Modern London*. Manchester: Manchester University Press, 2001.

Jones, Norman. *God and the Moneylenders: Usury and Law in Early Modern England*. Oxford: Oxford University Press, 1989.

Kermode, Jenny, and Garthine Walker (eds), *Women, Crime and the Courts in Early Modern England*. London: University of London Press, 1994.

Kowaleski, Maryanne. "Women's Work in a Market Town: Exeter in the Late Fourteenth Century." In *Women and Work in Preindustrial Europe*, (ed.) Barbara Hanawalt. Bloomington: Indiana University Press, 1986.

Lane, Penelope. "Work on the Margins: Poor Women and the Informal Economy of Eighteenth and Early Nineteenth-Century Leicestershire." *Midland History* 12 (1997): 85–99.

Lawson, Peter. "Patriarchy, Crime, and the Courts: The Criminality of Women in Late Tudor and Early Stuart England." In *Criminal Justice in the Old World and the New*, (ed.) Greg Smith, Allyson May, and Simon Devereaux. Toronto: Centre of Criminology, University of Toronto, 1998.

Lemire, Beverly. *The Business of Everyday Life: Gender, Practice and Social Politics in England, c. 1600–1900*. Manchester: Manchester University Press, 2005.

Loats, Carol. "Gender, Guilds, and Work Identity: Perspectives from Sixteenth-Century Paris." *French Historical Studies* 20, no. 1 (1997): 15–30.

Manning, Roger B. *Village Revolts: Social Protest and Popular Disturbances in England, 1608–1640*. Oxford: Clarendon Press, 1988.

McIntosh, Marjorie Keniston. "The Benefits and Drawbacks of *Femme Sole* Status in England, 1300–1630." *Journal of British Studies* 44 (July, 2005): 410–38.

———. *Working Women in English Society, 1300–1620*. Cambridge: Cambridge University Press, 2005.

McKendrick, Neil, John Brewer, and J.H. Plumb. *The Birth of a Consumer Society: The Commercialization of Eighteenth-Century England*. Bloomington: Indiana University Press, 1982.

Mendelson, Sara and Patricia Crawford. *Women in Early Modern England 1550–1720*. Oxford: Clarendon Press, 1998.

Muldrew, Craig. "Credit and the Courts: Debt Litigation in a Seventeenth-Century Urban Community." *Economic History Review*, new series, 46 (Feb., 1993): 23–38.

———. "Interpreting the Market: The Ethics of Credit and Community Relations in Early Modern England." *Social History* 18 (May 1993): 163–83.

———. "The Culture of Reconciliation: Community and the Settlement of Economic Disputes in Early Modern England." *Historical Journal* 39 (Dec., 1996): 915–42.

———. *The Economy of Obligation: The Culture of Credit and Social Relations in Early Modern England*. London: Macmillan, 1998.

———. "'A Mutual Assent of her Mind?' Women, Debt, Litigation and Contract in Early Modern England." *History Workshop Journal* 55 (2003): 47–71.

Newman, Karen. *Fashioning Femininity and English Renaissance Drama*. Chicago and London: University of Chicago Press, 1991.

O'Connell, Laura Stevenson. "Anti-Entrepreneurial Attitudes in Elizabethan Sermons and Popular Literature." *Journal of British Studies* 15 (Spring, 1976): 1–20.

Ogilvie, Sheilagh. *A Bitter Living. Women, Markets, and Social Capital in Early Modern Germany*. Oxford: Oxford University Press, 2003.

Outhwaite, R.B. "Dearth and Government Intervention in English Grain Markets, 1590–1700." *Economic History Review*, new series, 34 (August, 1981): 389–406.

———. (ed.), *Marriage and Society: Studies in the Social History of Marriage*. New York: St. Martin's Press, 1981.

Oxford English Dictionary, 2nd edn.

Pennington, David. "Beyond the Moral Economy: Ideology, Economic Change, and the 1621 House of Commons." *Parliamentary History* vol. 25, no. 2 (2006): 214–31.

———. "Taking it to the Streets: Huckstering and Hucksters in Early Modern Southampton, *circa* 1550–1651." *Sixteenth Century Journal* 39 (Autumn, 2008): 659–79.

Perry, Mary Elizabeth. *Gender and Disorder in Early Modern Seville*. Princeton: Princeton University Press, 1990.

Phelps-Brown, E.H. and Shelia V. Hopkins. "Seven Centuries of Building Wages." In *Essays in Economic History*, (ed.) E.M. Carus-Wilson. 2 vols, London: Edward Arnold, 1962.

———. "Seven Centuries of the Prices of Consumables, Compared with Builders' Wage-Rates." In *Essays in Economic History*, (ed.) E.M. Carus-Wilson. 2 vols, London: Edward Arnold, 1962.

Phillips, Richard. "Grassroots Change in an Early Modern Economy: The Emergence of a Rural Consumer Economy in Berkshire." *Southern History* 11 (1989): 23–39.

Price, Richard. *British Society, 1680–1880*. Cambridge: Cambridge University Press, 1999.

Prior, Mary. "Women and the Urban Economy: Oxford 1500–1800." In *Women in English Society*, (ed.) Mary Prior. London and New York: Methuen, 1985.

———. (ed.), *Women in English Society*. London and New York: Methuen, 1985.

Reay, Barry (ed.), *Popular Culture in Seventeenth-Century England.* New York: St. Martin's Press, 1985.

Reed, Michael. "The Urban Landscape 1540–1700." In *The Cambridge Urban History of Britain* vol. 2, *1540–1840*, (ed.) Peter Clark. Cambridge: Cambridge University Press, 2000.

Roper, Lyndal. *The Holy Household: Women and Morals in Reformation Augsburg*. Oxford: Clarendon Press, 1989.

Rublack, Ulinka. *The Crimes of Women in Early Modern Germany*. Oxford: Clarendon Press, 1999.

Scott, Joan. "Gender: A Useful Category of Historical Analysis." *American Historical Review* 91 (Dec., 1986): 1053–75.

Shammas, Carole. *The Pre-Industrial Consumer in England and America*. Oxford: Clarendon Press, 1990.

Shapiro, Ann-Louise (ed.), *Feminists Revision History*. New Brunswick: Rutgers University Press, 1994.

Sharp, Buchanan. *In Contempt of All Authority: Rural Artisans and Riot in the West of England, 1586–1660*. Berkeley: University of California Press, 1980.

Sharpe, J.A. "'Such Disagreement Betwixt Neighbours': Litigation and Human Relations in Early Modern England." In *Disputes and Settlements: Law and Human Relations in the West*, (ed.) John Bossy. Cambridge: Cambridge University Press, 1983.

———. "Social Strain and Social Dislocation, 1585–1603." In *The Reign of Elizabeth I: Court and Culture in the Last Decade*, (ed.) John Guy. Cambridge: Cambridge University Press, 1995.

Sharpe, Pamela. "Continuity and Change: Women's History and Economic History in Britain." *Economic History Review*, new series, 48 (May, 1995): 353–69.

Shepard, Alexandra. "Contesting Communities? 'Town' and 'Gown' in Cambridge, c. 1560–1640." In *Communities in Early Modern England: Networks, Place, Rhetoric,* (ed.) Alexandra Shepard and Phil Withington. Manchester and New York: Manchester University Press, 2000.

———. "Manhood, Credit and Patriarchy in Early Modern England c. 1580–1640." *Past and Present* 167 (2000): 75–106.

———. *Meanings of Manhood in Early Modern England.* Oxford and New York: Oxford University Press, 2003.

———. "Litigation and Locality: the Cambridge University Courts, 1560–1640." *Urban History* 31, no. 1 (2004): 5–28.

Shepard, Alexandra and Phil Withington (eds), *Communities in Early Modern England: Networks, Place, Rhetoric.* Manchester and New York: Manchester University Press.

Shepherd, Simon. *Amazons and Warrior Women: Varieties of Feminism in Seventeenth-Century Drama.* New York: St. Martin's Press, 1981.

Slack, Paul. *Poverty and Policy in Tudor and Stuart England.* London: Longman, 1988.

Smith, Greg, Allyson May, and Simon Devereaux (eds), *Criminal Justice in the Old World and the New.* Toronto: Centre of Criminology, University of Toronto, 1998.

Smith, Richard M. (ed.), *Land, Kinship and Life-Cycle.* New York: Cambridge University Press, 1984.

Spufford, Margaret. *The Great Reclothing of England: Petty Chapmen and Their Wares in the Seventeenth Century.* London: Hambledon Press, 1984.

Stearns, Peter. "Stages of Consumerism: Recent Work on the Issues of Periodization." *The Journal of Modern History* 69 (Mar., 1997): 102–117.

Stevenson, John. "The 'Moral Economy' of the English Crowd: Myth and Reality." In *Order and Disorder in Early Modern England,* (ed.) Anthony Fletcher and John Stevenson. Cambridge: Cambridge University Press, 1985.

Stone, Lawrence. *The Family, Sex and Marriage in England 1500–1800.* 2nd edn. New York: Harper, 1979.

Stretton, Tim. *Women Waging Law in Elizabethan England.* Cambridge: Cambridge University Press, 1998.

Supple, Barry. *Commercial Crisis and Change in England, 1600–1642.* Cambridge: Cambridge University Press, 1964.

Swanson, Heather. "The Illusion of Structure: Craft Guilds in Late Medieval English Towns." *Past and Present* 121 (1988): 29–48.

Swanson, R.N. (ed.), *Studies in Church History*, 34 (1998).

Thirsk, Joan (ed.), *The Agrarian History of England and Wales*, vol. 6, *1500–1640*. Cambridge: Cambridge University Press, 1967.

———. *Economic Policy and Projects: The Development of a Consumer Society in Early Modern England*. Oxford: Clarendon Press, 1978.

Thirsk, Joan and J.P. Cooper (eds), *Seventeenth-Century Economic Documents*. Oxford: Clarendon Press, 1972.

Thomas, Keith. "The Double Standard." *Journal of the History of Ideas* 20 (April, 1959): 195–216.

———. "Numeracy in Early Modern England." *Transactions of the Royal Historical Society*, 5th series, 37 (1987): 103–32.

Thompson, E.P. "The Moral Economy of the English Crowd in the Eighteenth Century," *Past and Present* 50 (1971): 76–136.

Thwaites, W. "Women in the Market Place: Oxfordshire c. 1690–1800." *Midland History* 9 (1984): 23–42.

———. "The Corn Market and Economic Change: Oxford in the Eighteenth Century." *Midland History* 16 (1991): 103–25.

Tilly, Louise A. and Joan W. Scott, *Women, Work, and Family*. New York: Holt, Rinehart and Winston, 1978.

Tittler, Robert. *Architecture and Power. The Town Hall and the English Urban Community c. 1500–1640*. Oxford: Clarendon Press, 1991.

———. *Townspeople and Nation*. Stanford: Stanford University Press, 2001.

Todd, Barbara. "The Remarrying Widow: A Stereotype Reconsidered." In *Women in English Society 1500–1800*, (ed.) Mary Prior. London and New York: Methuen, 1985.

Underdown, David. "The Taming of the Scold: the Enforcement of Patriarchal Authority in Early Modern England." In *Order and Disorder in Early Modern England*, (ed.) Anthony Fletcher and John Stevenson. Cambridge: Cambridge University Press, 1985.

Valenze, Deborah. "The Art of Women and the Business of Men: Women's Work and the Dairy Industry c. 1740–1840." *Past and Present* 130 (1991): 142–69.

Vickery, Amanda. "Golden Age to Separate Spheres? A Review of the Categories and Chronology of English Women's History." *Historical Journal* 36 (1993): 383–414.

Waddell, Brodie. *God, Duty and Community in English Economic Life, 1660–1720*. Woodbridge: Boydell Press, 2012.

Walker, Garthine. "Women, Theft and the World of Stolen Goods." In *Women, Crime and the Courts in Early Modern England*, (ed.) Jenny Kermode and Garthine Walker. London: University of London Press, 1994.

———. "Expanding the Boundaries of Female Honour." *Transactions of the Royal Historical Society*, 6th series, 6 (1996): 235–45.

———. *Crime, Gender and Social Order in Early Modern England*. Cambridge: Cambridge University Press, 2003.

Walter, John. "Grain Riots and Popular Attitudes to the Law: Maldon and the Crisis of 1629." In *An Ungovernable People. The English and their Law in the Seventeenth and Eighteenth Centuries*, (ed.) John Brewer and John Styles. New Brunswick: Rutgers University Press, 1980.

———. "Public Transcripts, Popular Agency and the Politics of Subsistence in Early Modern England." In *Negotiating Power in Early Modern Society: Order, Hierarchy and Subordination in Britain and Ireland*, (ed.) Michael Braddick and John Walter. Cambridge: Cambridge University Press, 2001.

Walter, John and Keith Wrightson. "Dearth and the Social Order in Early Modern England." *Past and Present* 71 (1976): 22–42.

Wiener, Carol Z. "Sex-Roles and Crime in Late Elizabethan Hertfordshire." *Journal of Social History* 8 (1974–5): 38–60.

Wiesner, Merry E. *Working Women in Renaissance Germany*. New Brunswick: Rutgers University Press, 1986.

Wiesner Wood, Merry. "Paltry Peddlers or Essential Merchants? Women in the Distributive Trades in Early Modern Nuremberg." *The Sixteenth Century Journal* 12, no. 2 (1981): 3–13.

Wiltenburg, Joy. *Disorderly Women and Female Power in the Street Literature of Early Modern England and Germany*. Charlottesville and London: University of Virginia Press, 1992.

Withington, Phil. *The Politics of Commonwealth: Citizens and Freemen in Early Modern England*. Cambridge: Cambridge University Press, 2005.

Wordie, J.R. "Deflationary Factors in the Tudor Price Rise." *Past and Present* 154 (1997): 32–70.

Wright, Sue. "'Charmaids, Huswyfes and Hucksters:' The Employment of Women in Tudor and Stuart Salisbury." In *Women and Work in Pre-Industrial England*, (ed.) Lindsey Charles and Lorna Duffin. London: Croom Helm, 1985.

Wrightson, Keith. "Two Concepts of Order: Justices, Constables and Jurymen in Seventeenth-Century England." In *An Ungovernable People. The English and their Law in the Seventeenth and Eighteenth Centuries*, (ed.) John Brewer and John Styles. New Brunswick: Rutgers University Press, 1980.

———. *English Society 1580–1680*. London: Routledge, 1982.

———. *Earthly Necessities. Economic Lives in Early Modern Britain*. New Haven and London: Yale University Press, 2000.

Wrigley, E.A. and Roger Schofield. *The Population History of England, 1541–1871: a Reconstruction*. Cambridge, Mass.: Harvard University Press, 1981.

Theses and Dissertations

Cionci, Maria Lynn. "Women and Law in Elizabethan England with Particular Reference to the Court of Chancery." PhD diss., Cambridge University, 1974.

Goose, Nigel. "Economic and Social Aspects of Provincial Towns: A Comparative Study of Cambridge, Colchester and Reading, c. 1500–1700." PhD diss., Cambridge University, 1984.

Siraut, Mary Christine. "Some Aspects of the Economic and Social History of Cambridge Under Elizabeth I." M.Litt thesis, Cambridge University, 1978.

Websites

Bohstedt, John. "Riot Census." http://web.utk.edu/~bohstedt/.

Index

For Product Safety Concerns and Information please contact our
EU representative GPSR@taylorandfrancis.com Taylor & Francis
Verlag GmbH, Kaufingerstraße 24, 80331 München, Germany